CLIMB TO GREATNESS

The American Aircraft Industry, 1920–1960

CLIMB
TO
GREATNESS

The American Aircraft Industry, 1920–1960

John B. Rae

THE MIT PRESS

Massachusetts Institute of Technology
Cambridge, Massachusetts, and London, England

This book is dedicated to
Arthur Harrison Cole
*in appreciation of the encouragement and help he gave to me in my study
of the history of American industry*

Preface

The story of the American aircraft industry presents a unique intertwining of business, politics, and technology. The industry has depended for its existence on one major customer, the United States government. It has therefore been acutely subject to variations in national policy and has simultaneously had to keep pace with a rapidly changing technology. These conditions might well have led to domination of the industry by the procurement agencies of the government and a condition of cartelization or near-monopoly to the extent that the law would permit. Instead the aircraft industry is privately owned, vigorously competitive, and has attained a standard of technological performance that producers elsewhere have sometimes matched but seldom surpassed.

This is in fact a success story, or rather a series of success stories, in the best American tradition: of small beginnings, handicaps overcome by skill and persistence, and a climb to outstanding achievement. It is also an unfinished story; but there is a coherent and vital segment between the close of the First World War, when a makeshift manufacturing structure virtually disappeared and a new start had to be made, and the end of the 1950's, when a new era came along to require a new name, *aerospace,* for the industry.

When I first undertook this study, I was repeatedly advised that the aircraft industry is not historically minded. It is true that the leaders of the industry, by the nature of their business, have had to be much more concerned with the future than with the past, but the implication that I would find little assistance or interest happily turned out to be erroneous. I have received generous cooperation from organizations and individuals connected with the aircraft industry, as well as from others. My indebtedness is extensive, and if I have omitted from the following list anyone who should be on it, I apologize.

My thanks are due to Harl V. Brackin, director of historical services of The Boeing Company; Nelson Fuller, manager of research and historian, Convair Division, General Dynamics Corporation; Crosby Maynard, public relations department, Douglas Aircraft Company, Inc.; and A. J. Montgomery and W. E. Van Dyke, public relations staff, North American Aviation, Inc., for making available company histories and other materials. Charles T. Thum, vice-president of Lockheed Aircraft Service, Inc., and a friend and neighbor of long standing, not only provided material but assisted in making contact with key figures in the Lockheed organization. Valuable information was also contributed by officials of Beech, Bell, Chance Vought, Curtiss-Wright, Goodyear, Grumman, Hughes, Kaman, Martin, McDonnell, Northrop, Republic, Ryan, and United Aircraft.

Thanks are also due to H. Dana Moran, formerly of the Aerospace Industries Association, whom I met through the good offices of George I. McKelvey, director of development at Harvey Mudd College. Several individuals who have been part of the history of the aircraft industry generously took time to be interviewed: John L. Atwood, Frank R. Collbohm, Kenneth R. Jackman, Joseph S. Marriott, Richard Millar, John K. Northrop, Henry H. Ogden, Nathaniel Paschall, Arthur E. Raymond, Frederick Salathé, Raymond C. Sebold, Carl Squier, and Thomas Wolfe.

Special acknowledgment is due to Commander Eugene E. Wilson, who enabled me to travel across the country and be his guest while he discussed his own varied experiences in the history of aviation. These arrangements were made with the help of a mutual friend, Dr. Vernon D. Tate, then librarian of the United States Naval Academy, who also extended hospitality and gave me access to Commander Wilson's materials in the Naval Academy library. Lieutenant-General Laurence C. Craigie (USAF ret.) gave me his own account of the test flight of the first American-built jet plane, the XP-59A, in which he was a participant.

I am also grateful for assistance given in a variety of ways by Dr. Eugene Emme, NASA Historian; Dr. Robin Higham of Kansas State University; Dr. I. B. Holley of Duke University; and Dr. G. R. Simonson of the California State College at Long Beach. Drs. Rodman Paul of the California Institute of Technology and Seymour Chapin of the California State College, Los Angeles, were kind enough to make available the manuscript on pressurized flight prepared by Dr. Chapin and Thomas M. Smith under the auspices of the Garrett Corporation. Dr. John Niven of the Claremont Graduate School gave me the benefit of his acquaintance with the General Dynamics Corporation and introduced me to two of its officials, Charles Perrine and C. David Cornell, who gave valuable advice. The members of the Department of Engineering at Harvey Mudd College, especially Drs. Jack L. Alford, Arnold M. Ruskin, Harry E. Williams, and Warren E. Wilson, have been unfailingly helpful in trying to keep me straight on technical points. Dr. Joseph B. Platt, president of Harvey Mudd College, and Dr. Alfred B. Focke, chairman of the Department of Physics, have also gone out of their way to provide assistance, as have Mr. and Mrs. Howard Critchell of the Bates Foundation.

I also owe much to the courtesy of the staffs of the various libraries I have used: the Honnold Library of The Claremont Colleges; the Occidental College Library; the Library of Congress; the National Archives; the Library of the University of California, Los Angeles; the Doheny Library of the University of Southern California; the New York Public Library; the Pacific Aeronautical Library; the Pomona Public Library; and the Library of the Eleutherian Mills-Hagley Foundation. I wish to give special acknowledgment to Dr. Royal Frey of the Air Force Museum, Wright-Patterson Air Force Base; Mrs. Nell Steinmetz of the Pacific Aeronautical Library; Dr. Louis M. Starr of the Oral History

Research Office, Columbia University; Mrs. Lucille Bucher, Business and Industry Collection, Pomona Public Library; Dr. Marvin McFarland, Library of Congress; and Mrs. Shelton Beatty and Mrs. Malcolm Douglass of the Oral History Program of the Claremont Graduate School. In the course of research into the history of the British aircraft industry, I found some useful information on the American industry in the library of the Royal Aeronautical Society in London, and my thanks are due to Dr. A. M. Ballantyne and the staff of the Society for providing access to these resources.

I have a deep personal indebtedness to my daughter Helen and to Mrs. Glenn E. Thompson, secretary of the Department of Humanities and Social Sciences at Harvey Mudd College, for typing the manuscript, and to my wife for preparing the index, as she has done for each of my books. Dennis West made a substantial contribution as my research assistant in 1964–1965. Finally, my research was made possible by the financial support of the American Philosophical Society and the John Randolph Haynes and Dora Haynes Foundation.

JOHN B. RAE

Harvey Mudd College
Claremont, California

Contents

Tables

1. Rebirth

For the American aircraft industry the conclusion of the First World War was, to use one of Winston Churchill's famous phrases, "the end of the beginning." What had happened to the industry previously was of negligible importance for its future development. The Wright brothers invented the airplane, but their feat provoked an astonishingly sluggish response in their own country. The United States lagged well behind Europe in the development of aviation, both qualitatively and quantitatively. In 1914 there were sixteen firms important enough to be listed by the Census Bureau as aircraft manufacturers, and their combined total output for the year was 49 planes.[1] Apart from the achievement of the Wrights, the only major American contribution to aeronautical progress in the prewar period was Glenn Curtiss' pioneering work with seaplanes.

The war brought what would now be called a "crash program," a subject of bitter dispute at the time and for years afterward.[2] While the program was by no means the fiasco its critics alleged it to be, it did little either to win the war or to advance aviation. The principal accomplishment was the Liberty engine, and although the Liberty was a sturdy, dependable mechanism, it was no technological innovation. It was designed specifically for immediate large-scale production in existing automobile engine plants; its designers in fact were expressly enjoined to use only known and tested methods and techniques, and what they achieved has been described as "an excellent synthesis of the state of the art of its time." [3] The eventual record of production was impressive, if belated. Between April 1917 and November 1918, American industry delivered 13,894 aircraft and 41,953 engines.[4] A production rate of 21,000 planes a year was reached, and 175,000 people were employed in aircraft manufacturing.

Only a small part of this output could be credited to companies that had been in the aircraft business before the war. The engines, as had been intended, came predominantly from the automobile industry. The airframes were built by a variety of firms, some organized for the specific purpose of securing war contracts. Some 300 plants, including subcontractors with 20,000 workers, were involved in aircraft manufacturing before the war ended.[5] The final results of the program appear in Appendix A.

The whole structure collapsed immediately after the signing of the armistice. Contracts for aircraft and parts totaling $100,000,000 were canceled in a matter of days, with no notice or warning of any kind; by the end of 1918 the aircraft industry had been reduced to a small fraction of its wartime size. The precise extent of the shrinkage is difficult to measure. One contemporary observer, Howard Mingos, secretary of the Aircraft Manufacturers Association, estimated that the industry was cut to about 10 per cent of what it had been, while the distinguished aeronautical engineer, Charles L. Lawrance, later said, "No one knows how many millions of dollars were poured into the emergency aircraft industry hastily created during the World War, but we do know that by 1920 not more than $5,000,000 investment remained." [6]

The aircraft industry was by no means the only sufferer from the government's failure to plan for the return of peace, but it was in a peculiarly vulnerable position. The automobile manufacturers, for example, were able to turn without undue difficulty from military production and resume their accustomed function of satisfying a booming demand for motor vehicles; they withdrew from aviation without hesitation or regret, except to the extent that Packard continued to be a fairly important designer and builder of aircraft engines. The aircraft manufacturers, on the other hand, were left with the fragments of a military market and with no established civilian market to return to. There were, not for the first time in the history of the industry, sanguine expectations of a great expansion of private flying, but these hopes would be realized only very slowly and on a considerably smaller scale than the enthusiasts had predicted. Commercial air transport was a more solid prospect, but in 1919 it existed only in the form of experimental flying of mail between New York and Washington, D. C. Its further growth would require the development of airfields and navigational aids, along with legislation for the regulation of air commerce and the establishment of standards of safety. Even if all these had been provided promptly, the market for aircraft in the years immediately following the war was glutted with the thousands of planes and engines left over from the wartime program.

The war surplus blighted the military market also. With all this unused equipment on hand, neither Congress nor the public at large could see any need to spend money on new construction. Military aviation was still too novel for there to be any general understanding that most military aircraft are obsolescent when they come off the production line. In any case, to most Americans at that time "the war to end war" had just been fought, so that there was little interest in maintaining a large air force. The Army and Navy decided, wisely under the circumstances, to use their limited funds largely for experimental work, so that they could keep abreast of technical progress in aeronautics.[7]

The Survivors

The result of this combination of conditions was that aircraft production in the United States dropped from the wartime peak of 14,000 in 1918 to a low of 263 in 1922 [8] and the aircraft industry was thrown into a desperate struggle for survival. There was a drastic weeding-out process, in some respects healthy because it got rid of the incompetents and the misfits who had rushed into the field to get rich on war contracts.

Of the companies that emerged from the war, the strongest was the Curtiss Aeroplane and Motor Company, Inc., of Buffalo, New York. It could claim to be the oldest American aircraft company, tracing its origin to the Curtiss Motor Vehicle Company formed by Glenn Curtiss in Hammondsport, New York, late in 1907, to manufacture "engines, motorcycles, airships, aeroplanes, and low-priced automobiles." [9] This company was eventually merged in January 1916 with the Burgess Company of Marblehead, Massachusetts, to create the Curtiss Aeroplane and Motor Company. The Burgess firm was a family concern with an established reputation as designers and builders of racing yachts. Its head at that time, W. Starling Burgess, became interested in aviation and began to build airplanes in 1910. The purpose of the merger was partly to create a larger organization capable of meeting the increasing demand for aircraft generated by the war in Europe, and partly to consolidate patents held by the two companies so as to strengthen their position in the patent controversy between the Wrights and Curtiss. [10] During the war Curtiss Aeroplane and Motor concentrated its operations in Buffalo, where production facilities and labor were more plentiful than in either Hammondsport or Marblehead. It also became part of John N. Willys' automotive empire, with government approval, so that Willys could stimulate production while Curtiss devoted himself to design. [11] In 1920, however, Willys ran into financial difficulties and lost control of Curtiss Aeroplane and Motor. [12] These changes of management had no perceptible effect on the company's affairs. Even in this difficult period it was able to maintain a reasonable volume of production of both airframes and engines. Its outstanding achievement at this time was to build the NC Navy seaplanes that crossed the Atlantic in 1919. [13]

The Curtiss claim to seniority among American aircraft companies might have been disputed by the Wright Aeronautical Company, which could claim a somewhat circuitous descent from the Wright brothers; but since the two would eventually combine, the question of priority is not particularly relevant. The original Wright Company was organized late in 1909 and operated on a small scale for the next five years, building some planes and running two flying schools. After Wilbur Wright's death in 1912, Orville became dissatisfied with the management of the company and finally sold it in 1915 to a syndicate that merged it with the Glenn L. Martin Company of Los Angeles, California, and the Simplex Automobile Company of New Brunswick, New Jersey, to form the Wright-Martin Aircraft Corporation.[14]

The purpose of this combination was to create an organization big enough to handle a French government order for 450 Hispano-Suiza aircraft engines. The new company was therefore oriented toward engine production from the beginning. Martin withdrew in 1917, and two years later the Wright-Martin firm was reconstituted as Wright Aeronautical Company, devoted exclusively to the design and manufacture of aircraft engines.

The Martin association with Wright-Martin was very tenuous. The original Glenn L. Martin Company was founded in Los Angeles in 1912 and was doing reasonably well when the merger took place. Why Martin took this step is not clear. He continued to operate in Los Angeles, with 500 people on his payroll, until 1917; the Aircraft Production Board then closed his factory as "not suitable," because, although he was then delivering a plane a day, Martin could not promise more than three a day in six months.[15] Martin promptly left Wright-Martin and formed a new Glenn L. Martin Company in Cleveland, Ohio, with support from local businessmen. It was a small company, but it played a unique role in the subsequent growth of the aircraft industry. The twin-engined Martin MB bomber was probably the best combat plane designed in the United States during the war; although it was not ready for wartime service, it became the Army's first-line bomber for a good many years. Its design was not in any way radical, but it was ahead of its competitors and was well adapted to quantity production.[16]

More important, however, was the company's role in producing future leaders of the aircraft industry. The chief engineer and designer of the Martin MB was Donald W. Douglas; his assistants were Lawrence Bell and James H. "Dutch" Kindelberger.[17]

The other major holdover from the prewar period was the Boeing Airplane Company in Seattle, Washington. It was

founded by William E. Boeing, a product of Yale's Sheffield
Scientific School who had done well in the timber business and
become interested in flying about 1910. He was one of Martin's
first customers and began to build his own planes in 1915. He
organized his first company a year later.[18] By the end of the war
the technical work of the company was in the hands of two
young engineers from the neighboring University of Washington, Philip Johnson and Claire Egtvedt. It is said that when
William E. Boeing telephoned the Engineering Department at
the University to inquire about possible assistance Johnson, then
a graduate student in the department, happened to answer the
call and promptly recommended himself and Egtvedt although
neither knew anything then about airplanes.

The cancellation of war contracts left the Boeing company in
a very difficult position. It took to building sea sleds and furniture in order to keep the factory in operation, but this venture
was not successful; what really saved the company was an order
to recondition 50 De Havilland 4's for the Army.[19] Boeing also
experimented with air transport, a field in which William E.
Boeing and his company maintained an unbroken interest. A
flying boat, the B-1, was built in 1919 with space for two passengers as well as mail or cargo.[20] It was used successfully to carry
mail between Seattle and Vancouver, Canada, the first international U.S. mail flight, logging 350,000 miles in seven years; but
the surplus of planes from the war discouraged the building of
more B-1's. It was a useful experiment, nevertheless, because it
gave the Boeing organization data that proved valuable in bidding on mail routes when the firm later went into the air transport business.

Other small firms remained in existence, most of them for
limited periods. The Aeromarine Plane and Motor Company continued until the mid-1920's as a minor producer of aircraft engines. It was founded in 1914 by Inglis M. Uppercu, who had
made a fortune as the New York distributor for Packard cars.
Like Boeing, Aeromarine tried to stimulate business after the
war by establishing a passenger flying service,[21] but it did not
succeed. The other firms were products of the war, including the
Thomas-Morse Airplane Company of Ithaca, New York, which

appeared to have excellent prospects as a builder of fighter planes. This company was the creation of two Englishmen, namesakes but unrelated. William T. Thomas, a graduate of the Central Technical College in London (now part of the Imperial College of Science and Technology), joined the Herring-Curtiss Company in 1909 and a year later formed his own company with his brother Oliver.[22] When Oliver returned to England in 1913, William was joined by B. Douglas Thomas, who had learned his engineering at Vickers and worked for Curtiss assisting in the design of the famous "Jenny" (JN) trainer. His agreement with the Thomas Brothers firm was that he should supervise construction and get half the profits. He became chief design engineer when the company became Thomas-Morse and moved to Ithaca in 1916; he was therefore responsible for the Thomas-Morse MB-3, the principal Army pursuit plane of the early 1920's. Unfortunately, Thomas-Morse fell foul of the system of bidding employed for military orders at that time, whereby any aircraft manufacturer could bid on any other's designs. Thomas-Morse built 50 MB-3's but in 1920 lost an order for 200 to Boeing; as a result the company declined and was subsequently absorbed by the Consolidated Aircraft Corporation.

The Loening Aeronautical Engineering Corporation was founded in 1917 by Grover Loening, who was the first student at Columbia University to go into the field of aeronautics.[23] Loening possessed technical talent and, as one of the few trained aeronautical engineers in the country at the time, should have had a bright future in the aircraft industry. Yet he never quite arrived; apparently he was an individualist who preferred experimental work to regular production.

A more obscure firm at this period was the Lewis and Vought Corporation, which, like Loening, was established in New York. It was formed in 1917 by Chance Milton Vought, aeronautical engineer and pilot, and his friend Birdseye Lewis, who provided the capital and the business management. The company, whose original quarters were a third floor in a loft building in Astoria, Long Island, began by building trainers for both Army and Navy but soon specialized in naval aircraft, particularly reconnaissance planes designed for catapult launching.[24] Thus the company, while small, was making aircraft of a type that had not been produced in quantity during the war and was therefore not subject to competition from war surplus. It became the Chance Vought Corporation in 1922.

New Arrivals

A period when the market for new aircraft was virtually nonexistent hardly seems an appropriate time for newcomers to try to get established in aircraft manufacturing. Yet the early 1920's saw several significant entries into the industry. This step required a dedication to aviation and a profound faith in its future rather than any expectation of immediate gain. The founders of aircraft companies in those days conformed to the accepted pattern of the entrepreneur in that they assumed risks; they must have felt, indeed, that the business consisted entirely of risks. On the other hand, they deviated from the conventional entrepreneurial model in that they did not base their actions on the maximizing of profit; they seldom had profits to maximize. Their dominating motive was a passionate desire to design and build airplanes, or sometimes aircraft engines.

The first arrival was Donald W. Douglas, who was not, strictly speaking, a newcomer to aircraft manufacturing. He had become an aviation enthusiast while a midshipman at the United States Naval Academy and left Annapolis in 1912 at the end of his third year to study aeronautical engineering at the Massachusetts Institute of Technology. He graduated in 1914 with M.I.T.'s first S.B. degree in aeronautical engineering and remained for another year as an assistant in the field (at $500 a year). In his spare time he consulted for a small concern called the Connecticut Aircraft Company, which was trying to build dirigibles for the Navy.[25] Then he made his first acquaintance with southern California by going to Los Angeles in August 1915 as chief engineer for Glenn Martin. In November 1916, Douglas went to Washington, D. C. as chief civilian aeronautical engineer for the Signal Corps, which controlled such aviation as the Army possessed; this assignment ended less than a year later, when Douglas left in protest against a War Production Board order to put the 400 h.p. Liberty engine into the Bristol fighter, a British design meant for a 200 h.p. engine.[26]

When Martin reestablished his company in Cleveland, Douglas rejoined him. This association ended early in 1920, because Donald Douglas at the age of 28 wanted to be in the aircraft business on his own. He picked southern California as his location on the strength of his earlier acquaintance with the region, which made him aware of its climatic advantages for airplane manufacturing. He also believed that he had a better prospect of getting financial support. He arrived in Los Angeles with cash resources of $1,000 and launched what would become the Douglas Aircraft Company, Inc., by renting the back room of a barber shop.

Douglas was introduced to the Los Angeles business community by Bill Henry of the *Los Angeles Times*. The two had first met in 1919 when Henry, on the threshold of a long and distinguished journalistic career, was doing public relations work for Martin.[27] The first investor was a wealthy aviation enthusiast, David R. Davis, who put up $40,000 for the construction of a plane intended to make the first nonstop flight across the country. Davis and Douglas went into partnership as the Davis-Douglas Airplane Company, with Henry's name on the letterhead as vice-president although he was never an active participant. Douglas designed and built for Davis a biplane that they called the Cloudster, the first in a long line of Douglas aircraft. Completed early in 1921, the Cloudster crashed on a trial flight, and when an Army flyer made a successful one-day transcontinental trip in a De Havilland 4B, Davis lost interest and withdrew from the company. Yet the Cloudster was a significant step in the growth of the Douglas tradition. Powered, as were most of its contemporaries, by a 12-cylinder Liberty engine, it was capable of lifting a load equal to its own weight.[28] It was built in a hangar owned by the Goodyear Tire & Rubber Company and rented for $40 a month.[29]

Fortunately for Douglas, another and more important customer appeared in the form of the U.S. Navy. The Navy had decided that it wanted a plane capable of carrying a full-sized torpedo, and it happened that Jerome C. Hunsaker, who had known Douglas at M.I.T., was serving as head of the Material Division of the Bureau of Aeronautics.[30] At Hunsaker's suggestion Douglas was invited to Washington to discuss the matter, and he drafted the preliminary design for the DT-1 on the spare drafting table in Hunsaker's office—using some of the ideas he had put into the Cloudster. The result was an order for three at $40,000 each. Actually only one was built, but the DT-1 was the precursor of a continuing series that made Douglas the country's leading manufacturer of naval aircraft.

The departure of Davis, however, left the company without capital, and Henry provided the solution. He brought together Douglas and a group of fifteen Los Angeles businessmen, headed by Harry Chandler, publisher of the *Los Angeles Times*. The fifteen signed a promissory note for $15,000 on the strength of the Navy order. Since this yielded a profit of $40,000 and was followed by a larger order, Douglas's credit was sound. The company became the Douglas Company in 1922 and moved into an unused movie studio in Santa Monica.[31] It became the Douglas Aircraft Company, Inc., in 1926, after it achieved a major triumph by building for the Army the World Cruisers that made the first round-the-world flight in 1924.[32]

The successful establishment of Douglas Aircraft in southern California was an event of historic importance in the history of the American aircraft industry, far out of proportion to the size of the company at the time. It was the first effective step in the process of geographical concentration that by 1940 would give southern California 45 per cent of the nation's airframe manufacturing facilities.[33] California has a long history of aeronautical development,[34] including such famous names as John J. Montgomery, Glenn L. Martin, and the Loughead (subsequently Lockheed) brothers, Allan and Malcolm. But Montgomery's gliding experiments were largely forgotten, Martin moved east (or was moved), and the original Loughead firm in Santa Barbara folded in 1921. Douglas was the first to get into business in southern California and stay.

Donald Douglas also appears to have been the first airframe manufacturer to make a deliberate choice of location. Earlier companies were established where their founders happened to live, financial support was offered, or manufacturing facilities were readily available. Douglas chose the Los Angeles area and then sought his backing and his factory space. In the aircraft industry, accessibility to materials and markets is a negligible factor in determining location, and capital is usually procurable from local sources in a company's early days. A climate that permits year-round flying has been mentioned as one desideratum; the other major one is an adequate supply of skilled and semiskilled labor. Los Angeles had both, and a substantial part of Douglas' success must be credited to his appreciation of these factors as well as to his own talents as an aeronautical designer.

The next major arrival, comparable to Douglas Aircraft in terms of future importance, was the Consolidated Aircraft Corporation, the creation of Major Reuben H. Fleet, U.S.A. In contrast to Douglas, Fleet was not a trained engineer but rather an organizer and promoter. He had been a National Guard officer and had become an Army pilot in 1917. Then he served as contracting officer for the Army Air Service and as business manager for McCook Field at Dayton, Ohio, now the giant Wright-Patterson Air Force Base.[35] He was also supervisor of the flights that instituted air mail service between New York and Washington, D. C., in 1918.

At the end of the war Fleet was given offers by both Boeing and Curtiss, but he declined them in order to become vice-president and general manager of the Gallaudet Aircraft Corporation of East Greenwich, Rhode Island. Consolidated can therefore claim to be older than Douglas, because Gallaudet dated back to before the war. Edson Fessenden Gallaudet, son of the president of Gallaudet College for the Deaf in Washington, D. C., was a graduate in electrical engineering of Yale and Johns Hopkins. He became interested in aeronautics while an instructor in physics at Yale; he is reputed, indeed, to have left the teaching profession because he was given a choice between doing so and giving up his aeronautical experiments.[36] He became a consulting engineer and built some experimental planes until in 1917 the war stimulated the formation of the Gallaudet Aircraft Corporation.

Gallaudet himself had technical skill and a willingness to

experiment. In 1920 he secured a contract from the Navy to build the power plant for a projected triplane flying boat, the Pacific. Gallaudet's design envisioned three 18-foot propellers, each driven by three 12-cylinder, 400 h.p. Liberty engines.[37] How well this scheme would have worked was never determined, because the Navy abandoned the project and Gallaudet was unable to keep his company alive. He resigned in 1922, unsuccessful as an aircraft manufacturer but doing very well as a manufacturer of waterproof string for tennis racquets, made by coating silk fibers with airplane dope.[38]

Shortly after Fleet joined the firm he reported adversely to the directors on its prospects and offered to buy it. So the Consolidated Aircraft Corporation was founded (May 29, 1923) with an authorized capital of $60,000, of which $25,000 was actually subscribed, $15,000 by Fleet and the rest by his sister, Mrs. Lillian Fleet Bishop.[39] This was more than Donald Douglas had started with, and Fleet had a more definite prospect of business than Douglas. As business manager at McCook Field, Fleet had been in an excellent position to become familiar with the affairs of the Dayton-Wright Company. This concern had been formed in 1917, largely by men from the automobile industry, to take advantage of the opportunities offered by the wartime aircraft program. The Wright name was purely advertising. Orville Wright was a consultant to the company, but he had very little to do with its affairs. It did eventually build 3,500 planes under the war program, mainly De Havilland 4's,[40] but it came under severe criticism because one of its organizers was Colonel Edward A. Deeds, who shortly afterward became head of the Aircraft Production Board. Deeds became the scapegoat for the disappointing record of aircraft production and, among other things, was accused of having given special favors to his own company.

So Dayton-Wright emerged from the war very much under a cloud, although no misconduct by either Deeds or the company was ever actually proved. It was bought by General Motors in 1919 for $1,096,000 in debenture stock as part of William C. Durant's ambitious postwar expansion program.[41] Then, however, the expected boom in aviation failed to materialize, General

Motors went through a crisis in the 1920–1921 panic, and in the reorganization Dayton-Wright was dissolved. From the defunct company Fleet acquired the design rights to its planes, and the designer, Colonel V. E. Clark. Clark was a Naval Academy graduate who had transferred to the Army, gone into aviation, and received the first doctorate in aeronautics conferred by M.I.T.[42] During the war he was a member of the Bolling Commission, a group sent to Europe to get up-to-date information on military aviation.[43]

Clark brought to Consolidated the design for two trainers (TA-3 and TW-3) featuring steel-tube fuselage construction; Consolidated also assumed a contract for twenty TW-3's. Fleet and Clark then improved the design to create the Consolidated PT-1, which became the primary trainer for both Army and Navy until 1935. It retained the steel tubing, eliminated engine hoods, thereby both reducing cost and improving the pilot's view, and was so stable that it was virtually impossible to put it into a spin.[44] A contract for 50 of the planes in 1923 necessitated larger quarters for the company plus more skilled labor than was available in Rhode Island; Consolidated therefore moved in 1924 to Buffalo and occupied a large building that had been used by Curtiss as a temporary wartime factory.[45]

Two other entries of the early 1920's deserve attention. One was the Stout Metal Airplane Company, founded in Detroit, Michigan, in 1923. Its founder, William Bushnell Stout, had been both engineer and journalist.[46] He attended Hamline University in St. Paul and the neighboring University of Minnesota but because of eye trouble was never graduated. For a while he was aviation correspondent for the *Chicago Tribune* and edited a magazine called *Aerial Age*. In 1913 he became chief engineer of the Scripps-Booth Motor Company and during the war took charge of Packard's aeronautical division. His idea for a metal airplane came shortly after the end of the war when he saw the potential of duralumin, an aluminum alloy combining strength with lightness.[47] He then contracted to build an all-metal torpedo plane for the Navy for $50,000. It crashed on its test flight and the Navy lost interest, but Stout was able to raise $128,000 in thousand-dollar subscriptions to start his company, largely from Detroit automobile men. The list of subscribers included Walter Briggs, Edsel Ford, Charles F. Kettering, William S. Knudsen, Edward G. Budd, Roy D. Chapin, Walter P. Chrysler, R. L. Stranahan, Harvey Firestone, Paul W. Litchfield, and Ransom E. Olds—all, Stout says, duly warned by him that the chances were against their getting their money back.[48]

Stout's claim to have built the first American all-metal airplane appears to be valid, but he was only partially a pioneer. During the war the Air Service Laboratory in Pittsburgh, Pennsylvania, experimented with rolled steel as a covering for wings and fuselages, but steel thin enough to be usable for airframes buckled easily and was very difficult to handle.[49] Stout's design was basically similar to the existing German Junkers transport, an all-metal, cantilevered high-wing monoplane with a corrugated skin that was merely a covering and gave no structural support.[50] Neither Junkers nor Stout tried to use the fully stressed smooth metal skin already developed by Dr. A. K. Rohrbach in Germany.

A year after Stout's company was organized it was acquired by Henry Ford, to the accompaniment of much fanfare and anticipation that Ford would perform the same kind of miracles in aviation as he had in highway transportation.[51] Stout's plane thereupon became the famous Ford trimotor, the Tin Goose, one of the most popular transport aircraft of the 1920's. It had the merits of durability and ease of handling; it could take off and land on short runways, a quality that kept it in service in remote parts of the world long after more modern types had replaced it on the regular airways. As a passenger carrier, however, it had definite limitations. The vibration of its metal skin caused a deafening racket inside the small cabin. With Ford to back it, Stout's company was in a securer position than most of its competitors, but Stout himself soon found, as did a good many others, that Henry Ford was a difficult man to work for. Ford persistently interfered with design until in 1930 Stout gave up and left. Two years later the manufacture of Ford planes became so unprofitable that Ford abandoned it.

Less highly publicized at the time than the Ford-Stout operation was the appearance on the American aviation scene of the great Dutch aeronautical engineer, Anthony Fokker. He had dominated German aircraft design and production during the First World War but afterward found opportunities in Europe limited, and in 1922 came to the United States. He established the Atlantic Aircraft Corporation in 1924 and put a three-engined transport plane on the market.[52] It had a plywood stressed skin on a frame of welded steel tubes and enjoyed considerable success, but the main part of the Atlantic Aircraft story has to come later.

The astonishing rise of Wichita, Kansas, as the nation's principal center for the manufacture of private planes started in the early 1920's. Wichitans attribute the rise to the city's location in the heart of a vast plain constituting the largest natural airport in the country,[53] but this claim could be made for any number of places in the same approximate longitude. The Wichita achievement was fundamentally entrepreneurial. A well-financed beginning attracted talent to the city and became the stem from which other companies proliferated.

Commercial aircraft manufacturing in Wichita began with a partnership in 1919 between Jacob M. Moellendick, a Wichita oil man, E. M. Laird, a Chicago, Illinois, banker who had been experimenting with airplanes since 1910, and William A. Burke, an Oklahoman who had been a flight instructor during the war and who then became an exhibition flyer.[54] Moellendick and Burke subscribed $15,000 each, and Laird contributed designs and equipment he had been working with in Chicago. They were initially the E. M. Laird Company, but soon purchased (for $19,000) the name and property of an unsuccessful flying service called the Wichita Airplane Company, of which Moellendick was also the principal stockholder. Its first product, designed by Laird, was a three-seater, open-cockpit biplane with a 90 h.p. Curtiss OX-5 engine.

It performed well enough to justify expanding the firm. Among those added to the technical staff were Lloyd C. Stearman, a student in architecture who became a naval aviator during the war, and Walter H. Beech, also a product of military aviation training.[55] The enterprise was successful enough commercially and technically, with output reaching four planes a month in 1922, but Moellendick, who ultimately put $300,000 into the business, seems to have had a capacity for antagonizing his associates. Laird left in 1923, and the company was reorganized as the Swallow Airplane Manufacturing Company. A year later Beech and Stearman left because Moellendick refused to adopt metal construction.[56] They founded a new company, Travel Air, with a new partner, Clyde V. Cessna. A former garage mechanic from Enid, Oklahoma, Cessna had been successfully in business in Wichita for some years and in 1917 had actually made the first plane built in Wichita, a small monoplane with a 6-cylinder air-cooled engine.[57] In 1925 Wichita was not as yet the center of the private plane industry but could be considered as securely established in the field.

Perhaps the most obscure of the new entrants was the Sikorsky Aero Engineering Company, incorporated March 15, 1923, by a small group of Russian refugees led by one of the world's most brilliant aeronautical designers, Igor Sikorsky. He had already distinguished himself as the builder of the world's first multi-engined aircraft, a four-motored bomber constructed for the Russian Army in 1913.[58] It had four 100 h.p. engines and a gross weight loaded of 10,340 pounds. It was the prototype for 70 such bombers built and successfully used by the Russians during the First World War. Sikorsky left his country during the Revolution and made his way to the United States; he founded the aircraft company in an attempt to make a living for himself and some of his fellow exiles. Most of the capital came from Arnold Dickinson, a Fitchburg, Massachusetts, businessman, and there was one subscription of $5,000 by Sergei Rachmaninoff, who became a vice-president of the company.[59] The first aircraft undertaken was an all-metal, two-engined transport, put together on a farm belonging to a friend near Roosevelt Field, Long Island.

The Outlook

This influx into the airframe industry gives a somewhat misleading picture of activity. The market for new airplanes of all types never exceeded 800 a year between 1920 and

1925—enough to keep an aircraft industry alive, but just barely. Besides the firms mentioned, there were many others that appeared briefly and obscurely, most to vanish with no trace. Competition for the slender volume of business was intense, and a company's future could easily turn on winning or losing a single contract. Boeing's success in securing an order in 1921 for 200 MB-3A Thomas-Morse planes has already been mentioned. It was the largest single order given to an airframe manufacturer since the war; Thomas-Morse was crippled, but Boeing was established as one of the country's principal builders of military aircraft.[60] At the same time Glenn Martin was complaining that awards to others to build Martin bombers had compelled him to discharge 300 employees, keeping only a development staff of 90.[61] Curtiss had an order for 50 Martin bombers at $18,900 each, plus $220,000 worth of spare parts, and L. W. F. (Lawson, Willard, and Fowler of College Point, Long Island) was making 35 for $23,000 each. Martin himself had bid for 50 at $22,485; he did not believe the work could be done at the contract price and regarded L. W. F. as unreliable. Whether he was right or not is immaterial. His experience offers an illustration of the hit-or-miss system in use for the awarding of military contracts.

The experience of Grover Loening offers another example of the problems confronting the airframe manufacturer. He won the Collier Trophy in 1921, an award made annually for the greatest achievement in American aviation as demonstrated by actual use during the year, with a design for an "aerial yacht," a seaplane with an enclosed cabin for three or four passengers.[62] The plane sold well as a private plane for several years. Despite this distinction, Loening complained that lack of government orders might compel him to stop commercial work, and he pointed out a feature of the aircraft business that would in time be recognized as fundamental: no private company could bear the cost of development work on commercial planes unless it had support from government contracts.[63] He eventually got his government contracts by designing the Loening amphibian, a plane following the general lines of the De Havilland 4 but with a flying-boat hull and the novel feature of retractable landing gear.[64]

Production figures for the period 1920–1925, as shown in Table 1, tell their own story.

Table 1. Aircraft Production, 1920–1925

Year	Total Aircraft	Military	Civilian
1920	328	256	72
1921	437	389	48
1922	263	226	37
1923	747	687	56
1924	377	317	60
1925	784	447	342

Source: *Aerospace Facts and Figures, 1964*, p. 24.

There was no systematic pattern on which the manufacturers could plan. The industry was perforce living hand to mouth, even the stronger firms.

Yet for those willing and able to stay in the aircraft industry there were some encouraging signs. Public interest in aviation was gradually reawakening. The transatlantic flight of four Curtiss-built Navy seaplanes in 1919 dramatized the potentialities of aviation, both military and commercial. So did the first round-the-world flight, made by Army planes in 1924. The four that started the trip were DWC's (Douglas World Cruisers), biplanes built by Douglas with a single 420 h.p. Liberty engine. Two of these completed the journey. One crashed in Alaska early in the expedition, and near the end, one fell into the sea between Scotland and Iceland and was replaced by a fifth aircraft of the same series.[65] The trip required 172 days, although actual flying time was 15 days, 11 hours, and 7 minutes.

This growing public consciousness about aviation was brought to a head by General William S. "Billy" Mitchell. First there were the much-disputed bombing tests off the Virginia Capes on surrendered German warships and on the unfinished U.S.S. "Washington." The arguments over these tests need not be revived here. It was regrettable that the technical and tactical lessons that should have been learned were obscured by the superficial and meaningless "bomber versus battleship" quarrel.[66] The bitterness was intensified by Mitchell's intemperate attacks on his service superiors at the time of the disaster involving the Navy dirigible "Shenandoah" in 1925, and by the subsequent court-martial proceedings against him. From the historian's point of view, in the interest of having the history of American aviation presented accurately, it is unfortunate that the publicity given to the Mitchell controversy has overshadowed the solid work then being done to advance military aviation by men such as Admiral William A. Moffett, chief of the Navy's Bureau of Aeronautics, and Generals Mason Patrick and Andrew A. Foulois, Mitchell's own associates in the Army Air Service.[67] Nevertheless Mitchell's flamboyance and assertiveness did serve a useful public purpose: they impressed on the American people the fact that the United States had no aviation policy and urgently needed one.

2. Toward Stability

If, as General Mitchell's admirers believe, he deliberately sacrificed his career in order to get the plight of American aviation before the government and people, then he achieved his purpose. The results undoubtedly fell short of his hopes, since the policies eventually adopted rejected the extreme air power doctrines that Mitchell shared with the Italian General Giulio Douhet. However, any reasonable consideration of what was practical and acceptable in the middle 1920's indicates that aviation policy at this time was formulated wisely and well.

President Calvin Coolidge was not, after all, a man to be stampeded into hasty action and inadequately considered remedies. The country demanded an aviation policy, and the country would get one, but only after thorough investigation. The Aircraft Board appointed by Coolidge was a body of exceptional quality. At its head was his Amherst classmate, Dwight W. Morrow, then at the height of a distinguished career in business and public service. Its secretary was William F. Durand, one of the country's leading aeronautical engineers, a member of the National Advisory Committee for Aeronautics since its inception in 1915 and chairman from 1916 to 1918. The other members were General James G. Harbord, Rear Admiral Frank E. Fletcher,

Howard E. Coffin, distinguished automotive engineer, Senator Hiram Bingham of Connecticut, formerly professor of political science at Yale, Congressmen Carl Vinson, for many years chairman of the House Committee on Naval Affairs, and James E. Parker, and Judge Arthur C. Denison of the U.S. Circuit Court. The Morrow Board, as it came to be called, held extensive hearings and published its report late in 1925.[1]

The condition of the aircraft industry as it emerged from the Board's findings revealed its problems in the postwar years. Since 1917 it had undergone twenty investigations by various government bodies, all without result.[2] The system of bidding on military contracts, as described in Chapter 1, gave no protection to any right in design, and on experimental work the manufacturers usually lost money. In civil aviation the Post Office was offering coast-to-coast air mail service by the end of 1925, but provision for passenger transport was negligible, and no private operator could remain in business at that time without subsidy. This fact was already recognized in Europe. France, for instance, was spending about $12.5 million annually on civil aviation and Great Britain $2.5 million.[3] General Hugh A. Drum, assistant chief of staff, testified that the United States had fifteen to twenty aircraft factories and three firms making aircraft engines.[4] Current production was 40 to 50 planes a month. In the event of war the general estimated that by converting other suitable plants, output could be raised to 400 a month in six months and 3,350 a month at the end of a year.

The industry itself was asked to state its position and submitted a four-point program:

1. Formulation of a long-range procurement policy to secure continuity of production.
2. Ending of competition by government plants. This point referred less to outright manufacturing than to extensive repair work done in government establishments, some of it amounting to complete rebuilding.
3. Ending of destructive price policies. This was a protest against the system of awarding contracts, which the manu-

facturers claimed was under unduly inflexible regulations that made contracting officers of the government over-exacting.

4. Recognition of proprietary rights in design.[5]

This program was reinforced by testimony from individuals. Reuben H. Fleet advocated a ten-year policy of development and procurement, placement of orders to keep factories operating, plus support for building airports and providing navigational aids.[6] C. L. Lawrance claimed that repair work done by the Post Office amounted to new building and argued that government construction should be limited to experimental models.[7] He was opposed to having a finished production model handed over to a manufacturer, because then there was no incentive to make improvements. C. M. Keys, president of Curtiss Aeroplane and Motor, pointed to the retardation of design work under the existing bidding system: no one was going to continue design on a model whose production had been awarded to a competitor.[8]

These contentions admittedly had a large element of special pleading; yet the only alternative to accepting the substance of the industry's proposals was socialization of aviation, a solution hardly likely to commend itself to American opinion of the Coolidge era. No aircraft industry anywhere in the world has been able to exist without a substantial measure of governmental support. The only real choice has been between outright public ownership and operation and the use of public funds to maintain some degree of competitive private enterprise. The United States was already committed to the latter policy—fortunately so, because subsequent experience among countries engaging in aircraft manufacturing would show that it yielded far more satisfactory results in terms of technological advance. The Morrow Board's achievement was to provide for effective implementation of this policy.

The first step in the development of a comprehensive national policy for aviation came early in 1925, ahead of the Morrow Board's work but clearly foreshadowing the direction that subsequent policy would take. This was the Kelly Air Mail Act of 1925, providing for the transfer of the actual operation of air mail lines from the Post Office to private enterprise. This step in itself was a stimulus to aircraft manufacturing, because while the Post Office might be satisfied to keep its aircraft (principally De Havilland 4's) operating as long as possible, with a minimum of replacement, private carriers would be in the market for improved planes with low operating costs.[9]

The Morrow Board's recommendations produced three important pieces of legislation. First was the Air Commerce Act of May 1926. It established a Bureau of Air Commerce in the Department of Commerce, with authority to establish safety regulations, provide for airways and navigational aids, encourage the building of airports, and regulate civil aviation generally, except for the allocation of mail routes and the award of mail contracts, which were the responsibility of the Post Office. The other two were five-year military procurement programs whereby the Army would have 1,600 first-line aircraft and the Navy 1,000 by 1931.[10] The demand of the Mitchell partisans for a separate air force was rejected, although the Air Corps Act, in which the Army program was incorporated, sought to give the air arm more status and autonomy within the existing military establishment. This decision, however, did not affect the aircraft industry. An independent air force might have ordered somewhat different types of aircraft, but in the middle 1920's the range of possible alternatives was limited.

It would be overstating the case to give the Morrow Board the entire credit for the manifest improvement in the condition of American aviation, and the aircraft industry in particular, from 1926 on. There were other factors. The doubling of Federal expenditures on aviation, from $6 million in 1922 to $12 million in 1926, before the five-year programs were put into the budget, was bound to have a stimulating effect, as was the simple fact that by the middle of the decade, war-surplus engines and planes were at last wearing out.[11] In addition, the research work of the National Advisory Committee for Aeronautics (NACA) and the military services was yielding beneficial results for the industry. Nevertheless, the formulation and implementation of a rational, coherent national policy was necessary to provide a secure foundation for future growth.

Aeronautical Research

In the area of aeronautical research, as in the field of aviation generally, the United States moved slowly after the great achievement of the Wrights. The major powers of Europe all had government-supported aeronautical research establishments before the First World War, whereas the NACA was created in 1915 only after prolonged agitation by leaders of American science and technology, including, for example, Alexander Graham Bell.[12] Even then the charter got through Congress as a rider to the Naval Appropriation Bill and was accepted reluctantly by President Wilson, who was concerned that establishing an organization for aeronautical research while war was raging in Europe might reflect on American neutrality. However, once the step was taken Wilson and his successors in the White House saw to it that the caliber of the NACA membership was of outstanding quality.[13]

For its first few years the NACA was necessarily absorbed by the specific problems raised by the First World War, and since it had no research facilities of its own its role was purely advisory. It acquired its first laboratory in 1920, at Langley Field, Virginia. The Committee was also asked for advice on matters such as the regulation of air traffic; it was only after such functions were assigned to the Bureau of Air Commerce that the NACA was able to devote itself to research. Consequently the flow of technical information from the NACA to the aircraft industry increased markedly after 1926.

At this period the greater part of its effort went into aerodynamic research. This policy was adopted because the agency had to operate within a limited budget and it was calculated that greater returns would accrue from a concentration on aerodynamics than from concentration on such items as power plants and structures, both of which require elaborate and expensive equipment.[14] In any event, the military services and industry were doing a considerable amount of work on power plants and structures, so that it made good sense to avoid unnecessary duplication.

In its chosen field the accomplishments of NACA research

were impressive. Two examples can be selected as outstanding and understandable. First, the NACA cowling for radial air-cooled engines brought the agency the Collier Trophy in 1928. The cowling essentially gave a streamlining effect while still permitting a free flow of cooling air around the engine. As described in the agency's report for 1928, it increased the speed of a Curtiss AT-5A pursuit trainer from 118 to 137 m.p.h., the equivalent of an additional 83 h.p. without extra weight or cost.[15] Second, in the early multi-engined monoplanes of the 1920's the engines were hung from, or sometimes mounted above, the wings. By 1930 NACA research had made it clear that much better performance could be obtained by fairing the engine nacelles into the leading edge of the wings.[16] The engine compartments, that is, were built into the wings.

The other fields of aeronautics were by no means ignored. There were useful contributions to the development of engines and fuels, and a very interesting exploration of jet propulsion. A report made in 1923 for the NACA by Dr. Edgar Buckingham of the Bureau of Standards made it clear that the jet engine was technically possible, but that at the flying speeds then attainable (a maximum of 250 m.p.h. was envisioned) the jet would be heavier, more complicated, and would consume much more fuel per horsepower than the piston engine.[17] Subsequent studies by the NACA and others pointed to the same conclusion: in the existing state of the aeronautical art jet propulsion would be more expensive and less satisfactory than the piston engine driving a propeller.

As was stated before, however, the bulk of the government's research and development work on aircraft power plants was done by the Army and Navy. Dr. Robert Schlaifer, the outstanding American scholar in this field, believes this division of responsibility between the two services yielded excellent results for the United States. For one thing, it avoided the neglect of the special requirements of naval aviation that had occurred in Great Britain and was painfully evident at the beginning of the Second World War.[18] For another, to quote Dr. Schlaifer:

The existence of two independent agencies meant that the mistakes of one were corrected in a surprisingly large number of instances by the actions of the other. Whatever may be the merits of the case for unification of the military services in other respects, there can be no doubt that the sponsorship and direction of development by two separate agencies brought results worth very much more than the cost.

The basic policy of both services was to finance research and development by the private engine manufacturers. The Air Corps engineering center at McCook Field made some attempts during the 1920's to carry engine development all the way to the prototype, but these efforts were unsatisfactory.[19] The manufacturers themselves preferred to include research and development in their overhead costs and count on recovering them from quantity sales of a successful design. The McCook Field contributions were in the form of research on specific problems such as improved cylinder design and the use of sodium and potassium nitrate in exhaust-valve stems to prevent overheating.[20] There was also important fuel research done at McCook Field. California gasolines gave better performance than others, but no one knew why. The research on the properties of gasoline was done by several people and not necessarily for aviation. The work of Charles F. Kettering, T. R. Midgley, and W. O. Boyd in developing ethyl gasolines, for example, was aimed primarily at eliminating knock in automobile engines. But the octane scale, discovered by Graham Edgar in 1926, found its first and most important application in aviation fuels, and much of the research on octane ratings and the establishment of Performance Numbers was done in Air Corps laboratories.[21]

The services also influenced the direction that aircraft engine manufacturing would take by policy decisions on the type of engines they wanted, specifically, in choosing between liquid and air cooling. The merits of the two types can be and have been argued at inconclusive length. All that needs to be said here is that each has its specific advantages, and the choice has to be made on the basis of the qualities desired in a particular plane, that is, on the emphasis to be given to such factors as performance at high altitudes, rate of climb, and so forth. The in-line liquid-cooled engine predominated at the end of the First World War and continued to be favored in Europe. In the United States the Army, while willing to encourage the development of air-cooled engines, continued to regard the liquid-cooled type as more suitable for fighter planes. The Navy Bureau of Aeronautics, on the other hand, committed itself fully to the air-cooled engine because it was more practical for carrier-borne aircraft, offering compactness and easier maintenance since there was no elaborate (and vulnerable) cooling system.[22]

The pioneer in American development of the radial air-cooled engine was Charles L. Lawrance, who began with an experimental 2-cylinder opposed engine in 1916. Three years later he designed a 3-cylinder engine with the cooperation of the Navy's Bureau of Steam Engineering, which was then in charge of aircraft as well as marine power plants.[23] Next, Lawrance brought out a 9-cylinder engine in 1921, which was described by a leading authority on the internal combustion engine as "definitely the prototype for the modern American radial air-cooled engine."[24] It had cast-aluminum cylinders with steel liners, a cast-aluminum crankcase, and was rated at 200 h.p. Its development was assisted by an order for 200 from the Navy. By this time responsibility for aircraft engines had been transferred to the Navy's Bureau of Aeronautics, and there, under the supervision of Admiral Moffett, it was in the hands of Captain Bruce Leighton, a man with positive ideas on what the Bureau's policy should be. He believed implicitly that the air-cooled engine best filled the Navy's needs, and he also believed that the primary responsibility for design as well as production should be left to the manufacturers.

Lawrance had the engine, or at least the basic design, that Leighton wanted, but the Lawrance Aero Engine Company was not equipped to manufacture in quantity. Consequently the Bureau of Aeronautics, whose fixed policy in any case was to have competing producers, undertook to interest the two large firms already in the aircraft engine field, Curtiss Aeroplane and Motor and Wright Aeronautical. Neither showed any marked enthusiasm. Curtiss already had a commanding position in the market with the 400 h.p. water-cooled D-12 and saw no reason to make a radical change. Wright was still manufacturing Hispano-Suizas, with a 200 h.p. water-cooled model as its principal product. Since, however, this engine was bought almost exclusively by the

Navy for ship-based airplanes, Leighton was able to push the company into air-cooled radials by refusing to buy any more Hispano-Suizas.[25] Wright Aeronautical made its move by the simple expedient of buying Lawrance's company. Then, with Lawrance as chief engineer and later as president, Wright Aeronautical more than made up for its initial reluctance by developing the Lawrance designs into a series of highly successful air-cooled radials, including the J-5 Whirlwind that powered Charles A. Lindbergh's "Spirit of St. Louis" across the Atlantic.[26]

The Wright-Lawrance merger meant that the Navy still had only one supplier of air-cooled engines. Curtiss remained aloof, except for an unsatisfactory development contract with the Army for an engine called R-1454.[27] The development work was divided between the company and McCook Field, and by the time the prototype was approaching completion better engines were already in production.

Competition came from within the Wright organization itself. In 1924 Frederick B. Rentschler, president of Wright Aeronautical, resigned because the directors decided to allocate to dividends funds that Rentschler wanted to apply to research and development.[28] Rentschler was one of the many people who had turned toward aviation because of the First World War. After graduating from Princeton in 1909, he had gone to work for his father's firm in Hamilton, Ohio, building stationary engines. When the war came he joined the Army, became a lieutenant in the Signal Corps, and found himself inspecting engines at the Wright-Martin factory. He stayed on and became the first president of Wright Aeronautical. It was paradoxical that after having had to be pushed by the Navy into switching from the Hispano-Suiza to the Lawrance engine he should resign because he felt his company was not putting enough effort into air-cooled engine research; Lawrance took his place at Wright Aeronautical.

Rentschler and a group of engineers who accompanied him out of Wright Aeronautical then founded a new company to concentrate on radial air-cooled engines. Financial support came from the Niles Tool Company (subsequently Niles-Bement-

Pond) in the form of a loan of $250,000, an agreement to underwrite the operation for another half million if necessary, and a lease of the company's idle Pratt and Whitney machine tool plant in Hartford, Connecticut.[29] The willingness of Niles Tool to support Rentschler's experiment was largely due to the fact that its president at this time was Edward A. Deeds, who retained an interest in aviation in spite of his harrowing experiences in the First World War. Since the name Pratt and Whitney had an established reputation for mechanical precision, Rentschler simply took it over for his company. The other inheritance from the earlier concern was that Hartford had a supply of skilled labor available for the exacting task of building aircraft engines.

The Niles Tool advance was definitely risk capital. All Rentschler had in prospect was knowledge that the Navy wanted an improvement on the Wright Whirlwind. Actually the initiative came from Chance Vought. He had a contract for scout planes expiring, and he proposed to the Bureau of Aeronautics the building of a new scout bomber capable of being used as a fighter if he could get an engine capable of 350 h.p. but weighing not more than 650 pounds.[30] Naturally Wright Aeronautical was asked to meet this challenge and in response designed the Wright R-1200 Simoon. But the Simoon never got beyond the prototype stage, because in the meantime Rentschler had asked to be allowed to compete. Admiral Moffett was anxious to encourage competition in the building of air-cooled radials, but he could not legally award a contract to a firm that existed only on paper, even if the paper included a promising design. However, the Bureau of Aeronautics did have $90,000 available for experimental purposes. Moffett agreed to use this money to buy six experimental engines from Pratt and Whitney; this covered about half the development cost of the Wasp engine.[31] The first Wasp was ready for trial on December 24, 1925, just six months after the founding of the company. It met the 650-pound weight requirement and delivered 425 h.p.

The qualities of the Wasp were clear enough for the Navy to place an immediate order for 200, even though production costs for this quantity of a novel design were so uncertain that the price was fixed by taking the price of the Packard 1500 liquid-cooled engine. The Wasp was used for Vought's plane, the O2SU Corsair; the Boeing FB6 and F28-1, carrier-borne fighters; and the Boeing Model 40, the mail plane that started a new era in commercial air transport.[32]

Industrial Growth

The effects of these legislative and technical developments would require time to make themselves fully manifest in the design and manufacture of aircraft. The industry had to adapt itself to changed economic conditions and digest the constant advances in aeronautical science and technology. It took just about ten years to combine the aerodynamic advances and the improvements in engines and fuels into operational airplanes,[33] and in the interim, especially at the beginning, there was necessarily a good deal of trial and error. The airplane of 1925 was still predominantly the fabric, strut, and wire creation of its pioneering days, with some indication of future trends in types like the Ford trimotor. The airframe industry was just learning the techniques of working with metal; it is significant of the state of the art that Fokker, with all his skill, preferred to use plywood for his fuselages rather than follow Stout's example. Yet 1925–1926 is selected by a recognized authority as the period when American transport aircraft finally began to match and even go ahead of European.[34] Military aircraft are more difficult to judge because of the greater specialization and consequent variety of types.

Just as it took time for technological advances to be incorporated into aircraft design, so it took time also for improvement in the economic condition of aviation to have noticeable effects on the structure of the aircraft industry. Between 1925 and 1928 the most conspicuous change was the appearance of new competitors. Of these, the most important in terms of subsequent growth was the Lockheed Aircraft Company, incorporated in December 1926.[35] This marked the return to aviation of one of the two Loughead brothers who had been aircraft builders in Santa Barbara, California, between 1913 and 1921. When this company was liquidated, Malcolm Lockheed (the spelling of the name was legally changed at this time) had already turned his talents to the automobile industry as the designer of the first effective four-wheel hydraulic brake system. Allan dabbled in real estate, a standard procedure for a California businessman, but his heart was still in aviation, and he returned to it as soon as the prospects brightened. The earlier Loughead company had been working on a plane, the S-1, designed by John K. Northrop. It was a single-engined biplane with a monocoque plywood fuselage.[36] It was intended as a sports plane, but it could not push its way into a market crowded with war surplus Curtiss Jennies.

Northrop, with Allan Lockheed's help, went to Douglas as a designer and remained there until 1926, when he rejoined Lockheed to work out a design for a transport plane based on the S-1. They succeeded in interesting Fred S. Keeler, a brick and tile manufacturer, in their project. He put up $25,000 for 51 per cent of the common stock and all the preferred stock in the new company, and with this they put the first Vega on the market in 1927. It was a small plane, carrying only three or four passengers, but it represented a significant step in design. It was a high-wing, wooden monoplane, with a monocoque fuselage and the wings cantilevered so as to reduce the amount of external bracing required.[37] The first Vega was sold to George Hearst, son of the publisher, for $12,500—actually at a loss, but the Hearst name was good advertising. So, too, was the use of a Vega by Captain George Hubert Wilkins in a flight from Alaska to Spitzbergen in 1928 and in subsequent aerial explorations of Antarctica. A successor to the Vega, the Lockheed Orion of 1931, was the first American transport equipped with retractable landing gear.[38]

A second important newcomer was the Fairchild Engine and Airplane Corporation. It began in 1920 as the Fairchild Aerial Camera Corporation, founded by Sherman M. Fairchild to make cameras for aerial photography and to conduct aerial surveys.[39] Then, partly because he could find no planes suitable for his aerial surveys, Fairchild established two companies in 1925, the Fairchild Airplane Manufacturing Corporation and the Fairchild Engine Corporation. The latter was located in Hagerstown, Maryland, home of the parent company; the airframes were built in Farmingdale, Long Island, convenient to Roosevelt Field. The prototype Fairchild, FC-1, was test-flown in 1926.[40] It was designed as a single-engined, high-wing monoplane, with the unusual feature for a landplane of folding wings.

The third noteworthy newcomer was the Ryan Aeronautical Company, which evolved from a sightseeing and charter flight business established by T. Claude Ryan in San Diego, California, in 1922.[41] Early in 1925 Ryan converted some war surplus Standards into five-passenger planes and began regular service between San Diego and Los Angeles, later adding to his fleet the original Douglas Cloudster, remodeled to carry ten passengers, a large load for that day. Shortly afterward Ryan began to do his own manufacturing, aiming for the potential market opened by the transfer of air mail routes. He produced the Ryan M-1 high-wing monoplanes, best known through the one that became Lindbergh's "Spirit of St. Louis." Ryan, it may be pointed out, was the second airframe manufacturer to go into business and stay in it in southern California. Lockheed was third, in terms of continuing corporate organization. This was hardly evidence of a trend, since only Douglas at the time could have been rated as a major producer. As of 1925, indeed, California had only four firms making aircraft or parts, other than engines and tires, compared with fifteen in New York.[42]

In the middle 1920's the established airframe firms were leading a slightly less hand-to-mouth existence, but only slightly. Orders were bigger; capital investments in 1926 had trebled from the $5 million of 1920.[43] Nevertheless, although the Morrow Board reforms would bring some improvement, the industry remained subject to the uncertainties of the government's contracting system. An experience of Consolidated is illuminating. The incident is best narrated directly from the company's own history: [44]

The Air Corps Act of 1926 marked a turning point for military aviation. It set up a five-year purchasing program for both services, and spurred many advances in plane and engine design.

The Army's initial appropriation would let it purchase 150 or more trainers, depending on the cost. (The price paid for Consolidated planes had declined steadily as output increased—from $9,800 for the first PT's to $7,750 in the fall of 1926, and further reductions were projected.) Fleet proposed to Major General Mason Patrick, the Air Corps chief, that a single contract for 150 trainers be negotiated. This would let Consolidated order material in quantity, maintain production without letups, and share the savings from mass production with the Air Corps. Patrick would make no commitment beyond an order for fifty.

Fleet gambled on his own judgment—"I knew nobody had a better trainer, and nobody could design a better one." He ordered steel tubing, spruce and other materials for 250 aircraft and kept the production line humming. The orders kept coming in; from the Army at intervals of sixty and ninety days, until its contracts totaled 170 planes; and from the Navy (which continued holding competitions that Consolidated always won).

By the middle of 1927, Consolidated showed a cumulative profit of $867,000 on the service trainers it had built since 1923. The Air Corps asked to see the company's books (a privilege not yet granted by law), and followed up with a demand for a $300,000 refund of excess profits.

Fleet and the directors felt that the company had no alternative, since the services were their sole customer. Fleet negotiated one practical compromise which benefitted customer and company alike, however. He pointed out that a $300,00 payment would vanish into the general fund of the U.S. Treasury. Patrick agreed to "take it out in trade" by letting Consolidated build fifty trainers, currently priced at $6,000 for a nominal charge of one dollar each.

Admiral Moffett refused to take part in this transaction, either in seeking a refund or accepting the share (26 per cent) the Navy might have claimed. Where the Air Corps would make successive contracts on the basis of a single design competition, the Navy held separate competitions for each order, no matter how small, and Moffett held that Consolidated had won each Navy contract fairly.

On the basis of performance Fleet was justified in his faith in his trainer, and it made sense for both the company and the services to take advantage of the economies of quantity production. Nevertheless, Major General Patrick had some justification for refusing Fleet's initial request for the 150-plane order. Fleet was really attempting a tour de force that would have given him a monopoly on training planes for the services in the conditions of the period. It may be argued that he already had this monopoly, but with a rapidly changing technology like aeronautics it was quite possible for someone to come along with a better trainer at any moment, and Patrick was quite right in refusing to commit his entire trainer appropriation in one contract. Douglas sold well over 200 of its O-2 observation planes to the Air Corps in the same way, the largest single order being for 75 in 1925.[45] The situations were not identical, since the O-2 was constantly modified, running in series through O-2K, but it does not appear that Consolidated was singled out for discrimination when Fleet's request was rejected. The claim for return of excess profits is another matter. The Air Corps took the position that while the contract price was calculated on an order for 50 planes, the company had actually been able to spread its costs from the beginning over several times that number. Fleet insisted that he had taken a risk and was entitled to his reward.

The technicalities of military contracts, however, were overshadowed by spectacular developments in the economic structure of the aircraft industry. The active promotion of commercial aviation provided by the Air Mail and Air Commerce Acts began to become operative just as the great bull market of the 1920's was reaching its peak and funds for speculative enterprises, as aviation still was, were more readily available than they had been previously. By the end of 1928 investment in the aircraft industry had risen from the $15 million of 1926 to $125 million and aviation securities were skyrocketing.[46] It was not just speculative mania, despite the number of would-be millionaires who bought Seaboard Air Line stock under the impression that they were getting into aviation. With air mail routes multiplying and more efficient aircraft types coming into production to offer increasing prospects of profitable operation, the future of commercial air transport was highly promising.

Changes in national policy and in aeronautical technology would not have meant much to the general public. Even the highly publicized Mitchell court-martial was of limited value in stimulating any general enthusiasm about the nonmilitary possibilities of aviation; the issues were misunderstood then and have remained so ever since. But in 1927 Charles A. Lindbergh flew from New York to Paris, nonstop and singlehanded. It was not the first nonstop transatlantic flight. That was achieved in 1919 by two British flyers, John W. (later Sir John) Alcock and Arthur W. Brown, flying from Newfoundland to Ireland in a twin-engined Vickers Vimy, a bomber of First World War vintage. Lindbergh, however, set the American nation on fire, even if there were very few capable of appreciating the superb technical skill that made completion of the flight possible. More than any other single factor, his flight sold the American people on commercial aviation. The solo flight without mishap from airfield to airfield (Roosevelt Field to Le Bourget) was a convincing advertisement for the future of travel by air.

Lighter than Air

The 1920's were also the period of greatest enthusiasm in the United States for the possibilities, both military and commercial, of lighter-than-air craft. There appeared to be every reason for the United States to take the leadership in airship development, which had so far been enjoyed exclusively by Germany. German design information became available at the end of the First World War. It became available to others as well, and Britain and France both had ambitions in this field; but the United States had the inestimable advantage of possessing the world's only supply of helium gas, which has the desirable properties of being both lighter than air and nonflammable.

American activity with airships began effectively with the building of a number of nonrigid "blimps" for antisubmarine use, following a successful British example in this field.[47] These, however, were far less glamorous than the big dirigibles that the Germans alone seemed to have the know-how to construct. At the end of the First World War the Navy was markedly interested in dirigibles because of their possibilities for long-range reconnaissance and became the principal agent of American dirigible development.

At the end of the war the Navy acquired three airships, all of German origin. ZR-1, the U.S.S. "Shenandoah," and ZR-2, built in Britain as R-38, were both based on a Zeppelin that had landed in France in 1916.[48] ZR-2 broke up on a trial flight in

England in 1922 and so never served in the Navy. The "Shenandoah" was designed at the Navy's Bureau of Aeronautics by Starling and Charles Burgess and built at the Naval Aircraft Factory in Philadelphia, Pennsylvania.[49] She made her first flight in 1923. The third, ZR-3, the U.S.S. "Los Angeles," was a reparations payment, built by the Luftschiffbau Zeppelin Company in Friedrichshafen and delivered in 1924.[50] The "Los Angeles," which survived until she was scrapped in 1940, was shorter and higher than her predecessors. It developed that to facilitate wartime production the Germans had adopted a pencil-shaped design that sacrificed some strength but allowed all the duralumin rings of the fuselage to be made the same size.[51] This structural difference probably helped to account for the loss of the first two ships.

In 1924 interest in dirigibles was accentuated by a favorable NACA report on their commercial possibilities. The report recommended adoption of the Zeppelin design, since nothing better was in sight.[52] Consequently, at the instigation of the government the Goodyear Tire & Rubber Company, which had already built over 1,000 observation balloons and 100 blimps for the Army and Navy, secured the American rights to the Zeppelin patents and formed the Goodyear Zeppelin Corporation.[53] Goodyear also acquired the services of Dr. Karl Arnstein, designer of the wartime Zeppelins. German-American cooperation in transatlantic airship service was contemplated. In addition, in 1924 the Navy began to plan an ambitious lighter-than-air program including two very large dirigibles, under the supervision of Commander Garland Fulton, who had studied under Hunsaker at M.I.T.

The disastrous wreck of the "Shenandoah" in the fall of 1925 dampened enthusiasm for these big airships, so that although the Navy persisted and got authorization for its two dirigibles in 1926, Congress did not appropriate the funds for another two years. The contracts were let late in 1928 to Goodyear Zeppelin; there was no practical alternative. The price for the first ship, the U.S.S. "Akron" (ZRS-4), was $5,375,000; for the second, the U.S.S. "Macon" (ZRS-5), $2,450,000.[54] The "Akron" was completed in 1931, the "Macon" in 1933. Except for the German "Hindenburg," they were the largest airships ever built: 785 feet long with 6,500,000 cubic feet of gas volume.[55] Their unique feature, apart from their size, was that they were flying aircraft carriers. Each had a hangar that would accommodate four small airplanes (Curtiss F9C's); there was a special "skyhook" gear for lowering the planes from the hangar for release and picking them up again on return.

The possibilities of the flying aircraft carrier were never to be adequately tested. The "Akron" was lost in a storm off the New Jersey coast in 1933 with almost her entire complement, including Admiral Moffett. Two years later the "Macon" was similarly wrecked off Point Sur, California, although this time with only two fatalities. Public opinion then turned against the big airships, which certainly had an unenviable record of disaster. At about this same time France's "Dixmude" disappeared over the Mediterranean without trace, and Britain's R-101 crashed on her maiden voyage with no survivors. The destruction of the "Hindenburg" in 1937 seemed to drive the point home.

The dirigibles had their defenders. It could be argued that they were not inherently unsafe; in each case where evidence was available there was human failure. The "Shenandoah" was sent on a barnstorming tour for publicity at a time when equinoctial storms were to be expected; the "Akron" was a victim of navigational error that sent her into instead of away from the storm; the "Macon" was lost because of faulty human reaction to a minor structural failure.[56]

Elsewhere, it was clear that the R-101 was a victim of political dogmatism. Her design was altered without adequate testing, her construction was rushed, and she set off for India in the face of adverse weather reports, all to demonstrate that the government could do a better job of building airships than private enterprise.[57] The R-100, sister but not identical twin of the R-101, was built by Vickers on a straight fixed-price contract. She went to Canada and back safely but was never allowed to fly again after the loss of the R-101. The "Hindenburg" disaster would not have occurred if helium had been available to the Germans, but this was refused by Secretary of the Interior Harold L. Ickes on the plausible enough ground that the Nazi government could not be trusted to use the gas only for peaceful purposes.[58]

However, whatever defense might be offered for the airships, the record of catastrophe stopped further construction. It would have stopped eventually anyway. Majestic and impressive as they looked, the giant dirigibles were still aeronautical dinosaurs. Jerome C. Hunsaker, who was as close to the heart of the American rigid-airship program as anyone, has characterized it as a false start, undertaken in mistaken imitation of the Germans and made obsolete while in progress by the development of airplanes and flying boats that would match the airship's range and payload and outdo it in speed and reliability.[59] With better luck, the big airship might have lasted some years longer but could not have avoided extinction. The American program did have one useful by-product. Duralumin, the copper alloy of aluminum first employed in Germany for airship frames, was not made in the United States until the Navy needed it for its own dirigibles and persuaded the Aluminum Company of America to manufacture it.[60]

The strictures on the large airship did not apply to the smaller nonrigid types. The familiar Goodyear blimps continued to be built. Apart from their advertising value, they were useful to train crews for the dirigibles and continued to have military value in the Second World War as antisubmarine weapons. The Goodyear Zeppelin Corporation itself was dissolved late in 1939 because the implication of German affiliation had become an embarrassment.[61] A new Goodyear Aircraft Corporation replaced it.

3. Aviation on Wall Street

The stimulation of interest in aviation by Lindbergh and the host of imitators who followed him coincided with the great boom period of the late 1920's. This circumstance, in conjunction with the advance of aeronautical technology, had far-reaching consequences for the organization of the American aircraft industry. For a time it appeared that aviation, both manufacturing and transport, would conform to the customary pattern of American business and come to be dominated by a few very large firms. The economic collapse and subsequent political complications retarded this trend. Some traces of the mergers survived, with lasting effects on the structure of the aircraft industry. These big combines, moreover, were involved in some significant technological and operational advances that might conceivably have come more slowly without this concentration of financial and technical resources. This part of the story will be discussed later. The formation of the mergers themselves has to be described first.

The Mergers

It was predictable in the light of American industrial history that, once the uncertainties of pioneering had been surmounted, a move to consolidate aircraft firms would be made, and by 1928 conditions were certainly ripe. Not only was the bull market eager to pour funds into almost anything labeled as "merger," but there was clear opportunity in a situation where, to quote J. H. Kindelberger, "There were three hundred aircraft factories, including those where you had to shove the cow aside to see the airplane." [1] The first major combination was solidly rooted in the development of the industry. It started in 1927 when Boeing Air Transport, Inc., instituted service between Chicago and San Francisco, using planes of the Boeing Model 40 series, designed for two passengers and 1,200 pounds of mail and powered by Wasp engines.[2] With these Boeing was able to underbid its competitors on this first privately-operated transcontinental air mail route. From this auspicious start Boeing's transport activities expanded, with beneficial effects on the business of the Boeing Airplane Company, and this relationship set the pattern for the combinations of the period. There was every indication of rapid growth in air transport, and it appeared to make sense for a manufacturer to assure himself a share of the commercial market by a corporate relationship to one or more airlines. From that it was a logical step to envision an integrated organization operating its own airlines and building its own airframes, engines, and components.

Some of this, if not all, was certainly in William E. Boeing's mind when he chartered the Boeing Aircraft and Transport Corporation in Delaware late in 1928 in order to raise capital for expansion. On February 1, 1929 the company was reorganized as the United Aircraft and Transport Corporation.[3] The original combination was Boeing Airplane, Boeing Air Transport, and Pacific Air Transport. The first capital issue in 1928 was 650,000 shares of common stock of no par value and 200,000 shares of cumulative preferred with a par value of $50.[4] The underwriter was the National City Company, a subsidiary of the National City Bank of New York, which had first become associated with Boeing through another affiliate, the Pacific National Company. National City took 90,000 shares of 6 per cent cumulative preferred for $4,500,000; 45,000 shares of common for $500,000; and 90,000 stock purchase warrants at $30 a share.

Early in 1929 the implications of the change of name from Boeing to United became manifest. Capitalization was increased to two and one-half million shares of common and one million preferred, of which National City took 100,000 common, 150,000 preferred, and 100,000 stock warrants entitling the holder to buy common stock at $30 a share before November 1, 1938. The rest of the issue was earmarked for expansion of the organization, beginning with Pratt and Whitney and Chance Vought. The initiative for this larger combination came from F. B. Rentschler, who had long-standing personal and business ties with Boeing and whose brother, Gordon Rentschler, was president of the National City Bank.[5] An exchange of stock brought Pratt and Whitney into the United fold, along with the Chance Vought Corporation, another Pratt and Whitney customer. William E. Boeing became chairman of United Aircraft and Transport and F. B. Rentschler, president. Before the end of 1929 the new company acquired control of two propeller manufacturers, the Hamilton Aero Products Company and the Standard Steel Propeller Company, both consolidated as the Hamilton Standard Propeller Corporation. The two were the principal American producers of metal propellers, which at this time were replacing the laminated wooden propellers of early days. Hamilton Aero Products was a Milwaukee, Wisconsin, firm, founded by Thomas J. Hamilton in 1921. Standard Steel Propeller was organized in Pittsburgh in 1919 to develop the work of two Westinghouse tool designers, Thomas A. Dicks and James B. Luttrell, who had begun making steel propellers in 1917.[6] By 1929 Hamilton was the stronger company, but Standard had a license to use a patent taken out by Dr. Sylvanus Reed for a propeller with "light alloy blades solid through the outer half of their length."[7] Reed's own company was absorbed by Curtiss-Wright, so United needed the Standard license to avoid patent troubles, although the Reed propeller was solid duralumin while both Hamilton and Standard made duralumin blades on a steel hub.

United also secured a foothold in private-plane production by purchasing the Stearman Aircraft Company of Wichita, formed late in 1927 after Stearman had left Travel Air in 1926 for an unsuccessful venture into manufacturing light planes in Venice,

California. The Stearman Aircraft Company attracted the interest of a Boston investment banker, Robert E. Gross, who invested $20,000 in it in 1928 and resigned from Lee, Higginson and Company to assist in the management of Stearman.[8] In addition, the United structure included the Sikorsky Aviation Corporation, the Avion Corporation, established in 1928 by John K. Northrop to design experimental planes; and three airlines besides the original Boeing properties: National Air Transport, Varney Air Lines, and Stout Air Services.

Hard on the heels of the United combination, almost simultaneously indeed, came North American Aviation, Inc., formed initially as a holding company pure and simple. Its creator was Canadian-born Clement M. Keys, formerly editor of *The Wall Street Journal* and *World's Work,* whom we have seen previously as the purchaser of Curtiss Aeroplane and Motor from John N. Willys.[9] Keys incorporated North American in Delaware on December 6, 1928, with financial backing from the investment house of Hayden, Stone and Company of Boston and the Bancamerica Blair Corporation. It was authorized to issue 6 million shares of no par value stock, of which 2 million were taken by the underwriters for $25,000,000.[10] The first major manufacturer to be included was the Curtiss-Wright Corporation, another Keys combination effected in August 1929 and predicted by F. B. Rentschler when he was founding Pratt and Whitney. Curtiss-Wright was in fact a merger within a merger. The principal participants were the Curtiss Aeroplane and Motor Company and Wright Aeronautical. In addition, the combine included the Curtiss-Robertson Airplane Manufacturing Company, created in 1928 to separate the commercial from the military manufacturing activities; the Curtiss-Caproni Corporation; Travel Air of Wichita; and two other Curtiss subsidiaries: the Moth Aircraft Corporation and the Keystone Aircraft Corporation, which a year earlier had bought the Loening Aeronautical Engineering Corporation.[11] The Curtiss-Wright organization by itself was the second largest seller of aircraft and engines at this time, United Aircraft and Transport being first (see Table 2).

North American was never as thoroughly integrated as United Aircraft and Transport. During its five years as a holding com-

Table 2. Aircraft and Engine Sales, 1927–1933

Companies	Government Sales	Per Cent of Total Government Sales	Commercial Sales	Per Cent of Total Commercial Sales	Total Sales	Per Cent of Total Sales
United	$ 50,184,443	39.7	$28,056,208	48.0	$ 78,240,651	42.3
Curtiss-Wright	44,755,590	35.4	26,813,517	45.9	71,569,107	38.7
Douglas	14,437,623	11.4	1,412,790	2.4	15,850,413	8.6
Glenn Martin	9,895,605	7.8	none	—	9,895,605	5.4
Consolidated	4,307,632	3.4	1,118,231	1.9	5,425,863	2.9
Great Lakes	2,451,993	1.9	905,719	1.5	3,357,712	1.8
Grumman	452,195	0.4	153,492	0.3	605,687	0.3
Totals	$126,485,081	100.0	$58,459,957	100.0	$184,945,038	100.0

Source: E. E. Freudenthal, *The Aviation Business: From Kitty Hawk to Wall Street* (New York, 1940), p. 120.
Without questioning the accuracy of these figures, it is possible to suggest that they present a somewhat clouded picture. The period 1927–1933 includes data before and after the formation of the mergers. Also, the totals are for both airframe and engine sales, but only the two leaders on the list made engines.

pany it became the owner of all or a majority of the stock in Pitcairn Aviation, Inc. (reorganized as Eastern Air Transport in 1930), the Sperry Gyroscope Company, the Ford Instrument Company, the Aviation Corporation of California, the Berliner-Joyce Aircraft Company, and the General Aviation Manufacturing Corporation; and of substantial minority interests in Transcontinental Air Transport, Western Air Express, and Douglas Aircraft.[12] It also formed an investment subsidiary, the Condor Corporation. There was a constant shifting of holdings. By the beginning of 1934 North American was out of Douglas completely. Its holdings in Curtiss-Wright, Sperry Gyroscope, and Ford Instrument were exchanged for stock in the Sperry Corporation, which in turn was distributed as a bonus to North American stockholders.[13] This transaction was part of a reorganization that brought North American into the General Motors orbit.

The role of General Motors in the aviation boom has been variously described. The common assumption is that General Motors participated in the original formation of North American,[14] but this is an ex post facto judgment. General Motors went into aviation on its own in 1929 because it appeared to be a promising field for expansion. It did so by buying a 40 per cent interest in the Fokker Aircraft Corporation for $7,782,000 in May 1929, followed by a 24 per cent interest in the Bendix Aviation Corporation for $15 million, and outright purchase, for $592,000, of the Allison Engineering Company of Indianapolis.[15] The Fokker Aircraft Corporation was a consolidation of the Atlantic Aircraft Corporation, Fokker's original American company, and such assets as were left of the Dayton-Wright Company, with the Fokker name used, it was hoped, for greater glamour. Unfortunately Fokker Aircraft came under a cloud because of the disastrous crash killing the famous Notre Dame football coach Knute Rockne. Investigation showed signs of rot in spars and ribs that had caused structural failure in the wing.[16] There was also disagreement between Fokker and General Motors over management policies, with the result that Fokker left the company and returned to Europe.[17] In 1930 General Motors organized the General Aviation Corporation to control its aircraft manufacturing activities, and three years later sold this company to another subsidiary, the General Aviation Manufacturing Corporation, whose stock in turn was exchanged for North American. The shares thus acquired, plus open-market purchases, gave General Motors a 29 per cent interest in North American Aviation.[18]

Thus, while Curtiss-Wright and General Motors were both involved in North American, they were not joint participants; Curtiss-Wright was out before General Motors came in. It is therefore technically correct to list Curtiss-Wright and General Motors as controlling separate groupings of aviation companies in 1929, but the General Motors holdings in that year hardly qualify it as a major power in the field.

The next of the combinations, the Aviation Corporation, has easily the most complex organizational story; because much of the corporate intricacy is at best peripherally related to aircraft manufacturing, no attempt will be made to trace it in complete detail. The abbreviation AVCO was commonly used for the corporation; since this later became the official name of the organization, it will be used here for convenience and simplicity. AVCO was founded in March 1929, with W. A. Harriman and Lehman Brothers underwriting an issue of 2 million shares at $17.50 a share.[19] E. L. Cord has been credited with being the creator of AVCO, but this is the same kind of error as making General Motors a founder of North American. Cord was a later complication. Besides the banking houses, the initial participants in AVCO appear to have been Juan Trippe, better known as the founder and president of Pan American Airways, Inc., and Sherman Fairchild. It was a characteristic move for Trippe, an aggressive graduate of Yale's Sheffield Scientific School. In the Naval Reserve Flying Corps during the First World War, he established in 1923 an air taxi service called Long Island Airways, and in 1925 founded Colonial Airways, later absorbed into Eastern Airlines, Inc.[20] Fairchild was a normally conservative businessman who started AVCO on its way in order to find financial support for a small, Cincinnati, Ohio, air service that was an agency for Fairchild planes,[21] and who then seems to have been carried away by the mania for corporate manipulation that characterized the finance of the bull market. One of his own company magazines states that between 1929 and 1931 the Fairchild corporate structure "went through a series of legalistic contortions that defy description by other than a Wall Street lawyer." [22] At one time Fairchild himself was the largest stockholder in AVCO. The organization controlled an assortment of small airlines but was not a large-scale manufacturer; the Fairchild companies, combined as the Fairchild Aviation Corporation, were the only manufacturing enterprises of any consequence. In this respect the AVCO structure was in marked contrast to both United and North American.

In 1931 AVCO came into association with the Cord Corporation, formed in 1929 by E. L. Cord to control a mixed automotive empire. It consisted of three automobile companies, Auburn, Cord, and Duesenberg; the Stinson Airplane Company of Detroit, a builder since 1926 of private planes and some trimotored transports; and the Lycoming Manufacturing Company of Williamsport, Pennsylvania, manufacturer of aircraft engines.[23] A contest for power followed which resulted in Cord taking charge of AVCO. Fairchild got out. He sold his company's Farmingdale, Long Island, plant to AVCO for $1,262,000 and used the money to buy back AVCO's holdings of Fairchild stock.[24] This transaction was completed in April 1931; Fairchild aircraft manufacturing was then concentrated at Hagerstown and engine manufacture was discontinued. In 1932, the Cord Corporation bought the Airplane Development Corporation of Glendale, California, founded in the same year by Gerard "Jerry" Vultee, who had been Northrop's successor as chief engineer at Lockheed.[25]

Finally, there was the Detroit Aircraft Corporation. Of the groupings formed at this time, none looked more impressive or was launched with greater pretentiousness. In effect, the automobile industry was going to take charge of aviation; "the General Motors of the Air" was one of the phrases used to describe the new company. Its aims were summarized as follows by the president, E. S. Evans, a Detroit businessman with varied automotive and aviation interests: [26]

The aviation industry has passed out of the state of infancy and is now prepared for a period of intensive development. The Detroit Aircraft Corporation will be among the leaders in that development. We will apply the famous Detroit industrial methods to the building of aircraft of every description—Further, because of the fact that the corporation will engage in the manufacture of lighter-than-air as well as heavier-than-air craft, we will be in a particularly advantageous position, participating in the growth of all branches of air development and not entirely dependent upon any outside source for a supply of motors. In short, the Detroit Aircraft Corporation will be probably the most self-contained unit in the industry.

Capitalization of $20 million was talked about, although the first authorized issue was 2 million shares of no par value, to be marketed through H. W. Noble and Company of Detroit, August Belmont and Company of New York, and Knight, Dysart and Gamble of St. Louis. The list of directors reads like a Social Register of the automobile industry, including such names as Charles F. Kettering and Charles S. Mott of General Motors, William B. Mayo of Ford, Roy D. Chapin of Hudson, and Ransom E. Olds, then chairman of Reo. These were not men to be carried away by or lend themselves to any fly-by-night or blue-sky stock promotion. Their presence in Detroit Aircraft is strikingly revealing of the atmosphere of 1929: completely sanguine about the continuity of the economic boom, and in this case, as with other mergers, convinced that a great expansion of aviation was immediately in prospect. There was nothing wrong with this assumption except that "immediately" was a little farther off than had been estimated. There was also an attitude, expressed for neither the first nor the last time, that the techniques of manufacturing and selling motor vehicles could be readily applied to aircraft and would produce a similar quantitative miracle.

The Detroit Aircraft holdings hardly justified the company's glowing claims; they were respectable enough, but not to be compared with those of United or North American. The most important was Lockheed, in which Detroit Aircraft acquired an 87 per cent interest in July 1929 by exchange of stock, a transaction so disliked by Allan Lockheed that he left the company.[27] The others were the Mahoney-Ryan Aircraft Corporation of St. Louis, an affiliate of Ryan Aeronautical Company; the Aircraft

Development Corporation, a Detroit company with no relationship to Vultee's Airplane Development Corporation; the Eastman Aircraft Corporation; the Blackburn Aeroplane Company; the Marine Aircraft Company; the Aviation Tool Company; the Grosse Isle Airport; and a part share in the Winton Aviation Engine Company.[28] Given time, this assortment might have been developed into something; but the Detroit Aircraft Corporation was not to have the time.

The result of all this activity was that in 1929 capital flotation in aviation increased to $255 million and aviation stocks rose to heights that distinguished them even in the speculative market of that year.[29] What would have happened if the boom had lasted longer can only be conjectured. United, North American, and AVCO showed a respectable staying power after the crash, so that under brighter conditions the trend to combination and consolidation might have become stronger. As it was, even during the boom major airframe manufacturers such as Consolidated and Martin were untouched by the mergers, and Douglas was only marginally involved. There was also an assortment of smaller competitors, any one with the potential to increase its share of the market in an industry with a rapidly fluctuating technology. In Wichita, Clyde Cessna left Travel Air in 1927 to establish his own company because he wanted to build monoplanes while the Travel Air management preferred to stick to biplanes,[30] thereby giving Wichita still another manufacturer of small planes. A year later Giuseppe Bellanca, Italian-born aeronautical engineer, started his own company, the Bellanca Aircraft Corporation, in New Castle, Delaware. He was already known as a designer of planes with an enviable record in speed and endurance competition.[31] The Grumman Aircraft Engineering Corporation in Long Island was solidly established in 1929 as a manufacturer of naval aircraft. Its founder, Leroy R. Grumman, was an aeronautical engineer from Cornell and M.I.T. with experience in the Navy as an aircraft constructor and also as factory manager for Loening.[32] The list of minor companies could be extended, but few of them would survive the depression; the essential point is that the big companies were not in an oligopolistic position in 1929.

Boom and Collapse

The rosy production picture for the aircraft manufacturers in 1929, as well as what happened afterwards, can be put into figures (see Table 3):

Table 3. Aircraft Production, 1926–1933

Year	Total	Military	Civil
1926	1,186	532	654
1927	1,995	621	1,374
1928	4,346	1,219	3,127
1929	6,193	677	5,516
1930	3,437	747	2,690
1931	2,800	812	1,988
1932	1,396	593	803
1933	1,324	466	858

Source: *Aerospace Facts and Figures, 1964*, p. 24.

This table runs from the start of the aviation boom to the low point of the depression. In 1926 production topped the thousand mark for the first time since 1918. The total output for 1929 would not again be surpassed until the nation began serious preparation for another war in 1940. The phenomenal increase in civil aircraft amply explains the confidence of both the industry and the investing public in a forthcoming great expansion of air transport and private flying. Admittedly there is some distortion in giving the data in numbers of aircraft manufactured. Airframe weight or dollar value would show that the private planes accounted for less than a fourth of either. But with aircraft sales rising from $21 million in 1927 to $71 million in 1929,[33] it did not seem to make much difference what set of figures was consulted.

The dream ended, as did so many others, with the collapse of the great bull market in the fall of 1929. For the aircraft industry the shrinkage came in stages. As the table shows, the market for military aircraft actually increased until 1931, when the five-year procurement program of 1926 came to an end. Conse-

quently the companies engaged predominantly in military production (Consolidated, Douglas, Martin) were less seriously affected than the builders of civil aircraft. Transport aircraft were
in an exciting phase of development that kept production active,
although it would take several years for the benefits to be realized in the form of profits. The demand for private planes
dropped first and farthest, with the result that the small companies were the worst hit.[34]

The newly-formed combines, as we have said, showed considerable strength, with one exception. The Detroit Aircraft Corporation had had very little to begin with; it even lost $733,000
in 1929. It went bankrupt and disintegrated in 1931, pulling
Lockheed into receivership in the process although Lockheed had
been the one solvent member of the combination. According to
an analysis made by Robert E. Gross, Lockheed showed a total
deficit on March 31, 1932, of $803,127.29, but after expenses
billed by the Detroit Aircraft Corporation were deducted, the
actual Lockheed deficit for the previous three years was $2,557.[35]
The margin by which Lockheed remained in business was criti-
cally narrow. The Detroit Aircraft Corporation had sent Carl B.
Squier to the company as general manager, with the idea that he
would move it to Detroit. Squier, however, became convinced
that Lockheed should stay in Burbank.[36] He continued to manage
Lockheed in the grimmest part of the depression. At Christmas
in 1931 he borrowed $2,500 on his personal credit to give in tens
and twenties to the employees as they left the plant, none of
them knowing if the next payroll would be met or indeed if they
would have jobs to come back to. Their credit matched his; all
but $65 was repaid. In 1932 Lockheed earned $23,000, all in
repairs and spare parts, and had a net loss of $10,000.[37]

The other groupings, United, North American, and AVCO,
weathered the depression with varying degrees of difficulty.
North American and AVCO were overcapitalized. In 1932 North
American gave its common stock a par value of $5 a share,
compared with the initial selling price of $12.50, and a few
months later wrote the stock down to a dollar a share.[38] AVCO's
financial troubles led directly to the involvement with Cord. Both
companies might have followed the Detroit Aircraft Corporation

into oblivion if, like it, they had been exclusively manufacturing enterprises. Employment in North American's manufacturing subsidiaries dropped from 1,300 in 1932 to 200 in 1934.[39] However, commercial air transport continued to grow even during the depression, and both North American and AVCO controlled valuable airline properties; a North American subsidiary, Transcontinental and Western Air, formed by combining Transcontinental Air Transport and Western Air Express, launched the first coast-to-coast all-air passenger service between New York and Los Angeles on October 25, 1930.[40]

United was the strongest of the combines. It seems to have had a lower proportion of water in its financial structure than did its rivals. Not that United escaped the effects of the depression altogether. A picture of the condition of United's eastern manufacturing operations, that is, omitting Boeing itself, is provided by Eugene E. Wilson, who resigned from the Navy in 1929 to accept an offer from Rentschler to become head of the combined Hamilton Standard Propeller organization. When Wilson actually began his new duties in January 1930, he visited the Hamilton plant in Milwaukee and the Standard plant in Pittsburgh to determine where operations should be concentrated. Both cities offered a gloomy pattern of empty factories and cold chimneys. It was decided to select Pittsburgh as a more convenient location, but labor trouble resulted in Hamilton Standard finally being moved to Hartford.[41] Then Wilson was asked to take charge of the financial affairs of the Sikorsky Aircraft Corporation. In 1929 Sikorsky had sold some 56 aerial yachts at $28,000 each to people who were largely connected with the stock market, so that Sikorsky had acquired a sizable stack of unpaid bills. The company also lost a million dollars on three flying boats for Pan American Airways.[42] Sikorsky himself was a genius at aeronautical design, but he was no match for Juan Trippe as a bargainer. His assistants were mainly Russian refugees of similar temperament: technically capable but casual about accounting, so that, as Wilson expressed it, United found itself engaged in a form of Russian relief. Wilson then added the Vought company to his responsibilities, but this was due to Chance Vought's death rather than to depression troubles.

Politics and the Air Mail

It is quite clear that most of the aviation combines would have survived the depression if economic factors had been the only consideration. Their dissolution was the result of political pressures, culminating in the arbitrary cancellation of air mail contracts not long after the administration of Franklin D. Roosevelt came into office.

The background to this occurrence was exhaustively, if not impartially, investigated at the time and has been gone over several times since, so that the facts are readily available.[43] The essential part of the story is simple enough. President Hoover's Postmaster General, Walter F. Brown, foreseeing a great expansion of air transport, wanted to use his authority over air mail routes and contracts to establish a nationwide network of soundly organized and financed airlines. He particularly wanted to keep out what he regarded as the shoestring operators, the little companies that were springing up with secondhand equipment bought on credit, and seeking mail contracts by cutting their bids to figures that Brown considered unrealistic, with the probable result that the contract could not be fulfilled. To achieve his objective Brown used to the full his legal power to award air mail contracts to the lowest *responsible* bidder, and to avoid wasteful competition among these he held periodic conferences with the established airline operators at which mail routes were allocated.

These conferences were the foundation for the subsequent charge of collusion between the Post Office and the big operators to keep the small fry out. Actually the airline executives had little choice but to go along with the Postmaster General; without a mail contract no airline could live. Passenger travel was still far too slight to support commercial air operations; mail and cargo, principally mail, were the major sources of revenue. In the 1920's, indeed, passengers were considered something of a nuisance, requiring special attention that inanimate payloads did not need; there are even well authenticated cases of passengers having to ride on top of the mail sacks. So Walter Brown was in a position to dictate his terms, and as a matter of fact the worst criticism that can be made of him is that he was dictatorial and arbitrary in his methods. A hostile investigating committee later went over every detail of his activities and was unable to find that he had exceeded his legal authority or that there had been any taint of corruption in what he had done. He genuinely wanted to build a sound and substantial air transport network, but he chose an unfortunate way to go about it.

Shortly after the beginning of the New Deal, a newspaper columnist, Fulton Lewis, Jr., opened the campaign against Brown by publishing the grievances of an airline operator whose low bid for a mail contract had been rejected. The air mail contracts were played up as a major political scandal; without any serious effort to find out what had actually happened, they were arbitrarily canceled (February 9, 1934) and the carriage of air mail turned over to the Army, effective ten days later. The results were not exactly felicitous. The Army pilots were not trained for night flying over a prescribed route on a fixed schedule, and after several of them had been killed flying the mail, the public outcry forced the administration to begin returning the mail routes to private operation.[44]

In the meantime a senatorial committee whose principal spokesman was Senator Hugo L. Black of Alabama did its best to find scandal in the air mail contracts. It found nothing that could be taken into court, but its investigations produced the Air Mail Act of 1934, whose most important provision was to require the separation of manufacturing and transport in aviation.[45] This much was desirable in order to promote healthy competition in aviation. It is a little more difficult to justify making companies that had held air mail contracts under the Brown regime ineligible to bid on the reallocation of contracts, since no wrongdoing was ever established against these firms. It is still more difficult to make a case for stipulating by law that none of the participants in Postmaster General Brown's conferences could be an official of a company holding an air mail contract. To condemn them by statute when they had not been convicted of anything illegal, or even charged with anything, suggests the Bill of Attainder rather than due process of law.

In conformity with the Air Mail Act, United separated into three segments. The transport subsidiaries became United Airlines; Boeing resumed its independence and absorbed Stearman; the eastern manufacturing divisions, Pratt and Whitney, Hamilton Standard, Chance Vought, and Sikorsky, became the United Aircraft Corporation.[46] North American reorganized its airlines into two companies, Transcontinental and Western (TWA) and Eastern, and was itself reconstituted as a manufacturing concern, representing a consolidation of Berliner-Joyce and General Aviation.[47] At first the manufacturing was concentrated in the Berliner-Joyce plant near Baltimore, Maryland, under the name of the General Aviation Manufacturing Corporation until December 1934. Then, however, the company decided that more favorable manufacturing conditions were to be found in southern California and in March 1935 leased a site near the Los Angeles Airport for $600 a year.[48] James H. Kindelberger was persuaded to leave Douglas to become president of the reorganized North American Aviation, Inc., and another Douglas engineer, John Leland Atwood, went with him. The new company devoted itself exclusively to the design and manufacture of military aircraft.

AVCO followed the same general pattern. Its transport companies emerged as American Airlines, Inc., while its aircraft manufacturing divisions became the Aviation Manufacturing Corporation. The principal components of this concern were Stinson and Vultee's Airplane Development Corporation, neither a major producer. Stinson had shown promise in the commercial field, selling 1,100 planes, including 100 trimotored airliners between 1926 and 1936,[49] but it failed to achieve further distinction. Vultee became a fairly important military producer, but not on a large scale. AVCO became a diversified corporation, partly in and partly out of the aircraft industry. The corporate reshuffling brought about, among other things, the departure of E. L. Cord from both the aircraft and the automobile industry.

So ended the first series of attempts at combination in aviation. There can be no question that separation of manufacturing from transport operations was desirable. The leaders of the industry themselves have been in general agreement on this point.

The means employed to attain the end are another matter altogether. It is difficult to agree with the complacent attitude of the New Deal's semi-official historian that blundering or arbitrary actions by the administration can be overlooked because everything came out all right in the end.[50] The evidence is that President Roosevelt ordered the arbitrary cancellation of the air mail contracts without knowing or understanding what had really been going on. He acted essentially on impulse. In those hectic days of 1933 it was easy, and politically advantageous, to take it for granted that a member of the Hoover Cabinet had been corruptly associated with "big business." Postmaster General James A. Farley was far better informed about the actual situation. He clearly did not approve of the President's decision but carried it out as a loyal subordinate. His reward was to be made the scapegoat when things went wrong and the toll of Army flyers began to mount ominously.

The performance of the Air Corps naturally evoked criticism also. General Mitchell, living in embittered retirement, remarked that he hoped future enemies would attack the United States only in good weather. The criticism was largely unfair. Techniques for flight control in darkness and bad weather were still elementary. The commercial airline pilots were able to fly their routes as safely as they did because they accumulated a substantial body of experience and "feel" for the country they traversed. The Air Corps pilots were thrown on short notice into an assignment for which they had no previous training, and their problems were accentuated by their natural eagerness to show that they could do anything a civilian pilot could do.

The deaths of the pilots may have saved private enterprise in American aviation. Roosevelt probably had no intention of effecting a fundamental change in the status of the industry, and Farley certainly had none. However, there was a substantial body of New Deal opinion that wanted to see both aircraft manufacturing and air transport nationalized.[51] This was not only the period of turmoil over air mail contracts; it was also the "merchants of death" era, when there was a strong agitation to abolish the private manufacture and sale of weapons of war, including aircraft. But the Army's unfortunate experience in flying the mail produced a public demand to return the operation to the professionals; that is, the privately owned airlines. So the sponsors of the Air Mail Act had to accept private enterprise. To the extent that it was considered necessary to justify the cancellation of the contracts, the act did so by a proscription of companies and individuals.

The whole controversy was forgotten rapidly once the mail contracts were reallocated. It was an unpleasant episode, and there was possibly more unpleasantness in it than appears in the standard accounts. According to E. E. Wilson, shortly after the election of 1932 Edward J. Flynn, the Democratic boss of the Bronx, visited Rentschler and proposed that Flynn's law firm be retained for a high figure to represent United.[52] When Rentschler replied that the company already had legal counsel, Flynn countered that he was offering special representation that an ordinary law firm could not give. Rentschler, however, rejected the proposal. What influence this incident might have had cannot be definitely established. United had taken part reluctantly in Postmaster General Brown's conferences because it was already well established in the air mail business and stood to gain nothing from a policy directed at turning small competing airlines into big ones. Yet the Black Committee singled out United as an organization and Rentschler personally for especially vitriolic criticism, and the pressure on the company made it the first of the combinations to be dissolved. By comparison, North American retained its holdings in Eastern Airlines until 1938 without anyone in the government getting excited.[53] The purge of airline officials was particularly harsh on Philip G. Johnson, who had become president of United in mid-1933, when William E. Boeing decided to retire from active management.[54] He had not approved of Brown's actions but was nevertheless driven temporarily into exile. The American aviation industry was closed to him; he spent the next several years manufacturing trucks in Seattle and then operating Trans-Canada Airlines, now Air Canada.

One event passed almost unnoticed except by aviation enthusiasts, but it had a greater long-range significance than the political imbroglio. When the air mail contracts were canceled, the last privately operated trip before the Army took over was made by Jack Frye, then vice-president and later president of TWA, with Eddie Rickenbacker as copilot. It was a deliberate gesture of defiance. The trip from Los Angeles to Newark was a record-breaking 13 hours and 4 minutes; the plane that accomplished the feat was the first production DC-2.[55]

4. The Airframe Revolution

The spectacular performance of the DC-2 on the Frye-Rickenbacker flight symbolized a decade of phenomenal progress in aircraft design. Engine development can be credited with coming first, in the form of the radial air-cooled engine that came into production in 1924–1925 and that was subsequently subjected to constant refinement by the competition between Wright Aeronautical and Pratt and Whitney. But better engines, along with greatly improved aviation fuels, would have been of limited value by themselves; as John K. Northrop once pointed out, no feasible engine could have propelled the Wright airplane at modern speeds.[1] Other factors had to be incorporated also in order to produce the revolution in design and construction that occurred approximately in the decade from 1925 to 1935.

These factors revolved about the introduction of all-metal monocoque airframes, built of aluminum alloy, with cantilevered, internally braced wings, and the smooth stressed-skin employed by the German, A. K. Rohrbach, and presented to American designers in a paper read to the Society of Automotive Engineers in 1927.[2] To this were added various aerodynamic refinements giving greater lift and less drag.[3] The controllable-pitch propeller and retractable landing gear complete the principal ingredients of change. As is frequently, indeed usually, the case with technological innovation, most of the techniques had been experimented with before the innovating process began. Monocoque construction (with wood) and an all-metal monoplane were both tested in Europe before the First World War.[4] As we have seen, there was further development along both lines in the 1920's. Retractable landing gear was used successfully by Grover Loening on his amphibians, and on the Lockheed Orion, but it had not been generally accepted because on the standard strut-and-wire planes of the period it did not give enough aerodynamic advantage to justify its added weight and cost. The same limitation applied for some years to the controllable-pitch propeller, whose principle was well understood and which was being experimented with at least as early as 1925.

These ideas and techniques came from many sources: the NACA, the military services, the universities, the airlines, and the aircraft manufacturing companies themselves. Some vital contributions, like the stressed-skin technique, came from Europe. Their over-all effect can be summed up, at least in part, by the fact that in the ten years we are considering it was possible to increase wing loadings from less than 15 pounds per square foot to 20, and to decrease power loading from 20 to 15 pounds per horsepower,[5] in other words, to get substantially more efficiency and economy of operation from the same weight of airplane.

What was required, and was in due course achieved, was a design that would synthesize these various features and create an airplane markedly superior to anything then in existence. This result could presumably have been attained in the course of time by simply adding one technological improvement to another, but this process would hardly have constituted innovation, which implies a certain amount of conscious direction of the pattern of change. Instead, it is possible to identify certain forces and choices which determined that the introduction of the modern airplane should occur in the United States within a specific period of time and under clearly identifiable circumstances.

There were two sources from which an impetus to innovate could have come: the military services, seeking constantly higher performance; or commercial demand for aircraft with greater earning capacity. Both forces were present, with the growth of civil air transport as the more decisive factor. I. B. Holley pinpoints the passage of the Kelly Air Mail Act in 1925 as the factor that started a new period of aeronautical advance, arguing that because the act put the carriage of air mail into private hands, it gave the carriers an incentive to keep looking for planes that would maximize profits by operating more economically and efficiently.[6]

The influence of the Army and Navy, to say nothing of the NACA, needs proper acknowledgment. The development of the new aircraft was materially assisted by the research work of the Air Corps in engines and fuels, and by the activity of the Navy's Bureau of Aeronautics in promoting the development of the radial air-cooled engine. Both services, in addition, did what they could to encourage the development of new designs. The aerodynamic research of the NACA likewise made indispensable contributions ranging from specific items like using fillets at the junction of wings and fuselage to reduce interference, to general refinements in airframe and wing design that had a cumulative effect in improving performance.

Nevertheless, the impetus for the innovation we are considering did not and could not have come from governmental sources. On the military side this was the era of isolation and limitation of armaments, when budgetary restrictions precluded any major expansion of aviation by either the Army or the Navy. Conditions improved markedly after the adoption of the recommendations of the Morrow Board in 1926, but development work still had to be carried on with extremely slender resources. During the twenty years between the First and Second World Wars the expenditures of the Air Corps for research and development ranged from a low of $2,184,000 in 1927 to a high of close to $6 million in 1936; the average was about $4 million a year.[7] Nor was the NACA any better off. In an era of massive government support for research and development in aerospace activities, it is astonishing to realize that as late as 1939, with the Second World War on the doorstep, the total staff of the NACA was 523, of whom 278 were classed as "technical people."[8] It is perhaps even more astonishing that these agencies accomplished as much in the way of research and experiment as they did.

The immediate incentive for the introduction of a radically new aircraft type emerged therefore in the "private sector," specifically in the form of competitive pressures between airlines and between aircraft manufacturers. Some of the competition, given the nature of the industry, was for military contracts. The significant new element, however, was the possibilities that improved aircraft design offered in the field of air transport.

The Competitors

The new ideas on aircraft design and construction were absorbed by a fiercely competitive industry, operating under conditions where a quite minor advantage in design or technique could make the difference between getting or losing a contract, or even between survival and extinction for the firm in question. At the same time, American aircraft manufacturers displayed an ability to cooperate in the exchange of information that was noticeably lacking in their European counterparts.[9] Despite, or perhaps because of the competitive pressures, American companies unhesitatingly dropped their own ideas and adopted their rivals' if these proved to be demonstrably superior.

In the implementation of these ideas four concerns stand out: Boeing, Douglas, Lockheed, and Martin. They are not entitled to exclusive credit, because other companies in the industry contributed significantly. Nor did they constitute, in the strict sense of the term, an oligopoly. They did not administer prices or dominate the market. Indeed, they were not even the largest firms in the airframe industry at the time: as a producer of military aircraft, the Curtiss-Wright combination outranked both Martin and Lockheed.[10] Nevertheless, as events worked out, these particular companies had the largest role in translating the advances in aeronautical science and technology into operating aircraft during the years from 1925 to 1935.

Consolidated has perhaps some claim to priority in that its Fleetster of 1929, an eight-passenger, high-wing monoplane, was the first American transport plane to have an all-metal monocoque fuselage.[11] The Fleetster, however, belongs properly among the forerunners of the new development, like the Lockheed and Northrop types of the late 1920's. The first real breakthrough was the Boeing 200 Monomail, begun in 1928 and flown two years later. It was an all-metal monocoque, single-engined, cantilevered low-wing monoplane with retractable landing gear and the then phenomenal speed for a transport plane of 158 m.p.h. (cruising speed was about 135 m.p.h.).[12] Initially intended to carry only mail and cargo, it was modified to accommodate six to eight passengers. It was a bold step in design, but the Monomail did little service flying. Its tests showed that it needed a controllable-pitch propeller to be both efficient and economical; in fact, with a propeller setting that worked well in Seattle the plane could barely get off the ground at high-altitude airports such as in Cheyenne, Wyoming.[13]

United was able to provide the requisite propeller. As with most great inventions, the origin of the controllable-pitch propeller is open to dispute. The idea of varying the pitch of propeller blades in order to give optimum performance under changing conditions was an obvious one, and propellers did exist whose blade settings could be adjusted in advance. But this was not enough. What was needed was a propeller whose pitch could be changed while the plane was in operation, particularly so that with constant speed rotation it would be possible to get both full power for take-off and economical cruising speed. Experimentation on this problem was fairly widespread. There is an NACA report, undated but clearly 1926, on a controllable-pitch technique designed by Spencer Heath, who had been one of the principal manufacturers of wooden propellers, under the trade name of Paragon, during and immediately after the First World War. Heath's mechanism was described as "experimental rather than finished," and the investigator recommended that it be redesigned so as to be lighter, more compact, and less complicated.[14] In 1927 Curtiss Aeroplane and Motor secured the rights to an electrically operated controllable-pitch propeller invented by a Canadian, W. R. Turnbull. Hydraulic control systems, however, proved more satisfactory. The first practical hydraulic device, the Hele-Shaw Beacham propeller, was successfully tested in Britain in 1928, but it was too advanced for contemporary airplanes to use.[15]

Credit for the effective development of the controllable-pitch propeller belongs to Frank Caldwell, who worked on it first at McCook Field and finished it as an engineer for Hamilton Standard.[16] Before the Monomail came along, his work was tested by the military services and rejected because the controllable-pitch propeller failed to give enough improvement in performance to justify the added weight and cost. What had been overlooked was that the tests were made on planes designed for fixed-pitch propellers, and putting new technologies on old airplanes is as unsatisfactory as putting new wine into old bottles. The new devices of the era, like the controllable-pitch propeller and the retractable landing gear, needed to be coordinated in design with the new aerodynamic knowledge. In other words, aircraft had to be designed for higher wing loadings and lower drag if these devices and techniques were to be properly utilized. Parenthetically, after the Army and Navy had rejected Caldwell's propeller, they then refused to allow it to be exported, on the ground of its military value.

The Caldwell propeller remedied the problems of the Monomail, but the plane itself was never produced in quantity. The day of the single-engined transport was over, so that the Monomail's principal service was to provide lessons for further development. The experience gained on it was incorporated into several new Boeing models, both military and civilian in accordance with the continuing and successful Boeing practice of using the same basic design for both military and nonmilitary planes. The military types were the P-26 and P-29 fighters and the B-9 bomber.[17] Of these only the P-26 was produced in quantity, and it still had wire-braced wings and fixed landing gear. Much was expected of the B-9, a twin-engined, low-wing monoplane, but it lost out in competition with the Martin B-10.

The most successful Boeing development from the Monomail was the 247 transport, which almost, but not quite, synthesized the new trends in aeronautical design. The 247 was a twin-engined, metal monocoque, cantilevered low-wing monoplane. It carried two pilots, a stewardess, and ten passengers, plus 400 pounds of mail; with a cruising speed of 155 m.p.h. it could provide coast-to-coast service in twenty hours, with seven intermediate stops.[18] It first flew in February 1933 and was manifestly superior to any existing transport in the United States or elsewhere.

Yet with all its merits the 247 emerged with a size limitation that severely curtailed its promise. The 247 was to have been a 16,000 pound plane powered by two 600 h.p. Pratt and Whitney Hornet engines. However, the pilots on the United Aircraft and Transport system, who would be the first to use the 247, had no experience in handling anything of this weight and objected to the proposed design as being too heavy and powerful to land safely.[19] Their concern had some foundation; one notable omission from the 247 was wing flaps. At any rate, in deference to the pilots' misgivings, the 247 as built was 12,650 pounds with two 550 h.p. Pratt and Whitney Wasp engines. It was done from the best of motives but cost Boeing the competitive advantage its innovation in design should have given it.

What Boeing could do, others could do also. There was no monopoly on aeronautical knowledge or engineering skill, and Boeing was being pushed by competition by the time its new designs were airborne. As has been mentioned, Boeing's first effort to incorporate the new design features into a bomber, the B-9, was outmatched by the Martin B-10. The B-9 was somewhat the larger of the two, but the Martin entry had an advantage in speed of about 35 m.p.h. and a service ceiling some 5,000 feet higher.[20] Some of the B-10's superiority was attained by the simple but at that time novel expedient of putting the bomb racks *inside* the fuselage. The B-10, including improved versions, became the standard Army bomber from its introduction in 1932 until 1936, and it was still being used by the Netherlands Air Force in Indonesia in 1941. It was faster than most of the fighter aircraft of its period (the same was true of the B-9) and was enough of an advance in aeronautics to be awarded the Collier Trophy for 1932. The Martin Company has justification for its assertion that the B-10 revolutionized military aircraft.[21] It certainly affected military design as decisively as the 247 affected transport planes.

Martin did not exploit its advantage. Part of the reason was that the company was engaged in a major relocation, moving from Cleveland to Baltimore late in 1928. This step was prompted by the growth of the company's business, which was going to require plant expansion anyway, plus the fact that part of the new business, present and prospective, was naval aircraft. Cleveland, or for that matter any Great Lakes city, was not a good site for testing flying boats because of the long winter periods when the Lakes were frozen. The Baltimore site was chosen after detailed investigation as offering an optimum combination of favorable weather conditions and proximity to the source of contracts in Washington, D. C.[22]

The timing of the move gave the company some anxious years financially. It had planned to raise the necessary funds by additional issues of stock, but the collapse of the stock market in 1929 ruled out this possibility for a company engaged in as speculative an enterprise as aircraft manufacturing, and Martin had to borrow about $3 million.[23] The onset of depression then cut the company's earnings, with the result that reorganization proceedings under the Federal Bankruptcy Act became necessary in 1934. Martin recovered, but the incident illustrates sharply the slender financial margin on which even the best-established aircraft companies operated.

When Martin left Cleveland the vacant plant was occupied by a locally sponsored successor, the Great Lakes Aircraft Corporation. It had a few years of success as a builder of naval torpedo planes, very similar to contemporary Martin planes of the same type. However, the company failed to keep up with the advances in design of the early 1930's and was out of business by 1935.[24]

The competition pressed on Boeing with equal vigor in the field of transport aircraft. One challenge came from the revival of Lockheed. In June 1932 the Lockheed Aircraft Company was sold at a receiver's sale for $40,000. The bidders were Carl Squier, Robert E. Gross, and Lloyd Stearman. Half the money came from Walter T. Varney, $10,000 from Cyril Chappellet, and $5,000 each from Robert C. Walker and Thomas Fortune Ryan III.[25] Varney was an airline operator, Squier was the manager of the Lockheed company at the time, Stearman had built airplanes in Wichita, and Chappellet was a former Army and airline pilot. Gross had been associated with Stearman in Wichita, and with his brother Courtlandt had formed the Viking Flying Boat Company in New Haven, Connecticut, in 1929, to manufacture flying boats of a French design. The depression killed this venture in 1931. Walker and Ryan were friends and business associates.

The company, reorganized as the Lockheed Aircraft Corporation, continued to build the existing Lockheed models, but its hopes were staked on the development of an all-metal transport plane to be named the Electra. The gamble succeeded, but only after two years of stress. Orders for the Electra came to half a million dollars by the end of 1934, but development costs proved unexpectedly high. To begin with, the Electra was initially to be single-engined, but, as with the Boeing Monomail, it became obvious that there was no future for a single-engined transport. So the Electra was redesigned for two engines, and then tests made at the aeronautical laboratories of the University of Michigan showed that twin rudders would be needed to give effective steering control with only one engine operating.[26] But the company got a loan of $200,000 from the Reconstruction Finance Corporation, and Lockheed stock was sold persistently in southern California by the Los Angeles investment firm of Brashears and Company.[27] The Electra was test-flown early in 1934: an all-metal biplane with two 450 h.p. Pratt and Whitney engines and a capacity for two pilots, ten passengers, and 350 pounds of mail or cargo.[28] The plane was principally the creation of Hall L. Hibbard, an M.I.T. graduate who became chief engineer in 1934, and Clarence L. "Kelly" Johnson, who had done the testing at Michigan and joined Lockheed immediately afterward. The Electra was priced at $50,000 and sales flourished. They reached $562,000 at the end of 1934, with another million in orders.[29] The company still showed a loss of $190,000 because of the high development cost, but the first month of 1935 showed a profit of $8,000; from there Lockheed never looked back. Forty-five Electras were sold by the end of 1935, for a profit of $218,000 on sales of $2 million, and 148 were built between 1934 and June 1941,[30] so that the Electra enjoyed a better production run than the 247, which had a total sale of 75.

Nevertheless the Electra was not the answer to the competitive threat posed by United's prior claim on the 247. Its virtues were low operating cost (25 cents a mile) and high speed (180 m.p.h.), but it was a smaller plane than the 247 and consequently carried less payload. At this time, however, major airline operators were thinking in terms of bigger planes capable of carrying larger payloads.

So, as events turned out, the culminating synthesis of the advances in aeronautical technology was achieved by Lockheed's southern California neighbor, Douglas Aircraft. Douglas was in a strong position as the 1930's began. It was well established in the military market. In terms of total units delivered, Douglas at this time was the largest single supplier of aircraft to the United States military services.[31] The O-2 series of observation planes ran to over 500 units before it was superseded, orders for torpedo bombers were steady, if not in large quantities, and about 1930 Douglas also turned to naval flying boats. So far the company had done little in the commercial field except to produce a modification of the O-2, listed as M-1 to M-4, used in some numbers for flying mail during the 1920's.[32] Expansion was financed by incorporating the Douglas Aircraft Company in Delaware in 1928 with an authorized capital of a million shares, of which 200,000 were retained by Donald Douglas for the assets of the old Douglas Company and the rest offered to the public.[33] The new company also was able to secure the first revolving credit given to an aircraft manufacturing company in the United States.[34] It was arranged through the Security First National Bank, and it was a testimony to the financial community's faith in Douglas Aircraft, because it had been taken for granted previously that the aircraft manufacturing business was too unpredictable for this type of credit to be feasible.

The immediate stimulus to the Douglas achievement was the development of the Boeing 247, whose superiority over existing transport planes was so evident that the airlines were faced with the necessity of replacing their fleets with 247's or something as good. But in 1932, when work on the 247 was beginning, United Airlines had first claim on Boeing production, and Boeing in fact made it quite clear that United's order for 60 247's would be filled before deliveries were made to anyone else.[35] How the officials of the Boeing company would have responded if they had been told that this would be the only substantial order they would ever get for 247's can only be conjectured.

The result was that Douglas Aircraft, among others, received a letter from Jack Frye, vice-president of operations for Transcontinental and Western Airlines, on August 2, 1932, asking for bids on a transport plane to outdo the 247.[36] Frye asked for an all-metal trimotored airplane, although he was prepared to consider two engines, with a payload of at least 2,300 pounds, comfortable accommodation for 12 passengers, range of 1,080 miles, a cruising speed of 145 miles an hour and a maximum of 185, and the ability to operate between any two points on the TWA system with one engine out. Invitations were sent to others besides Douglas. General Aviation and Sikorsky responded with trimotored designs; Douglas took a deep breath and plunged for a twin-engined plane.

To put it simply, Douglas Aircraft undertook to meet the twin-engined Boeing 247 with a similar but superior design, taking advantage, as an initial step, of the one major error the Boeing designers made, or, more accurately, had imposed on them: namely, the limitation of the 247's size and power. The Douglas engineers began with the assumption that the new 710 h.p. Wright Cyclones would give them the power they needed to meet Frye's requirements with a two-engined plane.

It was going to take more than a bigger engine to accomplish all that was wanted, and the Douglas engineering staff had to devote its entire energies and talents to the variety of problems to be solved if they were to comply with TWA's request that the plane be ready for testing by the middle of 1933. From the participants in this operation it is still possible to get a sense of the excitement and challenge it offered. Douglas was undoubtedly attracted by the opportunity of developing a market for commercial planes as a hedge against the uncertainties of military contracts, but this was not the only consideration. It is quite clear that the engineering staff saw in the TWA requirement a demand for an aeronautical masterpiece and went all-out to achieve it.

The talent that could be applied was impressive. The chief

engineer of Douglas Aircraft was James H. "Dutch" Kindelberger. His assistant chief, and later his successor, was Arthur E. Raymond, a Harvard engineering graduate.[37] While the staff was too small for much specialization, a large share of the drafting design fell to E. A. Burton, who subsequently became chief engineer at the Santa Monica plant; the stress analysis was done by John L. Atwood, a civil engineer from the University of Texas who would go with Kindelberger to North American and succeed him as president. At this time also John K. Northrop returned to the Douglas organization. What had happened was that United Aircraft and Transport had decided to move its Northrop subsidiary to Wichita, but J. K. Northrop himself preferred to stay in Los Angeles and had provided in his contract with United for his release if his company should be moved away.[38] The result was that a new Northrop Corporation was formed with the stock divided between J. K. Northrop and Douglas Aircraft, for the purpose of designing commercial aircraft. It was located at El Segundo, California, and eventually became the El Segundo Division of Douglas Aircraft. The immediate importance of this step was that Northrop had been building single-engined, all-metal monocoque transport planes (the Alpha transports) using a multicellular system of wing bracing that reduced the danger of flutter [39] and at the same time saved weight.

Besides the Company's own staff, two distinguished aeronautical engineers from the California Institute of Technology, Clark B. Millikan and Arthur L. Klein, were called in for advice.

This combination produced the desired aeronautical masterpiece, the DC-1 (Douglas Commercial). Its characteristics, along with those of its competitors and its immediate successors, appear in Table 4. It will be observed that, in addition to the features previously discussed, the DC-1 was equipped with wing flaps. These had been tried as far back as the First World War, but were strictly experimental until Northrop introduced them on his Alpha transports.[40] By bringing down the landing speed to about 60 m.p.h. the wing flaps allowed the DC-1 to be handled safely at a weight and power rejected in the original design for the 247. The DC-1 was in fact 3,000 pounds over its initially specified weight of 14,000 pounds,[41] but it still met and in fact

Table 4. Characteristics of the First Modern Transport Aircraft

Aircraft Type	Engines	Take-Off Power (b.h.p.)	Maximum Take-Off Weight (lb.)	Wing Area (sq. ft.)	Wing Span (ft.)	(in.)	Length (ft.)	(in.)	Cruising Speed (50% Take-Off Power) (m.p.h.)	Stalling Speed (m.p.h.)	Type of Flaps	Number of Passenger Seats
Boeing 200	1 × P.&W.R-1860-7	575	8,000	535	59	1½	41	2½	135	57	Nil	6
Boeing 247	2 × P.&W.R-1340-S1D1	550	12,650	836	74	0	54	4	155	59	Nil	10
Boeing 247D	2 × P.&W.R-1340-53	600	13,650	836	74	0	54	4	160	60	Nil	10
Douglas DC-1	2 × Wright R-1820-F3	710	17,500	942	85	0	60	0	170	59	Split	12
Douglas DC-2	2 × Wright R-1820-F3	710	18,080	942	85	0	62	0	170	61	Split	14
Douglas DC-3	2 × Wright R-1820-G2	1,000	24,000	987	95	0	64	5½	170	64	Split	21
Lockheed L-10 (Electra)	2 × P.&W.R-985-13	450	10,100	458	55	0	38	7	180	65	Split	8

Source: P. W. Brooks, *The Modern Airliner* (London, 1961), p. 69.
Note: The 247D was not a new model. It was the designation for existing 247's that were modified to improve performance. According to Lockheed sources, the L-10 accommodated ten passengers.

outdid its performance requirements. It was test-flown on July 1, 1933, and on September 20th of that year the only DC-1 ever built flew the most difficult section of TWA's transcontinental route, from Winslow, Arizona, to Albuquerque, New Mexico, on one engine, passing en route a TWA Ford trimotor that had left Winslow ahead of it.[42]

By the time of this demonstration the Douglas design had been accepted by TWA and had attracted the interest of others. The DC-1 turned out to be a prototype. What was actually produced was an improved version, the DC-2, slightly larger and accommodating fourteen instead of twelve passengers. The development cost of these two types was $300,000, large for those days. The initial price was $65,000, also high, and the company calculated its break-even point at 75 planes.[43] It eventually sold 190. The DC-2 outclassed the Boeing 247; it carried four more passengers and its cruising speed was 170 m.p.h., 15 m.p.h. more than its rival and 25 more than had initially been requested.

Douglas then outdid itself by producing an enlarged model that became one of the best known and most widely used of all aircraft, the DC-3. It was made possible because engine development was keeping pace with aircraft design and by 1935 radial air-cooled engines of 1000 h.p. were available. The DC-3 seated 21 passengers and had a cruising speed of 190 m.p.h. With the DC-3 the airframe revolution was complete. It was most immediately apparent in the transport field, because it was now possible for airlines to earn profits by carrying passengers, without having to depend on mail subsidies. The DC-3 was described as the first airplane capable of supporting itself economically as well as aerodynamically. It was so successful, indeed, that within two years Douglas had sold 803, and DC-3's were carrying 95 per cent of the nation's civil air traffic.[44]

Douglas continued to be a major builder of military aircraft while the DC series was being produced; as with Boeing, the development of this new transport type had a significant and visible influence on the design of Douglas military aircraft. The twin-engined B-18 bomber, which replaced the B-10 in 1936, was based on the DC-3.[45] The A-17 attack bomber, built by the Northrop division, and the TBD-1 Devastator torpedo bomber also appeared in the mid-1930's as production types incorporating the now basic concept of the all-metal, low-wing monoplane.

The last military types to adopt this design were dive bombers and carrier-based fighters. With the former, the problem was to brake this aerodynamically clean plane during the dive. Split flaps did not work satisfactorily, nor did a propeller-brake system tried by Chance Vought on its SB2U-1, which came out in 1936 as the first low-wing dive bomber. Vought got the contract with a bid based on a production of 75 planes and lost money when the Navy bought only 54.[46] When reversing the propeller failed to provide the desired braking, a Chance Vought engineer found a temporary solution in having the pilot lower the landing gear to increase drag. However, the NACA made wind-tunnel tests that provided the most effective solution, namely, perforated flaps.[47] Douglas experimented with this technique as early as 1935, but there were other problems to be solved as well, so that it was not until 1939 that the SBD-1 Dauntless became fully operational.

With carrier-based fighters the difficulty lay in the high take-off and landing speeds of monoplanes. A good deal of experimentation was required in order to solve this problem. The first low-wing monoplane fighter to meet carrier requirements was the Brewster F2A Buffalo, produced in 1939 by the Brewster Aeronautical Corporation, which had some claim to being the oldest organization in the aircraft industry. The original company was founded by James Brewster in New Haven in 1810, to build carriages.[48] It moved to New York City ten years later, and in the twentieth century recognized the trend of the times by switching to automobile bodies. In 1920 the company got a contract to build seaplane floats for the Navy, and twelve years later it was formally reorganized as Brewster Aeronautical. The principal product continued to be floats, but in the next few years the company began to expand to become an airframe builder. It started by buying from Consolidated the manufacturing rights for the Fleet trainer (making trainers was almost a standard opening gambit for getting into the military aircraft field) and then progressed to combat planes.

The Impact

It would be misleading to claim exclusive credit for American aircraft designers in bringing about this airframe revolution. As we have seen, the contributions of Rohrbach and other Europeans were of vital importance, and there was certainly no American monopoly on skill and originality in aeronautical engineering. Nevertheless it is clear that the American achievements culminating in the DC-3 represented a major advance in aeronautical technology.

The all-metal, low-wing monoplane, with controllable-pitch propeller, retractable landing gear, and wing flaps was developed by American manufacturers into a practical airplane between 1930 and 1935, and it remained for the next twenty years the dominant design for both military and civil purposes. It increased in size, its engines grew from the 500–700 h.p. of the earlier models to the 3,000 h.p. engines of the 1940's and 1950's, and wing loading rose by a factor of four to five; but there was no fundamental change of design until the arrival of the swept-wing jet plane in the 1950's. It can even be argued that the next basic design change was the swing-wing plane of the 1960's.

Flattery through imitation came immediately. Boeing sold two 247's to the German Lufthansa, but they were not intended for service.[49] Their design and construction were studied intensively, and the Germans presently came out with two transports, the Junkers 86 and the Heinkel 111, generally similar to the 247. Both designs were carried over into the military aircraft built by the same firms. The British indebtedness was even greater. For twenty years British aircraft design remained stubbornly dedicated to biplanes, a policy dating back to several fatal accidents with monoplanes in 1912.[50] This policy had to be abandoned in 1934, when it became unmistakably clear that aircraft design was undergoing a major revolution, and British sources freely acknowledged that the lag in development was made up by borrowing from abroad—in particular, that most of the new technical ideas in airframes had been tried out and embodied in American planes before they were adopted in Britain.[51]

It is very tempting to select the appearance in the mid-1920's of duralumin as the decisive step making the modern airplane possible. All-metal construction made bigger planes practicable and certainly made it easier to have cantilevered wings with internal bracing. Yet the record shows that designs incorporating monocoque fuselages and cantilevered wings came before the general use of metal construction. In this situation the material appears to have come in response to the potentialities of the design, rather than vice versa. Subsequently, of course, design concepts could expand because of the availability of suitable materials.

A major innovation is seldom produced by a single technological change; it is much more likely to grow from a complex of ideas and forces. This introduction of the modern airplane followed the customary pattern. It was a series of changes, no one of which was sufficient by itself. The unavoidable drag of the wire-and-strut biplane limited the utility of more powerful engines as well as of retractable landing gear and controllable-pitch propellers. On the other hand, without these devices the advantages of an aerodynamically clean airframe might not have been sufficiently great to justify the increased cost and more elaborate production techniques required to build it. The higher wing loadings that were actually adopted would not have been practical. Nor would they have been practical without wing flaps and wing slots (the latter a contribution from the British firm of Handley Page), and these in turn were a product of extensive research into the properties and behavior of the boundary layer.

It is arguable that the distinctively American role in this innovation was limited to the airframe. There was certainly a recognizable American superiority also in radial air-cooled engines and high-performance aviation fuels, but this was partly a matter of good fortune with respect to resources in petroleum and partly of concentration on what appeared to be best suited to the nation's requirements in both military and civil aviation. American thought was understandably dominated by the idea of moving heavily loaded bombers and transports over long distances, and for this purpose the radial air-cooled engine had no real competitor in the 1930's. On the other hand, the powers of

Europe had to think in terms of fighter aircraft in which speed and ability to operate at high altitudes were more important than range; therefore they were ahead of the United States in the development of liquid-cooled engines. In addition, there was no American counterpart to the experimental work on jet engines being done in Britain and Germany in the early 1930's.[52]

The difference was also reflected in the choice of superchargers. These were used on military aircraft in the 1920's, but the DC-3 was the first transport to be so equipped,[53] simply because it was the first transport with the performance potential to make supercharging worthwhile. Where American designers favored the turbo-supercharger because it gave the best results in providing high take-off power for large airplanes with heavy loads, European preference turned to the gear-driven supercharger as early as 1927 because it seemed to promise better performance at high altitudes.[54] Since the Americans continued to go their own way, and since in operation these two types of supercharger were not as far apart in performance as had been initially supposed, the design and construction of American airplanes was not affected.

There were other ancillary technologies contributing to the total result. The employment of bigger and faster planes was made more feasible by improvements in the techniques of instrument flying and the development of effective and reliable air-ground radio communication, the latter an achievement for which Herbert Hoover, Jr., was largely responsible.[55]

However, no matter how far afield we may take the discussion or what limitations and qualifications we may impose in order to define precisely what constituted the innovation, it remains abundantly evident that an assortment of advances in aeronautical technology produced radical changes in aircraft design and construction during the early 1930's, and that the result of these changes was a type of aircraft that may properly be termed the modern airplane. Its qualities and its performance represented so great an improvement over those of its predecessors that they ushered in a new era in aviation, both military and civil. It is also clear that the stimulus to effecting this innovation came primarily from the competitive forces in American aircraft manufacturing and air transport. During the years when the vital decisions were being made and implemented these industries had to contend with depression conditions as well as harassment by various elements in the government. Apart from the controversy over the air mail contracts, the aircraft industry was being subjected to criticism as "merchants of death," even though export of aircraft and parts could be made only under government license, and efforts were being made to curtail, in fact to eliminate, profits on government contracts. Under the circumstances, the industry's achievement has to be regarded as one of the most remarkable feats in the history of technology.

5. The Hungry Thirties

To all appearances the American aircraft industry should have been thriving by the middle of the 1930's. It had pioneered in a series of bold new developments that gave it a dominating position in the world market for transport aircraft, and the increase in air travel generated by faster, safer, and more comfortable planes made this a market with an encouraging potential for the future. Military demand was also rising although not as rapidly in the United States as elsewhere. To a substantial extent the appearances were correct. Technological advance continued at a satisfactory pace, and the industry's over-all financial condition was somewhat improved. Profit margins were higher; profits as percentage of sales rose from nothing in 1934 to eleven in 1938, and as return on investment from 3 per cent in 1935 to slightly over 15 per cent in 1938.[1]

However attractive this picture may have looked on the surface, and much was made of alleged enormous profits in aviation by those who classed the aircraft manufacturers as "merchants of death," there were adverse factors also. Progress is expensive. As aircraft became larger and more complicated, development costs mounted, and for most of this period these had to be borne almost entirely by the manufacturers.[2] Contracts in those days were fixed-price, with penalties for failure to meet specifications;

the cost-plus contract was uncommon in the aircraft industry until the Second World War.[3] Yet a company had to experiment if it was to stay in business, and if the experimentation failed to result in a production contract, then the manufacturer was faced with a substantial loss. Even with a successful bid it could easily happen that the production run was too short or the unit price too low to absorb the full development cost.

To complicate matters further, during most of this period the aircraft industry had to contend with influential elements in Congress and the administration who regarded the making of profit, especially on government business, as prima facie evidence of misconduct and who exerted a good deal of effort to insure that any such profits should be held to a minimum. As an outstanding example, the Vinson-Trammell Act of 1934 provided for a generous expansion of naval aviation but at the same time restricted profits on each contract to 12 per cent. In other words, the best a manufacturer could do on any one contract was to earn 12 per cent on a closely scrutinized cost of production; there was no guarantee that he would earn this much, and no assurance of any over-all profit on Navy business, since a loss on one contract could not be made up on another.[4]

As partial compensation for the uncertainties of the domestic market, exports of American aircraft and aircraft components rose during the 1930's. Exports of finished aircraft multiplied tenfold between 1927 and 1937, from 63 to 631; sales of engines and parts rose similarly.[5] The value of aeronautical products exported increased from $9,100,000 in 1929 to $39,404,000 in 1937, and in the latter year exports accounted for 26 per cent of the industry's total sales.[6] Part of the increase was due to the superiority of American transport planes; the DC-3 became standard airline equipment abroad as well as at home. Part was due simply to aggressive selling by the aircraft industry. Exports of military aircraft had to be licensed and as a rule a two-year delay was imposed on new designs. The manufacturers were inclined to feel that this restriction handicapped them needlessly without effectively preserving military secrets, but it is impossible to determine how valid this argument was. Until the close of the decade most exports of American military planes went to

Latin America and Asia. Whether the release of new models for sale to Europe would have stimulated exports or not is debatable, since the powers of Europe were trying to foster and protect their own aircraft industries. The export market had the attraction of not being subject to the limitation on profits of domestic military sales; on the other hand there was an element of risk in selling to financially shaky governments at this time. From its experience with export sales North American worked out a system by the end of the decade of requiring a down payment of 15 to 30 per cent on British contracts, with advances as the work progressed, and on other foreign contracts a larger down payment and an irrevocable letter of credit for the balance.[7] For the five years between 1934 and 1939, sales of American aircraft and parts divided 46 per cent to the United States government, 23 per cent to the domestic civilian market, and 31 per cent to export.[8]

The Organization of Production

One of the difficulties the aircraft industry has had to face in its relations with the public and to some extent with government has been misunderstanding, or ignorance, of the real nature of aircraft production. The problem is that one airplane cannot be compared to another in the way that, for example, one automobile can be compared to another. Aeronautical science and technology have changed too fast to permit very much standardization. Consequently figures showing merely the total number of aircraft produced during a given period are meaningless and may give a misleading picture of the state of the industry. Figures based on airframe weight or dollar value will indicate general trends more clearly but may still fall very short of giving an accurate picture.

The type of analysis required was made for 1931 by C. L. Lawrance. Although his production totals were estimated and were short of what was actually attained, his breakdown of the data shows some of the disparities that were seldom appreciated outside the industry. He estimated a total production for 1931 of 2,520 aircraft, of which 875 or 34.8 per cent were military, and 1,645 or 62.5 per cent, civilian.[9] In dollar value the proportions were exactly reversed: the military aircraft were worth $12,847,625 and the civilian, $6,441,820. The civilian aircraft fell into three categories: 740 light airplanes worth $1,256,894; 658 private planes worth $3,310,976; and 247 transport planes worth $5,100,550.[10] Lawrance's distinction between "light" and "private" planes is somewhat vague; presumably the "light" planes were in some form of commercial service, such as sight-seeing, charter flights, crop-dusting. The essential point is clear enough: the large transports constituted 15 per cent of the number of units but 52.7 per cent of the dollar value. For aircraft engines the same pattern prevailed: 1,866 for military use with a value of $10,197,690 and 1,700 for commercial use with a value of $3,226,600.

Lawrance derived from his data a conclusion that has remained valid for any period in the history of the aircraft industry:

70.4 per cent of the total value of our entire airplane and engine production is military, and 75 per cent of the individuals on our payrolls are engaged in military work. I know that engineering is vital to our progress and that it is prohibitive in its cost unless it can be stimulated by military production.[11]

This comparison of types was made before the completion of the revolution discussed in the previous chapter. One marked effect of this change was to make military and transport aircraft bigger and more complicated and to increase the disparity between them and the small planes. In 1937 (see Table 5) the aircraft industry sold 949 military planes for $37 million and 2,824 civilian planes, including commercial transports, for $19 million.[12] The transports had an average price of $63,000; the others, $3,500.[13] In terms of units, there were 10,836 nonmilitary airplanes registered in the United States in 1937; 386 of these were in scheduled airline service, about 100 *fewer* than the airlines had used in 1930 to carry a smaller volume of traffic over less mileage.[14]

It should have been clear, and was to those who knew the facts, that any assumption of a close relationship between aircraft and automobile manufacturing, based on little more than that both products used an internal combustion engine, was entirely unfounded. Even the relationship through the engine was negligible; by the 1930's aircraft and automobile engines scarcely had even a superficial resemblance to each other. The bulk of the aircraft industry's earnings came, not from the mass production of great numbers of virtually identical units, but from building a limited number of quite large, extremely complicated airplanes, whose total output seldom exceeded 1,000 units for any one year at this time and for which production runs of 100 or more for any given model were exceptional. Even if the

Table 5. Aircraft Production, 1932–1939

Year	Total	Military	Civil
1932	1,396	593	803
1933	1,324	466	858
1934	1,615	437	1,178
1935	1,710	459	1,251
1936	3,010	1,141	1,869
1937	3,773	949	2,824
1938	3,623	1,800	1,823
1939	5,856	2,195	3,661

Source: *Aviation Facts and Figures, 1956,* pp. 6 and 7.

small planes are included in the totals, the output of aircraft was in no way mass production. In 1935 the United States produced almost 4 million motor vehicles and not quite 2,000 airplanes, a ratio of 2,000 to 1.[15] Two years later, when aircraft output had doubled, the ratio was 1,500 to 1.[16]

It was therefore out of the question for the aircraft industry to use the production methods so successfully employed by the automobile industry. It had to develop its own specialized techniques, and in the 1930's these were undergoing some important changes in order to cope with new problems of production. Some distinction must be made between aircraft engines and airframes, since the trend to multi-engined planes and the need for spare engines required many more engines to be built over a given period than complete aircraft. In addition, there were fewer engine than airframe manufacturers, so that each individual engine company would have a larger share of the total output than was the case on the airframe side of the business. Nevertheless, with a total of 6,082 engines produced in 1937,[17] this phase of the aircraft industry was still not engaged in mass production.

With airframes, Glenn Martin pointed out in 1931, there was no possibility of continuous reproduction in the manufacturing process; the same plant had to be able to produce large and small types, both landplanes and seaplanes,[18] and this situation continued for the rest of the decade. It was impractical to use the expensive single-purpose machine tools that were commonplace in automobile manufacturing, because there was nothing in aircraft manufacturing comparable to performing the same operation on several hundred thousand identical units. The aircraft manufacturer, moreover, had to prepare to make frequent changes during the production process, whereas his automobile counterpart could count on freezing a design for an entire year.

On the other hand the processes of fabricating and assembling aircraft were too complex by this time to be done by simple handicraft methods. Glenn Martin refers to the introduction of metal construction as a step that necessitated major changes, specifically a sweeping and somewhat troublesome conversion of shop practices and comprehensive revisions of plant design and layout.[19] The industry met its production problems by ingenious adaptations of existing techniques. Standard machine tools were used with special jigs and fixtures, so that the same tool could be used for several different operations.[20] In airframe construction, where light metals were being worked, it was found that dies made of zinc, wood, or rubber were as effective as steel dies and had the advantage of being cheap and easily replaceable.[21] Drop hammers and mechanical and hydraulic presses were used for fabricating aluminum parts, and spot welding came to be widely utilized.[22]

The airframe companies made wings and fuselages and did the final assembly; in fact, in contracts with the United States government all components except the airframe and assembly —that is, engines, propellers, accessories, and armament—were purchased separately by the government and supplied to the manufacturer as "Government Furnished Equipment" (GFE).[23]

Normally GFE accounted for almost half the total cost of the finished airplane. In commercial sales the airframe manufacturer negotiated the contract on the basis of delivering complete aircraft, including all components. The industry therefore had associated with it an assortment of supplier firms, some directly affiliated with aircraft companies, others independent.

Subcontracting, as distinguished from procurement of parts, constituted less than 10 per cent of the industry's operations at this time.[24] A situation in which there was barely enough business for the major participants in the industry was not conducive to subcontracting. In addition, aircraft manufacturing involved special features that were a handicap to subcontracting:

Added to the usual cost and profit considerations found in all industries, airframe management must concern itself with the federal regulations affecting its commercial product and the noneconomic and political desires of the governmental agencies. At all times management must produce a product of outstanding excellence subject to fantastic quality and performance requirements.[25]

The writer of this passage goes on to point out that an ordinary manufacturing mistake could cause a disaster that would reflect adversely on the manufacturer, not on the subcontractor. There were therefore powerful incentives for the aircraft firm to keep production as much as possible in its own hands and depend for parts on a few suppliers of proven reliability.

Labor was not particularly a problem for most of the decade. The aircraft industry had a special situation in that it required a very high proportion of skilled and semiskilled workers, approximately 90 per cent of the labor force;[26] this consideration was a factor in determining location. However, there was seldom difficulty in finding the needed labor, largely because the industry was a comparatively small-scale employer. Employment in aircraft manufacturing in 1929 was 18,600, two-tenths of 1 per cent of all manufacturing employment in the United States; 9,600 in 1933, still 0.002 per cent; and up to 64,000 in 1939, or 0.007 per cent of total manufacturing employment.[27] Average weekly wages ranged from $30.16 in 1931 to $25.16 in 1935 and back to $30.56 in 1939.[28] These figures compare favorably with the earnings of automobile workers during the depression, but in the absence of accurate data on continuity of employment, it is difficult to make valid comparisons. It appears that aircraft workers were somewhat better paid than most industrial workers, no doubt because of the high ratio of skilled workers in the industry.

Nor was aircraft production during the 1930's appreciably affected by labor unrest. Strikes were rare before 1937, and union organization scarcely existed. Of the centers of aircraft manufacturing, southern California was notoriously hostile to union activity before the coming of the New Deal.[29] The hectic period of the NRA brought some gains among aircraft workers by the International Association of Machinists, but the industry managed to avoid formulating a code before the NIRA went out of existence. Douglas Aircraft was representative of the situation. It had a company union, the Douglas Employees Association, formed to try to stave off the threat of unionism posed by the NIRA.[30] The passage of the Wagner Act and the rise of the CIO brought a marked change. Douglas had a sit-down strike in 1937, which brought union recognition; Lockheed forestalled trouble in the same year by accepting the International Association of Machinists as the bargaining agent for its employees.[31]

New Competitors

On the surface it would seem that the limited volume of business, combined with the increasing burden of development costs, should have curtailed quite sharply the opportunities for new entrants to get established in the aircraft industry, and an arguable case could have been made for the emergence of a trend toward oligopoly. In the military market, where development costs were greatest and profit margins lowest, only about a dozen firms, including engine manufacturers, were effectively in competition, and the bulk of the business went to four airframe manufacturers (Douglas, Boeing, Curtiss-Wright, and North American) and two engine manufacturers (Curtiss-Wright and Pratt and Whitney).[32] Fundamentally, however, the fast-changing technology of aviation and the absence of any common and standardized aircraft type made it impossible for a few firms to dominate the industry and close it to newcomers.[33]

Getting into the aircraft industry was still a hazardous enterprise, and only men with a substantial amount of training and experience succeeded during the 1930's. Of those who met this requirement the first chronologically to establish and maintain a new airframe company was Major Alexander P. de Seversky, a Russian refugee with a flair for aircraft design, as well as a prolific if dogmatic writer on aviation. The Seversky Aircraft Corporation was organized in 1931, a year in which establishing a new business was an exercise in optimism, and located in Farmingdale, Long Island, where it shared facilities with Grumman and Fairchild.[34] The company began working on experimental designs and in 1935 developed one design into a monoplane trainer, the BT-8, that won an order for 30 from the United States Army. Further development along the same lines produced the P-35, the first American fighter plane to reach a service speed of 320 miles an hour and an operating ceiling of 30,000 feet. The P-35 put the company solidly on its feet; in 1939 it became the Republic Aviation Corporation, specializing in high-performance fighter planes.

A second important addition to the manufacturers of military aircraft came when Consolidated moved to San Diego. The vice-president of the company was Lawrence Dale Bell, who had left Martin to join Consolidated in 1928.[35] Bell had made his first airplane in Long Beach, California, in 1910; then he joined Glenn Martin as a mechanic and became shop superintendent at the age of twenty. According to Bell's own account, he was planning to start a company of his own as early as 1931–1932, but conditions then were definitely unpropitious. However, when Consolidated moved, leaving a factory and some experienced labor behind in Buffalo, Bell found his opportunity. The Bell Aircraft Corporation was formed in 1935 with a capitalization of $350,000. It took three months of virtually door-to-door selling to raise the first $150,000 needed to get started, but it was raised and Bell began work in the ex-Consolidated factory with 56 employees and $35,000 worth of secondhand machinery and used office equipment.

The new company kept itself alive by becoming a subcontractor for Consolidated to make wing sections for PBY flying boats while the design of its own first plane was being worked out.

This was the Airacuda (XFM-1), first flown on September 1, 1937. It was a twin-engined pusher, intended to give fighter escort to bombers. It carried two 37 mm. cannon and four 50-caliber machine guns, all remote-controlled, and required a crew of at least four.[36] The prototype cost $680,000 to develop, but in spite of the novel features incorporated into it the Airacuda was not a success and only fifteen were sold. Bell's next model did much better; it became the P-39 Airacobra, which, like Seversky's P-35, put its builder on a solid footing.

There were also smaller companies that entered the market for private planes, a market that rose appreciably after the worst of the depression had passed.[37] A substantial part of the rise in sales of light planes has to be credited to government assistance in the improvement and extension of facilities such as airfields and navigational aids.[38] The Bureau of Air Commerce even tried to promote development of a twin-engined six-place plane, which it hoped to be able to buy for $30,000 for use by its own inspectors.[39] Evidently it was expected that orders from the Bureau would induce one of the aircraft companies to adopt the design, but no one took the bait. The only indication of a response is a query from Robert E. Gross of Lockheed questioning the utility of a six-passenger plane and suggesting that eight would be much better.[40]

The number of firms engaged in the private-plane industry fluctuated: the membership of the Aeronautical Chamber of Commerce shows sixteen in 1938, excluding subsidiaries of larger companies.[41] Two may be singled out for attention. The absorption of some companies by the mergers of 1928–1929 and the effect of the depression left Cessna for a while as the sole independent in Wichita. However, in 1932 Walter Beech became tired of being an executive of Curtiss-Wright and returned to Wichita to start a new company of his own, the Beech Aircraft Corporation.[42] The first production, the Beechcraft Model 17, was a cabin biplane that performed so well that it continued to be built until 1948. Five years later (1937) Beech turned to the now classic pattern of the all-metal, low-wing monoplane in the form of the Model 18, a twin-engined "executive transport."

The other private-plane company to be noted here was the

Piper Aircraft Corporation, formed in 1937 by William Thomas Piper, a Bradford, Pennsylvania, oil man. It grew from a company organized in 1929 by C. B. Taylor, which became a depression casualty and was taken over by Piper. Taylor then founded Taylorcraft in Alliance, Ohio. When the Bradford plant was destroyed by fire, the Piper concern moved to Lockhaven, Pennsylvania, so that Piper could include float-planes among his products.[43] The Piper Cub, a small wooden monoplane, easy to fly and very maneuverable, rapidly achieved popularity and proved to be extremely useful for artillery spotting in the Second World War.

There was also an important addition to the aircraft engine manufacturers. This was the Allison Engineering Company of Indianapolis, Indiana, previously mentioned as a General Motors acquisition during the aviation boom of 1929. Allison had begun as a machine shop to service racing cars at the Indianapolis Speedway and had expanded to be a builder of marine engines and precision parts, including a steel-backed, lead-bronze bearing for aircraft engine crankshafts.[44] At the time of the General Motors purchase, the head of the Allison company, Norman H. Gilman, began to work on a design for a 1,000 h.p. liquid-cooled aircraft engine.

His timing was very good, because the Air Corps was becoming interested in developing an American liquid-cooled engine for fighter planes, and the number of firms in the field was limited. Packard had withdrawn in 1928 when the Air Corps cut off development funds in consequence of a disagreement over standards and policies,[45] and Curtiss-Wright was putting its emphasis on air-cooled engines. During the 1930's the Air Corps underwrote the development of liquid-cooled engines by the Continental Motors Corporation of Muskegon, Michigan, and the Lycoming Manufacturing Company of Williamsport, Pennsylvania, to the extent of about half a million dollars each. Allison put in some $900,000 of its own, or rather General Motors', money and received about as much again from the Army and Navy, with the result that its V-1710, 12-cylinder engine was ready in 1937, a year ahead of Lycoming's comparable O-1230, and two years ahead of Continental's O-1230, which was a flat, opposed-cylinder engine because the Army believed that engines should be enclosed in the wings.[46] Allison's successful emergence as an aircraft engine builder showed foresight and technical skill; having the financial support of General Motors helped also.

The Heyday of the Flying Boat

One of the most important consequences of the breakthrough in aircraft design achieved during the 1930's was the prospect of building considerably bigger planes, capable of operating economically at longer distances, higher speeds, and greater altitudes than had hitherto been feasible. This possibility had its first practical application in flying boats, which reached the apex of their development and use during this decade. The Navy had a long-standing and continuing interest in the development of flying boats, dating back to 1912, and naval demand provided the larger part of the market for them. In addition, a good deal of design and development work on the type was done at the Naval Aircraft Factory.

What was novel in the situation was the opportunity opened by large flying boats for transoceanic commercial operations. Aside from airships, the flying boat was the only satisfactory medium available. There were few commercial airfields in existence capable of handling landplanes large enough to carry adequate payloads on such long flights, and until the end of the 1930's there were no such landplanes anyway. On the other hand, a flying boat operated wherever there was a reasonable area of smooth water. Moreover, the hazard of forced landings at sea had to be faced, although in practice the risk proved negligible, and a flying boat offered a greater margin of safety. The full realization of its potential was predominantly the story of Juan Trippe and the growth of Pan American Airways.[47] Reaching first into Latin America, Pan American was spanning the Pacific by the mid-1930's and was prepared to cross the Atlantic, an achievement delayed far more by diplomacy than by technical problems. The extension of Pan American's routes required progressively larger aircraft. Trippe's first important supplier was Sikorsky, who as early as 1928 had designed and built a very successful twin-engined amphibian, the S-38. Over 100 were sold to various airline and private purchasers; the S-38, indeed, made it necessary for Sikorsky to reorganize his company as the Sikorsky Aviation Corporation, with a capitalization of $5 million and a new plant in Stratford, Connecticut.[48]

It was therefore natural for Trippe to turn to Sikorsky for large flying boats. Sikorsky's first response was the four-engined S-40, which went into service late in 1931.[49] It was not, as Sikorsky himself points out, as advanced a design as could have been attempted at the time; because he felt that safety was a prime consideration in a passenger-carrying plane, he based the S-40 on the S-38. Even so its size presented some novel problems. For instance, no conventional source of aircraft components could provide the springs for a landing gear that had to support a 17-ton load; the difficulty was resolved when it was found that what was needed was about the same as the springs used for railroad cars.[50] The location of the cockpit in a large plane also posed difficulties; the final decision was made on the strength of advice from Charles A. Lindbergh.

The S-40 paved the way for the ultimate Sikorsky Clipper, the S-42, designed to meet a Pan American request for a flying boat capable of carrying fuel for a 2,500-mile trip against a 30-mile wind, at a speed of 150 m.p.h., compared with the 115 of the S-40.[51] To achieve these qualities, it was necessary to go up to a wing loading of 30 pounds per square foot, and this in turn demanded wing flaps.

But while the Sikorsky Clippers were a technical success, they were a heavy financial loss to United Aircraft. The leap forward to these big four-engined amphibians meant a large development cost; the contract for the first three S-40's fixed the price at $125,000 each, and the preliminary design work alone cost more than that.[52] United Aircraft eventually concluded that the Sikorsky operation was too expensive to continue. It abandoned flying boats in 1938, but fortunately chose to finance Sikorsky himself in a return to a long-standing ambition—the design of a workable helicopter.

There were other firms in the field to carry on the development of flying boats. Douglas built some for the Navy, but not in any great quantity. Apart from Sikorsky, the two major competitors were Martin and Consolidated. Martin, as we have seen, moved from Buffalo to Baltimore largely because it needed better facilities for building and testing flying boats. Consolidated had a similar story, but without Martin's financial crisis.

During the boom period Reuben Fleet expanded his operations in several directions. There was the Fleetster transport, previously described. A modified version of the Fleet trainer was put on the market as a sports plane, first named the Husky Junior and later the Fleet. Its initial price was $7,500, and after a slow start it did very well, selling several hundred before the depression blighted the market for private planes.[53]

Consolidated also bought the Thomas-Morse Airplane Company for about $450,000 in 1929 (the actual purchase price was 10,000 shares of Consolidated stock).[54] This company came on the market because the Morse Chain Company had been acquired by Borg-Warner, which, however, did not want an aviation subsidiary that had been doing only experimental work for the Army and losing money on it. At the time of the sale to Consolidated the Army finally gave Thomas-Morse a production order for an observation plane (O-19) which eventually resulted in 170 being built between 1930 and 1932. This order helped Consolidated through the worst part of the depression.

Most important, in 1927 Fleet brought I. M. Laddon into the company to design large military aircraft. The first effort was a twin-engined bomber for the Army, built in cooperation with Sikorsky but withdrawn because it did not come up to specifications.[55] Consolidated then turned to the Navy, which was looking for a large flying boat with at least an 80-foot wing span and a 2,000-mile range. Laddon's entry, the XPY-1, had a 100-foot wing span and a metal hull that followed essentially the design of the Curtiss NC's of 1919.[56] It made its test flight successfully early in 1929, but the Navy contract went to Martin, leaving Laddon and his men with the grim satisfaction of discovering later that Martin lost heavily on the order.[57]

To help develop a market for flying boats, Fleet became one of the organizers in 1929 of the New York, Rio, and Buenos Aires Air Line (Nyrba). The new company bought fourteen transport versions of the XPY-1, named the Commodore. Nyrba was an early victim of the depression and was sold to Pan American in August 1930 for $4 million in stock, but it lasted long enough to establish Consolidated as a builder of flying boats. The experience gained on the Commodores was applied to a new design, XP2Y-1, which had the same 100-foot wing span but used a small bottom wing to replace the struts of its predecessor.[58] The Navy accepted it and ordered 23 in 1932. Its service designation was P2Y-1.

Thus, while Consolidated's business fell off sufficiently for the company to face deficits in 1931 and 1932,[59] recovery came rapidly through increased naval orders for flying boats. This part of the firm's business, indeed, became so important that it caused a relocation. Buffalo, like Cleveland, was not a good site for building and testing flying boats. When the prototype XPY-1 was finished, Lake Erie and the Niagara River were frozen over, and the plane had to be shipped by rail to the Washington Navy Yard.[60] The XP2Y-1 had to cut its test flight short in late March 1932 and a month later was unable to take off for Washington and almost unable to return to shore because of ice. Fleet had already begun the search for a new location and finally in 1934 leased a site in San Diego adjoining both the harbor and Lindbergh Field, the municipal airport. The new factory was ready for occupancy in the summer of 1935, and there Consolidated moved 157 carloads of machinery and other materials, plus 311 employees.[61] In contrast to Martin, Consolidated was able to finance its relocation from its own resources. The company arranged for a loan of half a million dollars from the Reconstruction Finance Corporation but did not have to use it.

Consolidated's move to San Diego had important implications both for the company itself and for the aircraft industry in general. Its arrival in San Diego a few months after North American had established itself in Los Angeles made southern California definitely the principal center of airframe manufacturing in the United States, with Consolidated, Douglas, Lockheed, North American, Ryan, and Vultee all concentrated in the area. If we consider the entire West Coast and add Boeing to the list, there was a clear preponderance over any other region. By 1937 California had become the leading producer of aircraft products, with a dollar output of $51,863,046 against second-place New York's $15,515,923.[62] The comparable figures for 1929 were New York, $17,225,764; California, $4,987,899. Since these totals include airframes, engines, propellers, and parts, the concentration of airframe manufacturing in California is all the more striking, because engine and propeller production remained in the Northeast.

For Consolidated itself the move implied a commitment to flying boats as the company's major product for the immediate future, and to the Navy as almost the exclusive customer. It is an interesting phenomenon that although the Commodore was reasonably successful and profitable, Fleet abandoned the commercial field entirely once his Nyrba operation ceased. Perhaps he was warned off by the losses Sikorsky and Martin were incurring. More likely he considered that since he was already working to capacity on naval orders and had the naval market for flying boats virtually monopolized, there was no need to get into the competitive transport market. Consolidated went to San Diego with an order for 60 flying boats of a new type, later to become famous as the PBY, or Catalina. It was a monoplane with a single pair of struts connecting the wings to the fuselage and no external bracing on the tail assembly.[63] In place of the fixed wing floats of earlier flying boats, the PBY had retracting floats. The first production model was flown on October 5, 1936.

The development of commercial flying boats beyond the point reached by Sikorsky was accomplished by Martin and Boeing, in that order. The Martin M-130, the China Clipper, was the successful response to Pan American's requirements for a plane to operate in transpacific service, not nonstop as yet but with long hops to Hawaii, Midway, Wake, Guam, and the Philippines. It was four-engined, weighed 52,000 pounds compared to the 40,000 of the S-42, and carried 48 passengers as against 32. The first of these craft was contracted for in November 1932 and the first trip from San Francisco to Macao was made just three years later.[64] As with Sikorsky, the Clippers gave Martin much publicity, valuable experience, and a substantial financial loss. By 1938 the company had abandoned the civilian market for the, by then, more promising military market. It was easy enough to shift from Clippers to flying boats for the Navy, and in 1937 Martin received an order for 21 of the type designated PBM amounting, with spare parts, to $5,299,538.[65] A year later Glenn Martin was able to report that the company had the best year in its history, with undelivered orders totaling $17,505,000.[66]

The climax of Martin's career as a builder of flying boats came with the Mars (XPB2M-1), the largest of the type ever built. Completed in 1942, it weighed 70 tons, had a wing span of 200 feet, a length of 117 feet, and four 2,000 h.p. engines.[67] Six others were built, designated JRM. Two were accidentally destroyed; the others were used as Navy transports until 1956.

The last builder of Clippers was Boeing. The B-314, designed for transatlantic service, weighed 82,000 pounds, had a cruising speed of 165 m.p.h. and carried 74 passengers.[68] Its construction brought out a number of problems indicating that knowledge of control surfaces for large aircraft was still fragmentary.[69] These were solved empirically, with the result, for example, that the Boeing Clipper started with a single but finally emerged with a triple tail. Twelve were built between 1939 and 1941, the first six went into service in 1939 with regular transatlantic commercial flights commencing on June 28th, and all remained in operation, some under military control, throughout the war.

The Clippers were magnificent feats of aeronautical engineering, markedly superior to the competitors produced elsewhere. They had much in common with the sailing ships for which they were named, in that they were spectacular, filled a transportation need which could not at the time have been met otherwise, and their career, brilliant while it lasted, was unavoidably brief because of the inexorable advance of technology. The Clippers were in the accepted pattern of the all-metal, cantilevered-wing monoplane; but a flying boat must of necessity have its wings above rather than below the fuselage, and the high-wing design has not been as satisfactory aerodynamically. Moreover, the flying boat's body is called a hull, for good reason. It must have some of the qualities of a ship's hull, because the plane must land on water, and it should be able to operate in water for considerable distances. It is therefore impossible to make a flying boat as aerodynamically efficient as a landplane of comparable size; while the Clippers were winging their way over the oceans, such landplanes were coming off the drawing boards and on to the production lines.

Four-Engined Landplanes

Leadership in this process was taken, understandably, by the companies that had already pioneered so brilliantly in the development of transport planes: Boeing, Douglas, and Lockheed. Douglas wanted to keep the advantage won by the DC-3; the other two were trying to regain their competitive position. The obvious step for all three was to go to a four-engined plane, because in commercial operations a large plane can operate more economically than a small one, provided there is sufficient density of traffic, and the large plane can make longer nonstop flights. During the last half of the 1930's the three companies were working on comparable designs, which would eventually emerge as Douglas' DC-4, Boeing's Stratoliner, and Lockheed's Constellation. It was more than a simple matter of enlarging previous models. The problems of control surfaces that had appeared on the Clippers existed on these big landplanes also. Moreover, with engines of increased power output (over 1,000 h.p.) now available, these planes could, by using superchargers, cruise at altitudes over 20,000 feet, thus meeting less air resistance and being able frequently to go over poor weather.[70] But at these heights an oxygen supply would be necessary, and for regular commercial passenger-carrying operations the only satisfactory solution was a system of cabin pressurization.

The problems of high-altitude flight had received some previous study, but intensive attention was delayed until it became clear that such flights were on the verge of becoming practical for both military and commercial aviation. By the mid-1930's, in addition to the three companies mentioned, Martin and Curtiss-Wright were also experimenting in this field, and the Air Corps, assisted by Professor John E. Younger of the University of California, was doing research on high-altitude cabins for military airplanes.[71]

Martin made some experiments but dropped out of the competition without building a pressurized plane. Curtiss-Wright developed a plane, the CW-20, with a unique double-arc fuselage design, instead of the circular cross section normally employed with metal monocoque construction.[72] The CW-20's appeared just in time to be taken over by the Army as nonpressurized cargo carriers, under the designation C-46, during the Second World War.

Douglas had a pressure system in 1935, including an indicator to show the oxygen concentration in the cabin patented by Frank R. Collbohm, then head of Douglas' research department and later president of the RAND Corporation.[73] This system was tested on a DC-2 but was abandoned because it used liquid oxygen and this was considered too dangerous. Douglas continued its experiments, but the war intervened here also, and the otherwise very successful Douglas entry in the four-engined transport field, the DC-4, never was pressurized. Like its competitors, the DC-4 appeared on the market just in time to be impressed into war service. Of the 1,200 that were built, most did the bulk of their flying as Army C-54 (Skymaster) transports.[74]

Boeing developed its own system, based on a cabin pressure regulator designed and patented in 1937 by a Boeing engineer, Nathan C. Price.[75] The Boeing system has more importance for the aircraft industry as a whole because the right to manufacture it under license was acquired in 1940 by the AiResearch Manufacturing Company of Los Angeles.[76] This company originated in a firm established by John E. Garrett in 1936 as a wholesale tool supply service for the West Coast aircraft industry. AiResearch, eventually a division of the Garrett Corporation, would grow after the war to become the principal manufacturer of high-altitude pressure systems.

But this was postwar. Boeing's principal achievement in the late 1930's was to develop the low-wing cantilevered monoplane into a four-engined bomber, the B-17, immortalized as the Flying Fortress. Considering what the plane later achieved, it had a surprisingly difficult time getting born. The concept of a giant bomber, a "battleship of the air," seems to have been implanted in the mind of Claire Egtvedt as early as 1928, as the result of a conversation with Admiral Joseph M. Reeves regarding the relative striking power of the battleship and the bomber of that day.[77] Nothing more was done until 1934, when the Air Corps asked Boeing, among others, to make design studies of an airplane weighing about 30 tons, to carry 2,000 pounds of bombs 5,000 miles.[78] The project was designated XB-15. It was completed in 1937, but its performance fell short of what had been hoped, and the experiment was discontinued. The initiative in this case came from the Army, but the next move was definitely Boeing's. In the fall of 1934 the Air Corps invited bids on a "multi-engined" bomber, with somewhat less ambitious characteristics than the XB-15. "Multi-engined" then ordinarily meant a two-motored plane, but the phrase was used in order to permit trimotored designs to compete. Egtvedt, however, decided to go the whole way,[79] utilizing the experience gained on the XB-15. Boeing, he felt, should specialize in big airplanes. He was already committed to planning a four-engined transport, and it was characteristic of Boeing policy to build military and commercial planes to the same basic design. So the company put $275,000 into the design and construction of a four-engined bomber, Model 299, temporarily holding up work on the transport, Model 300.

It was a bold and almost catastrophic decision. The prototype B-17 was successfully test-flown at Boeing Field in Seattle in July 1935, but when it flew against its competitors at Wright Field in the following October, it crashed because the pilot took off with the control surfaces locked. The production contract went to the twin-engined Douglas B-18. Fortunately the Air Corps could see beyond an accident due entirely to unfamiliarity with the complexities of planes of this size, and Boeing got a test contract for thirteen B-17's, although this must have seemed like very slender consolation to the company when compared with the sixty-five the Air Corps had planned to buy.[80] In time, of course, Boeing's risk paid off handsomely, and even this misfortune was not as bad as it could have been. Douglas also undertook an experimental project, the XB-19, which at 160,000 pounds was the biggest bomber prior to the postwar B-36, bigger even than Boeing's B-29.[81] It was finished in 1941, but only one was built. As with the XB-15, the expected performance was not reached, and the B-19's usefulness was limited to providing design and engineering experience for the future. It cost Douglas $4,039,000 and was sold at a loss of $2,644,000.[82] There was a good deal of opposition from the services to building these big bombers at all. It was argued that the same amount of money could procure more medium-sized bombers of the B-18 type which were fully capable of carrying out any mission then contemplated under existing policy.[83] So Boeing was perhaps luckier than it realized to be able to salvage the order for thirteen Flying Fortresses.

The Model 300, the fraternal twin of the B-17, had a similarly shaky start. Because the company had to concentrate on the bomber and the Clippers, the prototype 307 Stratoliner did not appear until late in 1938, and a test flight in the following spring ended in disaster, again because of unfamiliarity with control problems.[84] Nevertheless nine Stratoliners were built and delivered in 1940. Five went to TWA to become the first four-engined transports on domestic airlines, and the first pressurized passenger planes in regular operation.[85] They also became military transports (C-75), and in this service did not use cabin pressurization. Comfort was not a prime consideration on military flights; at high altitudes oxygen masks and pressure suits sufficed.

Lockheed was the last of the three rivals to produce a pressurized four-engined plane. It was the smallest of the three companies, and while the Electra was selling well, it took time to build up the company's resources after the painful receivership of 1932. One Electra was adapted in 1936 under an Air Corps contract as an experimental plane (XC-35) for investigating some of the problems of high-altitude flight,[86] but this was a minor part of Lockheed's activities. Until the company turned to military orders in 1938, its development work was concerned chiefly with the twin-engined Model 14 Super Electra, first tested in July 1937. It was noteworthy as introducing the Lockheed-Fowler wing flap design that increased wing area when the flap was lowered and permitted a wing-loading of 32 pounds.[87] An enlarged version became the L-18 Lodestar, introduced in 1939.

Lockheed also organized a subsidiary, AiRover, in 1937 to

build a twin-engined, six-passenger transport, with what was called a "Unitwin" power plant: the two engines had a single drive shaft and propeller.[88] It was intended for feeder-line service. First called the Starliner, it appeared in 1939; a year later both plane and company revived the historic Lockheed name of Vega.

It was therefore not until 1939 that Lockheed felt able to move into the construction of a four-engined transport, the L-049 Constellation. It was ready in 1943 and was taken over by the Air Force as the C-69.[89] It had the distinction of being the only one of the high-altitude designs to be flown in war service with pressurization, presumably because it came along so late that the Air Force decided to use the few that were available for testing this type of equipment.[90]

The Period Ends

By 1938 it was becoming obvious that the demand for military aircraft, both at home and abroad, was going to terminate the depression period for the aircraft industry. The decade of the 1930's had been an era of outstanding achievement. American transport planes, both landplanes and flying boats, dominated the world's airways both quantitatively and qualitatively. With military aircraft the situation was different, not because of any technical deficiencies but because American opinion continued in a mood of complacent isolationism, so that there was little of the urgency about developing air strength that existed among the other powers of the world. In some categories American military planes of the late 1930's were as good as or superior to their foreign counterparts; in other categories they were not.

Until its closing years the decade of the 1930's remained one of technical advance and economic struggle for the aircraft industry. Not even the major firms could be considered secure. Douglas had a near monopoly of the transport market and a strong position in naval aircraft, but Douglas needed help from the airlines to move from the DC-3 to the DC-4. In 1938 Boeing was borrowing every week to meet its payroll; it was losing money on the Clippers and heavily burdened with the development costs of the B-17's and the Stratoliners.[91] The year ended with a deficit of $500,000, and a threatened strike was called off when Egtvedt made it clear that the company would simply have to shut down. Lockheed in the same year reached the point where it had only one order left on its books: as it happened a Japanese order for Super Electras.[92] When Consolidated completed most of its PBY contract its work force dropped from a peak of 4,000 in 1937 to 1,200 in 1938.[93] A War Department decision in 1939 to buy liquid-cooled rather than air-cooled engines left Pratt and Whitney with the prospect of having to shut down when existing orders were filled in July 1939.[94] Military orders, both American and foreign, came along in time to forestall these threatened crises, but there is still a revealing picture of how even the strongest companies in the aircraft industry were living a hand-to-mouth existence.

The difficulties of the aircraft industry during the 1930's can be exaggerated. Figures are available (see Table 6) showing a

Table 6. Sales, Earnings, and Net Worth of Thirteen Leading Aircraft Companies, 1935–1939 (millions of dollars)

Fiscal Year	Net Sales	Earnings Before Taxes	Net Worth
1935	45	4	66
1936	72	7	83
1937	117	14	94
1938	152	22	111
1939	237	44	138

Source: W. F. Craven and J. L. Cate, *Men and Planes* (Chicago, 1955), p. 187.
Note: These are fiscal years, that is, beginning July 1.

constant increase in sales, earnings, and net worth for the thirteen leading American aircraft companies between 1935 and 1939, and the historians of the Army Air Forces show that in 1939 aircraft stocks were above the general industrial average and that assets were well ahead of liabilities.[95] However, analysis of the figures cited shows that the big increases came in the closing years of the decade, when military orders were mounting rapidly. Encouraging figures for the industry as a whole can hardly have impressed executives who had to worry about the high cost of keeping up with technical progress, the uncertainty of contract awards, and the prospect of labor difficulties emanating in part from rivalry between the United Auto Workers and the International Association of Machinists. These executives were the people who kept the industry going. What they were like as a group was described by Eugene E. Wilson, then president of United Aircraft, when he toured the industry in 1937 to discuss prospective requirements for engines: [96]

Out of this tour around the country, I not only collected every man's point of view as to power plants but got an interesting cross section of the industry as a whole. One-man shows for the most part, they were directed by engineer-executives, a combination hard to beat when manufacturing was involved. In contrast with the rather studied approach we had at United, they were bold and forthright. Averaging somewhat under forty-five years of age, they compressed into brief business careers the whole history of aviation. In a brief span of two decades they had created a whole new technology, and this had been accomplished in the face of many vicissitudes. Through doing business largely with a few customers like the government or the airlines, they had developed an outlook quite at variance with that of industries dealing with large numbers of individual customers.

6. The Approach of War

The years from 1938 to the attack on Pearl Harbor marked a watershed for the American aircraft industry. It was not just that the demand for aircraft climbed sharply, so that the financial hazards of the previous twenty years were at least temporarily eradicated. There were major changes in the structure of the industry. The opportunities and the pressures created by accelerating demand altered the position of firms within the industry, since the responses to the challenge varied markedly in effectiveness. In addition, important shifts in location were initiated, partly to reduce the concentration of aircraft production on the East and West coasts, where it was most exposed to possible enemy attack, and partly because plant expansion in the existing locations was handicapped by shortages of labor and housing. This process was not very far along at the time the United States entered the war, but it was important that the start had been made.

The Preliminary Stage

This start was made none too soon. As late as the fall of 1938, mobilization plans envisioned a maximum Air Corps of 12,000 tactical and 2,000 training planes.[1] A production rate of

1,000 planes a month was to be achieved by three months after M day, and a total output of 24,000 within a year. But these were just figures on paper. Neither the Air Corps nor the aircraft industry possessed the information needed to show if, or how, these requirements could be met.[2] There had been studies of industrial mobilization, as provided in the National Defense Act of 1920, but these were sketchy and inadequate. Apart from the chronic problem of severely limited funds, the Air Corps faced several special difficulties in planning for war, including a national policy based on the assumption that the United States would fight only a defensive war, differences between the Army and Navy regarding their responsibility for defense against invasion, and the rapid pace of technical change in aviation.[3] The result was that in 1938 there were still no clear-cut policies for the expansion of aircraft production, and except in a few quarters, not much sense of urgency about formulating them. "Educational" orders for industry were authorized by Congress in this year, but no funds were available until 1939 [4] so that their effect in facilitating conversion to military production was negligible.

Some attention was given to the British "shadow factory" system, whereby complete factory structures were put up near existing automotive plants, ready for key management personnel and technicians to move in and start operations when war came, but again nothing was done. It was highly unlikely that an isolationist Congress, essentially reflecting the attitude of the public, would have consented to spend money in this way, and the administration did not press the matter because it believed that, with depression conditions persisting, there was ample unused productive capacity to take care of expanded military production without interfering with normal civilian demand. Where aircraft production was concerned, there was a complacent assumption that the automobile industry could be converted overnight to the mass manufacture of airframes and engines, an assumption accepted unquestioningly by the automobile industry itself.

It is easy, and tempting, to present a picture of utter complacency and neglect of elementary preparation right up to the threshold of war; it is also unfair and inaccurate. In point of fact the administration and the military services did their best, within the limits imposed on them, to make adequate preparations for the world crisis that was impending. Almost every American airplane used in combat during the Second World War was at least on the drawing boards before the war began. Some of these preparatory steps have already been described: for instance, the development of the B-17 in the face of considerable opposition and misfortune and the Navy's persistence in seeking ways to adapt the all-metal, low-wing monoplane design to carrier operation. The success of the B-17 after its uncertain start led Boeing, with Air Force encouragement, to propose in 1938 an enlarged version with longer range and higher ceiling through pressurization.[5] However, there was still strong opposition to these big expensive bombers, so that for the time being Boeing could do no more than make design studies. As a matter of fact it was not until 1939 that funds were provided for additional B-17's beyond the original thirteen.[6]

Expenditures on military and naval aircraft at this time show awareness of growing need (see Table 7). Of $219,000,000

Table 7. U.S. Expenditures on Military Aircraft, 1934–1939 (millions of dollars)

1934	13 *
1935	23
1936	44
1937	58
1938	67
1939	68

Source: *Aviation Facts and Figures, 1958*, p. 30.
* Includes approximately $10 million allocated from the Federal Works Agency.

spent by the Air Corps between 1931 and 1939, $160,000,000 came during the period beginning with the fiscal year 1936.[7] For the Navy, the total was $169,000,000 between 1931 and 1939 and $83,000,000 after 1936, a somewhat more even distribution. This steady increase in expenditure by the United States government was helpful in stimulating production both qualitatively and quantitatively, but the rate of increase was not high enough to stimulate any appreciable expansion of the industry. Existing capacity could meet the government's requirements, especially in the prevailing atmosphere that there was no particular reason to hurry.

This attitude is reflected in the absence of any rush into aircraft manufacturing during this immediate prewar period, although it must have been clear that a major war, even if the United States were not directly involved, must produce an insatiable demand for airplanes. One deterrent, of course, is that aircraft manufacturing demanded, far more than in the First World War, a considerable investment not only in capital but in technical skill. The only important new entrants at this time came from well-established aeronautical backgrounds. One was Northrop Aircraft, Inc., founded in 1939 when John K. Northrop became restless in his association with Douglas and made a fresh start on his own, with the idea of concentrating on experimental aircraft.[8] The other was the McDonnell Aircraft Corporation, organized in St. Louis in July 1939. Its founder, James Smith McDonnell, Jr., was an engineer from Princeton and M.I.T. with a long background as an aeronautical engineer and test pilot.[9] McDonnell would become one of the most successful new ventures in the aircraft industry, but its impact would be felt after, rather than during, the war.

The preparation of the American aircraft industry for the burden of war production received as much stimulus from external as internal sources, specifically from the European democracies trying desperately and belatedly to make up for their own years of complacency and neglect. In 1938 British and French purchasing missions arrived in the United States with procurement of aircraft and engines as one of their major objectives. The effect was impressive. The aircraft industry accumulated a backlog of $680 million in orders during 1938 and 1939, and of this total $400 million represented foreign orders.[10] The Air Force historians estimate that the tooling and plant expansion financed by British and French funds advanced aircraft production in the United States by a full year.[11]

The incidence of these orders had a marked and lasting influence on the structure of the aircraft industry. Lockheed, for example, had reestablished itself as a successful builder of commercial aircraft on a moderate scale but until 1938 was not a factor in the military market. Then in April of that year a British military mission arrived in Los Angeles looking for a medium bomber and was attracted to Lockheed as a firm not heavily committed to United States government contracts. The company redesigned the L-14 Super Electra on five days' notice to meet the British specifications, creating the bomber that became known as the Hudson.[12] A conference in London followed, culminating with a contract on June 23, 1938, for 200 planes plus as many more as could be delivered by December 1939, up to a total of 250.[13] The initial price was $25 million. It was the largest single order received up to that time by any American aircraft manufacturer, and it has been identified by Cyril Chappellet as a major turning point in Lockheed's history.

North American had a comparable experience, except that North American had become established as a builder of observation and training planes for the Air Corps and made no commercial planes at all. When the company moved to Los Angeles it took with it two designs produced by its General Aviation predecessor. One was an observation plane, developed by the company as GA-15 and adopted by the Air Corps in 1936 as the O-47. It incorporated the now dominant design of the all-metal, cantilevered-wing monoplane and was described proudly by the company as "an observation plane built around the observer." [14] The observer's station was in the belly of the plane, with windows at the bottom and on each side. Over 200 were built, but they were already obsolescent when the war came and were allocated to training and general utility functions.

The other model, NA-16, was designed from the beginning as a trainer. It was accepted by the Army in 1935 as the BT-9, and two years later it appeared in revised form as the AT-6.[15] Both designs successfully combined close simulation of the handling characteristics of combat planes with the safety factors and ease of maintenance desired in trainers, so that the AT-6 became one of the most widely adopted of all military aircraft.[16] The initial Air Corps order was for 180. Then in 1938 Britain ordered 200, which likewise proved to be just an initial order. The British called the plane the Harvard; it became the standard advanced trainer for all the British Commonwealth Air Forces, as well as for the United States Army and Navy. What this did for North American can be judged by the fact that the 150 employees of 1935 increased to 3,400 by September 1, 1939.[17]

A third beneficiary of this mounting foreign demand for military aircraft was Gerard Vultee's Airplane Development Corporation in Glendale, California, later to become for a brief period Vultee Aircraft. Vultee himself was a product of the California Institute of Technology who had gone with John K. Northrop from Douglas to Lockheed and took Northrop's place as chief engineer at Lockheed when Northrop left in 1928.[18] He lost his job when Lockheed ran into its depression troubles, and for a time taught at the Curtiss-Wright Technical Institute in Glendale. Then he got support in 1932 from E. L. Cord to develop an eight-passenger transport, the V-1, and organized the Airplane Development Corporation, which became part of AVCO with the rest of the Cord interests. It was a minor operation; American Airways (later American Airlines) ordered twenty but actually bought ten.[19] The timing was bad, because single-engined, eight-place transports were a poor prospect in 1932. Vultee rectified the error by converting his design to an attack bomber, the V-11, in 1936 and did so well that the company, now the Vultee Division, Aviation Manufacturing Corporation, moved to larger quarters in Downey, California. Turkey bought 40 V-11's for $2,500,000; Brazil 26 for $1,700,000; Russia 9 for $2 million, plus jigs, blueprints, and manufacturing rights; and China 1 complete plane and parts for 29 for $1 million.[20] The company made a profit of $750,000 in the first half of 1938. In the meantime, however, Vultee had flown his own plane to Washington in an effort to sell a modified V-11 to the Air Corps, and on the return trip he crashed on Mt. Wilson in a snowstorm. The subsequent history of his company was part of the complex of relationships between AVCO and Consolidated. The Air Corps did buy nine of the planes, under the number YA-19, but the company lost $60,000 on the order.[21]

Finally Pratt and Whitney, as mentioned in the previous chapter, was rescued from a difficult situation by timely French and British orders. To recapitulate, early in 1939 the War Department awarded a $15 million contract to Allison for V-1710 liquid-cooled engines for fighter planes, which Pratt and Whitney had hoped to get for its R-1830 air-cooled engine.[22] Pratt and Whitney was left with a backlog of orders sufficient to keep the plant going until the middle of the year. After that it was faced with the prospect of closing down and probably seeing its trained staff disperse. The decision was not simply an arbitrary choice by the War Department. The Air Corps was well aware that while the United States was ahead of the rest of the world in the design and building of radial air-cooled engines, it was definitely behind in liquid-cooled engines, and this lag could be a serious handicap in war. The efforts of the Air Corps to encourage the development of liquid-cooled engines have been described. By 1938 the Allison V-1710 was the only satisfactory model in operation, and even in 1939 the Kilner Board put liquid-cooled engines between 1,500 and 2,400 h.p. at the top of the priority list for Air Corps development work.[23] Pratt and Whitney was not the victim of a whim, but of legal requirements for procurement that demanded competitive bidding and prevented the allocation of contracts in order to maintain or promote production facilities.[24]

However, the needs of France and Britain filled the breech. A preliminary French order for $2 million was placed in the fall of 1938, followed by a much larger contract signed on February 14, 1939, which not only resulted in orders totaling $85 million but provided financing for plant expansion to accelerate production of the engines.[25] By the spring of 1939 France was aware that it had very little time to rehabilitate its air power—too little, in fact. France fell before the engines could be delivered, and the order was taken over by Britain. The provision for plant expansion required prolonged negotiations with the Treasury Department, which was acting as intermediary for the Anglo-French purchasing missions and was urging the aircraft industry to accept French and British orders. The industry, including Pratt and Whitney, was willing enough, but it felt that where additional plant was required, some concession should be made with regard to existing tax regulations on depreciation. This was a reasonable precaution, because there was certainly no assurance that this additional capacity would remain in production for any extended length of time, and the Treasury, after some discussion, accepted the industry's position.

The Preparatory Phase

When war broke out in Europe in September 1939, therefore, the American aircraft industry was in a phase of rather low-pressure expansion. Its output in that year was 5,856 aircraft, the highest since 1929. Of these 2,195 were military and 3,661 civil, but airframe weights tell a more accurate story.[26] Military aircraft came to 10.1 million pounds, civil to 2.4 million.[27] The industry ranked 41st among American industries, with an output valued at $280 million and a working force of 64,000.[28] It had an estimated total capacity of 15,000 planes a year and 14,000 tactical engines (over 1,000 h.p.).[29] Expansion beyond these figures would call for both new plant and conversion of other industries, specifically the automobile industry. If events should call for such expansion, allowance would have to be made for the aircraft industry's poor location from the military point of view. Over 80 per cent was within 200 miles of either the Atlantic or Pacific Coast. The degree of concentration was quite remarkable. The Northeast had 24.2 per cent of the airframe, 80.7 per cent of the engine, and 81.8 per cent of the propeller floor space; the West Coast had 45.4 per cent of the airframe and 4.3 per cent of the engine floor space.[30] As it turned out, the risk of enemy attack never materialized, but this could hardly have been foreseen.

It was quite evident that some expansion was urgent. Apart from the pressing needs of the European democracies, the United States itself was inadequately equipped to face a world crisis. In August 1939 the Air Corps had some 800 first-line planes, compared with 3,750 for Germany and 1,750 for Great Britain.[31] The Navy added another 800 to the American strength, but many of these were obsolescent biplanes. There were qualitative factors also. The United States had a better heavy bomber than anyone else in the B-17, but only 23 of these were in service in September 1939. The standard bombers of 1939 were the B-18 and the Northrop A-17 attack bomber, both dating back to 1936. The worst situation was in fighters. The Air Corps was largely equipped with Seversky P-35's and Curtiss P-36's, its first fully cantilevered-wing, all-metal monoplane fighters, definitely inferior by 1939 to foreign competitors. They were just beginning to be superseded by the Curtiss P-40, an improved P-36 with the Allison V-1710 engine.[32] It was adopted in 1939 and saw widespread service with the American and Allied air forces, but whatever its virtues, no one ever put the P-40 into the same class with the British Spitfire or the German Me-109.

The fighter plane situation cannot be blamed wholly on budgetary limitations, because these affected all types. The qualitative lag in American fighter development has to be attributed primarily to the preoccupation, obsession is probably too strong a word, of the Air Corps with strategic bombardment. This, to a considerable extent, was the heritage of "Billy" Mitchell, an exponent of the extreme air power theories of the Italian General Giulio Douhet. However, while Mitchell had his disciples in the Air Corps, the prevailing policy in 1939 did not accept the complete mass-bombing doctrines of the Douhet-Mitchell school, but put an emphasis on high-altitude precision bombing. This called for big bombers, the type in which the United States excelled, and it was assumed that large formations of these planes would have the firepower to execute their missions without fighter escort. Consequently fighter aircraft were some way down the priority list.

The Navy appeared somewhat better off. Its Air Service was in much more satisfactory condition than the British Fleet Air Aim, which had spent most of the interwar period as an unwanted stepchild of the Royal Air Force. As far as could be judged at the time, American naval aircraft were at least as good as those of their principal rivals, the Japanese, and although the Japanese were underestimated, this appraisal was reasonably accurate, except for fighters. Most of the Navy's first batch of Brewster Buffaloes were diverted to Finland to help the Finns resist the Russians, and others went to Britain and its allies.[33] It was perhaps just as well, because the Buffalo demonstrated severe limitations in combat. Fortunately the Grumman F4F Wildcat was beginning to go into production.

While there were differences of opinion among the American people on their country's proper role with regard to the war in Europe, there was reasonably broad agreement on the desirability of strengthening the nation's defenses, so that the expansion of the previous two or three years accelerated somewhat, although on the whole modestly. Indeed, such acceleration of aircraft production as occurred was made possible, not by the outbreak of war, but by President F. D. Roosevelt's energetic support of a program to bring Air Corps strength up to 5,500 planes, which was approved by Congress in April 1939.[34] As a result new planes were on the way, at least on the drawing boards. For most of them the Army and Navy laid down the requirements they wanted and the manufacturers designed planes to meet them, but there was also a respectable degree of initiative from the industry.

In the heavy bomber category, Boeing was both stepping up its output of Flying Fortresses and also making improvements on the original design, a process that would intensify as the B-17 accumulated war experience. The company, as stated before, also proposed in 1938 a larger bomber with a pressurized cabin and longer range. The Air Corps was not ready for this yet, but Boeing continued design studies on the idea.[35] As a matter of fact, in 1938 the War Department had excluded production of any four-engined bombers from its projected budgets for 1940 and 1941, but this stipulation was overruled by the President. The Air Corps then decided that an additional source of big bombers was desirable and early in 1939 invited Consolidated to submit a design for a heavy bomber with a range of 3,000 miles, a speed over 300 m.p.h., and a ceiling of 35,000 feet,[36] a performance exceeding that of the contemporary B-17. Work progressed rapidly enough for the prototype XB-24, which became famous as the Liberator, to fly before the year was over. Since Consolidated also got a $20 million Navy order for 200 PBY's in December 1939, its production facilities were taxed, in fact overtaxed. It had to add 411,000 square feet to its plant at a cost of $2,470,000 under a contract whereby the government subsequently paid the company and took title to the addition.[37] Until the advent of the B-29, the Liberator was the longest-ranged bomber in existence. In this one respect it outdid the Flying Fortress. Combat experience showed that both planes needed more firepower and protection. Modifications for this purpose caused no difficulty with the B-17, but they affected the maneuverability of the B-24 and made it hard to handle.

There was more competition in medium bombers. The plane that became the A-20 Havoc, an attack bomber designed primarily to support ground forces, was initially designed by Douglas in 1937 for the French Air Force. Production on a French order for 100 was begun in 1939.[38] Much of the A-20 production eventually became the British Boston. The United States Army Air Forces (as the Air Corps became in 1941) made more use of the B-25 Mitchell and the B-26 Marauder. The former was designed by North American at its own risk early in 1938, with encouragement from the Air Corps, and after some modifications in the initial design, an order for 184 was placed in September 1939.[39] The B-26 was designed by Martin in response to an Air Corps specification of January 1939; it went into production simultaneously with the B-25.[40] It was significant of a change in outlook that both planes were bought "off the shelf," ordered from designs without taking time to build and test prototypes. It may also be significant that the North American plane, which was in preparation for a year longer, proved somewhat more satisfactory in service. The A-20, B-25, and B-26 were twin-engined metal monoplanes.

Fighter production in 1939 centered on the P-40. A first order for 524, at a total price of almost $13 million, was placed in May 1939. Two other fighters were under development at this same time. One was the Bell P-39 Airacobra, which got its first order, twenty planes for $2,839,000, in that active month of September 1939.[41] It was a good plane but, like the P-40, it lacked the altitude performance needed for first-rate Second World War fighters. An Air Corps decision against supercharging the P-39 was partially responsible for this handicap.

The other fighter was Lockheed's unique P-38 Lightning. It was designed in 1937 in response to an Air Corps request for a

fighter capable of reaching 20,000 feet in 6 minutes and a speed
of 360 m.p.h.,[42] and it was Lockheed's first major venture into
military aircraft. The prototype of this unique twin-engined,
twin-fuselaged plane flew early in 1939, and its speed actually
came to about 400 m.p.h. Although it was destroyed in a landing
accident, it made a good enough impression to produce a test
order, which was in due course followed by a production order in
September 1939.[43] When this first order for 66 planes was followed by another for over 600, Lockheed's production facilities
were overtaxed, and additional space for P-38 production was
found by buying an abandoned distillery.

The growth of Lockheed's business led to a pioneering step
among aircraft manufacturers in the formation of a separate
customer service department, which would eventually become
Lockheed Aircraft Service, Inc. It was organized in September
1937, and in its first year did $2,400,000 worth of business.[44]
The great increase of European sales due to French and British
orders made it advisable to establish an assembly and maintenance division in Britain. This operation was supervised by
Henry H. Ogden, who had flown round the world with the Army
planes in 1924, and it subsequently became the major British
depot for assembly and repair of all types of American
planes.[45]

These planes were all essentially prewar in conception, designed before any evaluation could be made on the basis of
combat experience. By early 1940 enough more was known of
what was demanded in a fighter plane to produce additional
designs. One, the P-47 Thunderbolt, brought the Seversky firm,
renamed the Republic Aviation Corporation in 1939, back into
prominence.[46] The design, in lineal descent from the P-35,
proved highly successful. The P-47 originally was to have a
liquid-cooled engine, but production problems caused a switch to
the Pratt and Whitney R-2800, giving the plane the additional
distinction of being the last American Air Force fighter to be
equipped with an air-cooled engine.

North American's P-51 Mustang had an origin all its own. It
began early in 1940 with a British proposal that North American
build P-40's so that Britain could get fighters in quantity in the

shortest possible time.[47] J. L. Atwood, then chief engineer of North American, believed that the plane could be improved by redesigning the cooling system so as to get better engine performance, and since this involved taking the radiator out of the cowling and putting it behind the pilot, the change would also put the pilot in a better position for visibility. Sir Henry Self, the head of the British purchasing mission, was reluctant to have North American undertake a complete new airplane, but eventually an agreement was reached whereby North American bought Curtiss' flight test reports and wind tunnel data on the P-40 for $56,000 to provide a foundation for redesigning, and in April 1940 was given a British contract for 320 of these modified planes at a cost not to exceed $40,000 each. The prototype Mustang was test-flown in the following October. It required some modifications, but essentially the design was sound.

Fifty Thousand Planes

The German blitz in the spring of 1940 brought about a complete reassessment of what was needed in American aircraft production. The reasons for the spectacular succession of German victories were certainly not fully understood, but it was manifest that German superiority in the air was a major factor; to most Americans it appeared to be the decisive one. Comparisons between German and American air strength and productive capacity were alarming, although German production was overestimated, and immediate large-scale action was obviously called for both to provide air strength for Britain and other nations still resisting the Axis drive, and to bolster the air defenses of the United States itself. At the same time there was deep uncertainty regarding just what could be done, or what ought to be done (by no means synonymous), and a continuing undercurrent of complacency that the war would not really affect us and that in any event American skill and know-how would take care of any crises that had to be faced.

This was a situation made to order for the talents of President Roosevelt. On May 16, 1940, he startled the nation, and most of all the military services and the aircraft industry, by calling for the production of 50,000 airplanes a year. The origin of this figure is still a matter of debate.[48] It definitely did not come from the services, still thinking in terms of available productive capacity and of Congresses notoriously unreceptive to military budget requests. Several of Roosevelt's associates, along with Lord Beaverbrook, British Minister of Aircraft Production, have claimed some of the credit; but the President may simply have taken Woodrow Wilson's First World War request for 25,000 airplanes and doubled it. This statement by an Army historian adequately summarizes what happened:

> But the 50,000 figure finally used was neither an Army nor a Navy figure—it was a Presidential figure concocted by the President and his political advisers. The President's big round number was a psychological target to lift sights and accustom planners in military and industrial circles alike to thinking big.[49]

To this the comment might be added that the 50,000-plane request had the great advantage of asserting bold and dramatic leadership with a minimum of political risk. It proved to be the kind of challenge that the situation required, and it was met. But if the figure had turned out to be unrealistic and the goal could not be reached, then blame for the failure could have, and would have, been laid on the aircraft industry.

It was one thing to ask for 50,000 airplanes, quite another to produce them. The figure had been pulled out of the air, and it gave no indication of the types of aircraft to be built. A hasty revision of plans two weeks later making an arbitrary allocation of 36,500 planes to the Army and 13,500 to the Navy did not help very much.[50] Nor was there as yet any effective organization for directing and coordinating production. The National Defense Advisory Commission (NDAC) was created at the end of May, and one of its members, William S. Knudsen, who left the presidency of General Motors to take this assignment, was responsible for production. The powers of the NDAC however were vaguely defined, so that Knudsen's function at this time was essentially advisory.

A contemporary estimate of the implications of the 50,000-plane program indicated that existing capacity for the production of airframes, engines, and propellers was about a fifth of what was needed.[51] The author calculated that over 75 million feet of floor space would be required, about 6 times what was then available, at a cost of $572,000,000.[52] To put the problem another way, the aircraft industry was being asked to turn out in a single year about as many planes as it had built in the entire period since the Wright brothers made their first flight in 1903, and this second 50,000 planes would be bigger and more complicated than the first.

There was no unused capacity in the industry itself. Besides the American orders placed under the 1939 program, there were the foreign orders, sharply increased during the crisis months of April and May 1940 when the Anglo-French Purchasing Commission ordered another 6,000 planes from Bell, Boeing, Consolidated, Curtiss, Douglas, Lockheed, Martin, and North American.[53] These contracts, all taken over by Britain after the fall of France were for up-to-date types just going into production such as the P-38, B-17, B-24, B-25, and B-26, and released for export by the United States as emergency assistance. By September of that year British orders mounted to 14,000 planes and 25,000 engines, for a total of $1.5 billion. While these purchases were made with the full approval of the United States government, they introduced an additional element of confusion, since there was no clear-cut system for deciding who got served first until a joint committee representing the interested parties began to function with reasonable effectiveness late in the year.

Neither new planes nor new factories could be created overnight by waving a wand, or even by appropriating millions of dollars. While additional facilities were being created, the aircraft companies had to make the most of their existing resources. What was being done can be illustrated by the experience of the major producers. North American had 3,400 employees on September 1, 1939, but J. H. Kindelberger foresaw that the demand for labor was going to rise. Consequently he established an apprentice training program and broke down jobs into smaller components so that inexperienced help could be trained in a minimum of time.[54] The company also established a methods department early in 1940 to study the improvement of production, one immediate result being the installation of overhead monorail conveyors on which components were moved by hand.[55] Neighboring Douglas and Lockheed expanded locally. Douglas not only took complete control of the former Northrop plant in El Segundo but added a new assembly plant at the Long Beach Municipal Airport.[56] Lockheed continued its successful adaptation of its designs to military uses by converting its L-18 Lodestar into a twin-engined bomber, named the Ventura by the British. Lockheed proposed this modification late in 1939 and received an order from Britain for 25 in February 1940.[57] The plane went into production in July in the Vega factory in Burbank.

Up in Seattle, Boeing's first move to stimulate production was to bring Philip Johnson back from his Canadian exile and reinstate him as president in September 1939, because Johnson was an excellent production man while Egtvedt, who now became board chairman, preferred to work on engineering design.[58] It was possible because the five-year period in which Johnson could not be an official of a company bidding on air mail contracts had expired, and in any case this ban did not apply to being president of Boeing. The new president found himself with an impressive backlog of orders and an alarming shortage of working capital. The backlog came to $28 million, including 38 B-17C's ordered in the 1939 program and an option for 42 more.[59] In addition, the Stearman division in Wichita had a $2,800,000 contract for trainers. On the other hand, Boeing had lost $2,600,000 for the first nine months of 1939 and the company's credit was exhausted. To complicate matters further, late in January 1940, the Air Corps asked for designs for a super-bomber, to outdo in every respect both the B-17 and the B-24.[60] Boeing was well placed to compete because of its two years of design work on just such a plane, but there would be more designing and development to do before a production contract could be expected.

Johnson took care of the company's immediate financial needs by an issue of 450,000 shares of new stock and a loan of $5,500,000 from the Reconstruction Finance Corporation.[61] By mid-1940 additional orders for Flying Fortresses assured Boeing of earnings to meet its obligations, and in September the Air Corps awarded a contract for the XB-29, the Superfortress. Four companies, Boeing, Consolidated, Douglas, and Lockheed, entered this competition, but Douglas and Lockheed withdrew. Consolidated was given a similar contract for the XB-32. The Boeing entry had the unprecedented wing loading of 58 pounds per square foot, and was designed for a speed of 400 m.p.h. (not reached in service because of modifications), a ceiling over 30,000 feet, and a range of about 5,500 miles. To expedite production the Air Corps took what was termed a "three-billion dollar gamble" by ordering over 1,600 B-29's before the prototype made its first flight.[62] This was a measure of the sense of crisis that emerged in 1940, because a large bomber like the B-29 posed serious problems of design, testing, and production.

Consolidated's entry, which became the B-32, had a less happy history. The experimental model was both ordered and test-flown at the same time as the XB-29, but the B-32 encountered serious production difficulties and was not ready for service until the war was practically over.[63] The Air Force evidently believed that it had to persist with an alternative big bomber in case the B-29 failed to come up to expectations, but since the NACA expressed doubts about the design of the B-32 as early as 1942, we are left wondering why the Air Force clung so long to an unpromising prospect. It is difficult to account for the failure on the company's side either. Except for Boeing, Consolidated had as much experience as any American manufacturer in designing and building large airplanes, except that most of this experience was with flying boats. The B-24 was its first four-engined landplane. Some of the explanation undoubtedly lies in the fact that at this time Consolidated was having management troubles, which would lead to a major reorganization during the next two years.

The total output of aircraft in 1940 was 12,813, of which just under half were military.[64] It would take another two years to reach the President's 50,000 level, which by then had been superseded by still larger programs.[65] First an enormous amount of groundwork had to be laid. The major steps were the construction of new plant and the involvement of the automobile industry in aircraft manufacturing, but the whole process was incredibly complicated. For instance, in 1940 only two companies in the

United States made oleo struts, the shock absorbers on the landing gear; [66] obviously something had to be done to insure that the output of oleo struts would keep pace with the output of planes. Similar conditions applied to an endless assortment of components. And to add to the over-all difficulties of industrial mobilization, the process was being undertaken in an economy still predominantly geared to peacetime production.

7. Mobilization

All planning for the mobilization of American industry for war had recognized the elementary fact that the peacetime establishment for manufacturing aircraft would have to be supplemented by direct expansion and by conversion of other industrial plant, specifically from the automobile industry. There was an easy assumption that the needed resources would be forthcoming without undue difficulty, and certainly that until the United States became an active belligerent the necessary scale of military preparation could be reached without disturbing the civilian economy. The plans were reasonable enough at the time they were formulated; their chief flaw was that they were based on considerably more modest estimates than the actual situation called for. With or without the President's 50,000-plane goal, the conditions that emerged in May 1940 created a demand for aircraft far in excess of any previous forecasts, and it was a demand that kept rising rapidly.

From the point of view of the aircraft industry it made no difference whether the production program adopted in 1940 was realistic or not. It was not the function of the manufacturers to decide how many airplanes or engines, or what kind, were needed. Their job was to produce what was asked for, and they had to try to maintain maximum output while they were simulta-

neously expanding at a geometric rate. To complicate matters
further, although the pressure for military production of all
kinds was increasingly creating shortages of materials and labor,
the government had no clear system of allocations or priorities
and in fact preferred to rely on exhortation and admonition.

The aircraft industry had an especially acute problem in that
its overtaxed facilities were congested with orders from the
Army, the Navy, and Britain and her allies, all clamoring for
immediate delivery. The Army-Navy-British board formed late in
1940 helped somewhat, as did a provisional allocation of companies between the services on July 3, 1940.[1] This was an agreement to settle which service took responsibility for sponsoring
expansion of facilities. Each company was allotted to the service
with which it did the greater volume of business. This agreement, as could have been expected, had to be modified later, but
it affords a useful and interesting checklist of the American
aircraft industry as it stood in July 1940. The allocation was as
follows:

Army	*Airframes:*	Beech, Bell, Boeing, Cessna, Curtiss, Doug-las, Fairchild, Lockheed, Martin, North American, Republic, Ryan, Stearman, Stinson, Vultee.
	Engines:	Allison, Continental, Jacobs, Lycoming, Menasco, Wright.
Navy	*Airframes:*	Brewster, Grumman, Spartan, Vought, Consolidated.
	Engines:	Pratt and Whitney, Ranger.

The organization of production was improved somewhat by
the creation of the Office of Production Management (OPM) in
January 1941 although the agency had neither the power nor the
structure to be fully effective. Like the NDAC before it, it had to
work largely by persuasion, since authority to impose priorities
or to allocate scarce materials was still lacking. Moreover, the
OPM showed a characteristic Rooseveltian administrative touch.
Responsibility was divided between a director (William S. Knudsen), an associate director (Sidney Hillman), and the Secretar-

ies of War and Navy, and the only effective decision-making power was retained by the President himself. That the agency functioned at all was due to the fact that Knudsen and Hillman were able, patriotic individuals who wanted above all to get the job done.

The passage of the Lend-Lease Act in March 1941 was another step forward in that it eliminated competition between American and Allied orders. Meanwhile, however, the backlog was still accumulating. Plant expansion took time and, as will be described later, involved some knotty financial problems. There were also major complications in placing contracts for airplanes and parts. It was quite clear that the leisurely peacetime procedures of design competition, submission of prototypes, and an eventual fixed-price contract would have to be discarded in a situation where the government wanted everything the aircraft industry could produce and wanted it as rapidly as possible. Yet Congress wanted to prevent profiteering and was reluctant to see the competitive contract given up for the negotiated contract; in June 1940 it even reduced the allowable rate of profit on aircraft contracts to 8 per cent from the 12 per cent of the Vinson-Trammell Act.[2]

But the pressure of events necessitated a change of policy. Just as it was unrealistic to go through the routines of competitive bidding when no one in the industry was competing with anyone else, so it was equally unrealistic to require fixed-price contracts at a time when costs and prices were being subjected to growing inflationary pressures. The limit on profits was repealed in October 1940, and procurement shifted gradually to negotiated contracts, with the cost-plus-fixed fee type predominating. In time these represented 55 per cent of all Air Force contracts over $10 million.[3] The fees in 1940 were 7 per cent of cost, but by late 1941 they had been reduced to 4 per cent. Ironically, in view of the suspicion of cost-plus contracts, the profit margin on them, at least where the aircraft industry was concerned, was about half that on the fixed-price contracts placed during the war period. These contracts were also arrived at by negotiation. It was the only feasible way when the Air Force was, as the North

American history expresses it, buying paper airplanes, that is, planes which existed at the time of placing the contract only in the form of design drawings and performance estimates.[4]

Expansion of Facilities

In addition to improving and extending their existing facilities, the aircraft companies had several other options available for increasing production; all were utilized.[5] The most important of these were as follows:

1. Construction of new plant. It was the most direct method of expansion, but from the industry's viewpoint it had the drawback of saddling it with excess capacity when the war ended.
2. Subcontracting. There was room for expansion here, because only 10 per cent of aircraft manufacturing was subcontracted prior to 1940.[6] The difficulty was to find new subcontractors who could work to the standards necessary for aircraft construction.
3. Licensing. This process had the same problem as subcontracting: finding licensees outside the aircraft industry with the requisite facilities and skills. It was the least used of the three methods, accounting for about 10 per cent of the airframe weight produced during the war as compared with about 35 per cent produced by subcontractors.[7]

Some of the steps toward the building of additional facilities have already been referred to. Until mid-1940 these were principally extensions to or in the vicinity of existing aircraft factories, and insofar as they were financed by other than the manufacturer's own resources, they were the product of foreign, mainly British funds. There was some continuing momentum to this process. By December 1940 the American aircraft companies had spent $83,000,000 of their own money on new plant and equipment, and an additional $74,000,000 had come from Britain.[8] A few months earlier these would have been staggering amounts to invest in aircraft manufacturing, but by this time they were clearly just a start. Equally clearly, the requisite new construction would be on a scale beyond the financial resources of either the manufacturers or Britain. It should be added that the expansion undertaken thus far was carried out with no definite assurance on the matter of depreciation. Not until October 1940 did Congress give legal sanction to five-year depreciation.[9]

These measures relieved but did not solve the problem of financing extensive new facilities. Governmental assistance was obviously essential in view of the magnitude of the operation and the rather considerable risks to be assumed. Even with allowance for more favorable amortization, there were bound to be increased and frequently unpredictable cost factors; in addition, no one could foresee the duration of the emergency or the future disposition of these structures and their equipment. The government's first remedy was the Emergency Plant Facilities (EPF) contract, an arrangement whereby the manufacturer financed his construction through the normal private capital market, or if necessary by loans from the Reconstruction Finance Corporation (RFC). The government reimbursed him over a period of five years and then assumed title, unless the manufacturer chose to purchase the plant at that time.[10] The manufacturer also had the option of borrowing from the RFC to build his plant on terms that gave him ownership from the beginning.

The EPF arrangement proved to be cumbersome and mutually unsatisfactory [11] and was replaced by a system whereby the RFC established a subsidiary, the Defense Plant Corporation, which built the new facilities itself and leased them to the aircraft firms. An alternative procedure, used more extensively for weapons and munitions than for aircraft and parts, was for the War or Navy Department to build the plant and have it managed and operated by one of the companies in the industry.

Financing was the first problem; after that came the question of where the new facilities should be located. The manufacturers understandably preferred to add to their existing plants or build in their vicinity,[12] and this was ordinarily the initial step. From the point of view of management and supervision, it was the most desirable arrangement, but there were other factors to be considered. The military planners, who were concerned about the concentration of aircraft production on the seacoasts where it was exposed to possible enemy attack, wanted dispersal into the "Defense Zone," that is, at least 200 miles inland. The fact that the danger never materialized does not affect the validity of the military case; it was a hazard that had to be taken into account and guarded against.

There were other reasons for dispersing aircraft manufacturing. One, stressed by Sidney Hillman when the NDAC was first considering the problem, was the desirability of using idle facilities and labor.[13] It was a sound idea, but it was of limited applicability for an industry like aircraft manufacturing with its highly specialized requirements in the nature of factory space and equipment; to cite just one point, building airplanes needs plenty of room. A more compelling reason for dispersal arose because the existing centers of production rapidly developed acute shortages of labor and housing as the industry mushroomed; it became simple common sense to locate new facilities in areas where these difficulties would be less acute.

The degree and character of the relocation varied from company to company. Boeing's new plant for B-29's was in neighboring Renton, Washington. It also made substantial additions to its Stearman subsidiary in Wichita, initially for trainers. Curtiss-Wright spread to Columbus, Ohio, Louisville, Kentucky, and St. Louis for airframes, and to Lockland, Ohio, for engines; Douglas operated plants in Oklahoma City, Tulsa, and Chicago; Martin had a branch in Omaha; North American had plants in Dallas, Texas, and Kansas City; there was also a Pratt and Whitney branch in Kansas City. Among the major producers Lockheed was an exception; it spread out around Burbank but had no branches elsewhere in the country. The construction of the new factories was still in its early stages when the United States entered the war. Eventually they represented an investment of close to 4 billion dollars, of which $3.5 billion came from the government.[14] Some became permanent additions to the aircraft industry.

For most of the principal aircraft companies this process of rapid expansion did not affect their corporate organization. The organization had to be stretched to handle a much larger operation than it had been designed for, and this situation demanded additional managerial and technical talent and skilled labor; but in one way or another the difficulties were resolved. Lockheed, for instance, invoked the aid of the California Institute of Technology to establish a sixteen-week training program in aeronautics for engineers and technicians from other fields.[15]

The expansion of North American Aviation affords a particularly instructive example of the variety of steps that one firm could take. In the 26 months between the outbreak of war in Europe and the attack on Pearl Harbor, North American increased its monthly production rate from 70 to 325 units, its employment from 3,400 to 23,000, and its factory floor space from 425,000 to 2.5 million square feet, including new factories in Dallas and Kansas City.[16] The total output for this period was 3,705 airplanes. In its Los Angeles factory, labor was trained by pre-employment courses in the public schools, an apprentice program in the factory, and special extension courses in the public schools for employees who wished to prepare for advancement. In Dallas the company set up a two-week pre-hiring training program; Kansas City already had municipally supported training schools from which North American could recruit.

The Defense Plant Corporation provided assistance by financing the Dallas factory and also leasing to North American the machinery and tools needed to expand production at Inglewood —another technique employed to relieve the manufacturers of the need to make heavy investments in what could be temporary equipment. The Kansas City plant was built by the Corps of Engineers with War Department funds. It was managed by North American to assemble components of B-25's made by the Fisher Body Division of General Motors.[17] In addition, by late 1940 North American had over 1,000 subcontractors.

Thus the onetime holding company had again become a large and complex operation, now exclusively concerned with the manufacture of military aircraft. With due allowance for the government's assistance, it was an impressive achievement, which established North American as a major producer in the airframe industry. There were difficulties in the process. The UAW local which represented the Inglewood employees came under the control of a left-wing element that indulged in endless obstruction and finally called a strike in the middle of 1941. There was an unexpected solution to this problem; the strike was called off the day after Germany invaded the Soviet Union.

This was an unusual case, but labor trouble was recurrent during this first burst of expansion. It was quite understandable. The work force in the aircraft industry rose from 63,200 in 1939 to 347,100 in 1941, and this was just a start.[18] The unions were naturally anxious to safeguard their position and avoid being swept away by this torrent of new and unorganized employees, and the need on the part of the industry to absorb this mass of untrained and inexperienced workers was bound to cause friction.

In contrast to the experience of most aircraft companies, Consolidated underwent a major change of management in the course of its expansion. It was a complicated story, beginning with two AVCO subsidiaries, Stinson and Vultee, that had no relationship to Consolidated. Stinson, whose founder was killed in an airplane crash in 1932, was reorganized in 1938 as a division of AVCO's Aviation Manufacturing Corporation.[19] It was doing reasonably well as a builder of light airplanes, well enough for the parent company, undoubtedly mindful of the probable rise in military demand, to build a new plant in Nashville, Tennessee. Meanwhile Vultee was having trouble. After Vultee's death Richard Millar, a Los Angeles financier, was brought in to take charge. He had previously been associated with both Douglas and Northrop and so knew the aircraft industry. In fact, in 1932 he had formed a syndicate and raised $125,000 to buy Lockheed at the receiver's sale but allowed himself to be talked out of it by Donald Douglas.[20]

Gerard Vultee had evidently been the design genius of his company because Millar found a mediocre engineering staff and had to see the company lose several contracts before a new chief engineer succeeded in getting an Army contract for 300 basic trainers (BT-13's) in August 1939. The company accepted an estimated loss on this contract of $3.5 million in order to get the business, and the gamble paid off when subsequent orders for the BT-13 totaled over 11,000.[21] From that Vultee moved on to a dive bomber, the Vengeance (A31 and A35). Initially designed for Britain, it brought $90 million in orders in 1940 and 1941.

To meet this expansion, AVCO did some reorganizing of its manufacturing subsidiaries. The parent company was now controlled by Victor Emanuel, an American financier, not the King of Italy, and Tom Girdler, president of Republic Steel, who had combined to buy E. L. Cord's AVCO stock in 1937 for $2,632,000.[22] Late in 1939 the Vultee Division, Aviation Manufacturing Corporation, became the Vultee Aircraft Corporation, largely to assist in financing. A fourth of the new company's stock was issued to the public; the rest was retained by AVCO.[23] A year later Vultee absorbed Stinson through transfer of stock within the AVCO structure.

The enlarged Vultee organization put on an impressive production performance. The Downey plant had the first powered assembly line in the industry, an overhead track that carried fuselage frames in cradles through 25 assembly stations.[24] It cut assembly time 75 per cent and costs 40 per cent. The Nashville plant was enlarged with British financial assistance to produce the Vengeance. By late 1941 this combination of two orphan companies had 10,000 people on the payroll and a backlog of $178,000,000 in orders.

While Vultee was aggressively moving up in the aircraft industry, Consolidated was encountering managerial complications. To all appearances the company was expanding as rapidly and effectively as any other manufacturer, and as the builder of both the PBY and the B-24, its position in the industry could have been considered enviable. Besides the extension of the San Diego factory built for the Navy late in 1939, there was a further addition in the spring of 1940 under an EPF contract and still another in the fall under the aegis of the Defense Plant Corporation.[25]

At the same time the War Department was promoting an ambitious program for accelerating the production of B-24's. Three giant new plants were projected: one, the eventual Ford Willow Run plant, to make subassemblies; the others at Tulsa and at Fort Worth, Texas, to do the final assembling. Consoli-

dated was assigned the Fort Worth plant for operation and Douglas the one at Tulsa.[26] Neither aircraft company started with
great enthusiasm for the idea, but they cooperated willingly.

At least it was more or less willingly. Reuben Fleet became
increasingly restive at the degree of control the government was
exercising over his business, to say nothing of being disgruntled
at what he considered excessive delay in reimbursement for
plant expansion along with confiscatory taxation.[27] On the other
side of the picture, it appears that Fleet attempted to maintain
one-man control of Consolidated's enlarged operations and
created a situation that had government officials worried. In
mid-1941 both Air Force and Navy sources sponsored a move to
have AVCO buy Fleet out, and at the end of November the
transaction was completed. Fleet's 440,000 shares (34 per cent
of the total) were bought by Vultee Aircraft for $10,945,000,
financed by selling 240,000 shares of Vultee preferred to the
public for $5,430,000, 150,000 shares of Vultee common to
AVCO for $1,500,000, and borrowing the rest.[28] The two compa-
nies were merged in 1943 as the Consolidated-Vultee Aircraft
Corporation, or Convair. In this process Millar found himself in
disagreement with Girdler, resigned, and was replaced by a Girdler man, Harry Woodhead. Millar himself rejoined his friend
John K. Northrop in the new Northrop concern formed when
Northrop left Douglas in 1939.[29] A minor transaction in this
operation was Vultee's acquisition in 1942, for $650,000, of the
Intercontinent Aircraft Corporation of Miami Springs, Florida,
interesting mainly because one of its founders in 1940 was
Commander Bruce Leighton, who had earlier been in charge of
engine development under Admiral Moffett in the Navy Bureau of
Aeronautics.[30]

Enlisting the Automobile Industry

There has been repeated reference to the role that the
automobile industry was expected to play in the expansion of
aircraft production. Mobilization plans were based on using this
vast reservoir of productive capacity, and there was in government circles, among the public, and not least in the automobile

industry itself an assumption that once these resources were brought to bear, quantities of airplanes would be pouring off the assembly lines in short order. It was not that easy. The capacity and the know-how to manufacture in quantity were most certainly there, and the automobile industry's total contribution to the war effort was staggering in its scope. But it took more time and effort than most people had anticipated to convert automotive facilities to aircraft production. In fact, few airplanes were ever built in an ordinary automobile factory; it turned out that there was more to the process than rolling the last chassis off the assembly lines and substituting airframes.

To begin with, the union of the aircraft and automobile industries was anything but a love match; it was, in fact, a wedding into which both parties were pushed by the government. The aircraft manufacturers were understandably reluctant to see a situation created in which the big automobile firms might become permanent competitors. In 1940, after all, the United States was still not a belligerent and there was no sure way of predicting how the situation would develop. On their side the automobile manufacturers were in no particular hurry to get into aircraft production. They were just emerging from the long slump of the 1930's and had a bright prospect in a brisk civilian and military demand for motor vehicles.[31]

The automobile industry, indeed, came under some criticism then and later for diverting large quantities of steel and other strategic materials to nonmilitary uses. This criticism is unfair. The automobile men were as patriotic and as willing to cooperate with the government as anyone else, and when they were given a clear lead they responded vigorously. But it was hardly reasonable to expect them to close down their extensive plants and lay off their considerable labor force until the government got around to deciding what to do with them. The real fault was the administration's belief that the armament program could be superimposed on the civilian economy without disturbance and its consequent needless delay in establishing priorities and allocations, and even in making clear to the public what needed to be done. Perhaps the people were not ready in 1940 to accept restrictions on their normal peacetime ways of living, but this still does not justify singling out the automobile industry for censure.

The man who had to try to resolve these conflicts was William S. Knudsen, who left the presidency of General Motors to serve his adopted country under rather thankless conditions. As the member of the NDAC "in charge" of industrial production he was in the unenviable position of having responsibility without authority. He was actually in charge of nothing. He could exhort and persuade, he could use all the personal prestige of a distinguished industrial career, but he could not command. Even when the OPM replaced the NDAC his position was not materially improved. The only thing he could be sure of was that he would be blamed for any failures in the production program.

Under the circumstances, Knudsen's work in bringing the two parties together was a creditable piece of business statesmanship. He allayed the fears of the aircraft manufacturers by making it clear that the automobile companies would be brought into aircraft production as subcontractors. He also had to reconcile two very different attitudes toward production: The automobile men were accustomed to freezing a design and turning it out in quantity, with maximum use of single-purpose tools; the aircraft men were accustomed to limited output and constant design changes during the process of production.

Understandably the most rapid progress in converting automotive facilities was in the manufacture of engines, which required a less drastic adaptation of concepts and techniques than did airframes. One difficulty that had to be surmounted was the desire of Secretary of the Treasury Henry Morgenthau to supervise the entire aircraft program. Morgenthau, who apparently felt that his Treasury post entitled him to take charge of industrial mobilization as well as foreign policy, had a plan for having the government build and operate its own airframe and engine factories in "distressed" areas. However, when E. E. Wilson of Pratt and Whitney and Guy Vaughan of Curtiss-Wright pointed out the high degree of skill required to make aircraft engines and asked Morgenthau if he would be willing to accept the responsibility for casualties due to faulty production, Morgenthau abandoned the idea.[32]

Wilson and Vaughan both advocated that the automobile firms

be brought into engine manufacturing. The first attempt to do so early in 1940 turned out unfortunately. The Ford Motor Company, through Edsel Ford and Charles E. Sorensen, agreed to build 9,000 Rolls-Royce Merlin engines, but the contract was rejected by Henry Ford because two-thirds of the engines were to fill a British order.[33] The contract was subsequently given to Packard. Ford was finally brought into the picture in August 1940 through a licensing arrangement to manufacture the Pratt and Whitney 18-cylinder R-2800. This involved a visit by Edsel Ford, Sorensen, and others to Hartford, where they arrived full of confidence that they could show Pratt and Whitney how to mass-produce aircraft engines. Before they left they asked for blueprints of the factory as well as the engine, since their existing automobile engine facilities were clearly inadequate.[34]

Ford built an addition to the River Rouge plant, financed by the government to the extent of $14 million, and began to turn out engines late in 1941. Some improvements were made in production techniques, most of which were accepted by Pratt and Whitney. The one major exception was a cast instead of forged cylinder barrel. It was used in the Ford-built engines, but not by the prime contractor.[35]

These efforts to utilize the resources of the Ford Motor Company met with intensive opposition from the UAW because of Ford's continuing opposition to unionization. The union argued that Ford was ineligible to receive government contracts because the company was not obeying the National Labor Relations Act; much was made also of Henry Ford's alleged "Nazi" sympathies.[36] Knudsen, however, insisted that the legal issue was something to be settled in court, and that in the meantime the needs of the defense program must be met. This problem disappeared by itself in 1941 when the UAW succeeded in organizing the Ford workers and won recognition after a spectacular strike.

Pratt and Whitney engines were also built under license by Buick, Chevrolet, and Nash. The fee was a dollar an engine at first; subsequently Pratt and Whitney dropped the fee altogether.[37] Dodge and Studebaker built Wright engines on similar terms. The licensees all had the same experience. They plunged into the job with great enthusiasm and complete confidence in their ability to produce in quantity and found that the techniques that worked with automobile engines did not necessarily apply to aircraft engines. Finally they worked out the snags and turned in an outstanding performance in quality as well as quantity.[38]

Airframes constituted a thornier problem. It was the airframe rather than the engine manufacturers who disliked the idea of bringing the automobile firms into their industry. The automobile companies for their part were sure that they could help with engines, but airframes were outside their experience. They were quite willing to try if the government so desired, but until late in 1940 the government's trumpet was giving off a markedly uncertain sound, so that the automobile industry could feel no pressure to give up its booming civilian market. There was ample confidence in the industry's ability to mass-produce airplanes. In May 1940 during the consternation caused by the German blitz, Henry Ford announced that his company could "swing into production of a thousand planes of standard design a day," given the advice of men like Charles A. Lindbergh and Eddie Rickenbacker and freedom from meddling by government agencies.[39]

Neither Lindbergh nor Rickenbacker was ever consulted about this proposal. It was probably within the capacity of the Ford Motor Company, but it would have been a waste of materials and labor, whose only consequence would have been to create a mass of airplanes that no one could use. The complete standardization and freezing of design necessary to reach this production figure was quite impractical for military purposes. Yet Henry Ford reflected, in extreme form perhaps, the way the automobile men thought. After all they had effected a technological revolution by producing in just such quantities. Knudsen, who was closer to the problem than most of his associates, spoke at about this time of General Motors building 1,000 planes a month,[40] and the same outlook on production appeared in the proposal made late in 1940 by Walter Reuther that idle automotive capacity be used to make 500 fighter planes a day.

The Reuther plan was based on a calculation that, since the automobile industry had a potential output of 8 million vehicles a year and was actually operating at a rate of 4 million a year, half its plant and equipment could be devoted to aircraft manufacture without any curtailment of civilian production. The goal could be achieved, according to Reuther, if the manufacturers gave up their annual model change in order to conserve tools and agreed to pool the machine tools in their possession. Administration of the program was to be vested in a nine-man board consisting of three representatives each from government, management, and labor.[41]

As with Henry Ford's proposal, it was easy to criticize the Reuther plan. The suggested administrative arrangement was certain to be unacceptable to the automobile companies, and it would have been clumsy at best to have the automotive industry run partly by its own management and partly by a board of the kind Reuther proposed. It was doubtful if automobile plants had the broad floor spaces needed for aircraft assembly, even for fighter planes, and in any event neither the United States nor Britain could have used 500 fighters a day.[42] On the other hand, the wide publicity given to the Reuther plan performed a useful function by calling public attention to the critical problem of machine tools. The most interesting feature is that Reuther's approach was identical to that of automobile management: a ready assumption that automotive production techniques would be readily adaptable to aircraft manufacture.

As it happened, the essentials of what Reuther was asking— the large-scale use of automotive facilities for airframe production and an effort to conserve machine tools—had already been initiated by Knudsen. The incentive came from the need for bombers, not fighters. On October 15, 1940, Knudsen spoke to the leaders of the automobile industry at a meeting of the Automobile Manufacturers Association in New York and appealed to them first to suspend any model changes requiring new machine tools, and second, in secrecy, to undertake the making of half a billion dollars' worth of airplane parts and subassemblies.[43] Ten days later he held another meeting in Detroit and presented the situation thus:

The present program calls for the delivery of some 33,000 airplanes by April 1, 1942. All plant expansion for this quantity is under way and the bottleneck is tools. Airplanes is a vague name for the product, as training planes weigh 4,000 lbs., and the biggest bomber, approximately 40,000 lbs. If we were to turn out 33,000 four-thousand-pound planes, there would be no problem, but only 30% are training planes, and the rest are combat planes and bombers.

Therefore you are asked to tackle the possible dies and stampings for four thousand 4-motor bombers, weighing 40,000 lbs. gross, and eight thousand 2-motor bombers weighing 24,000 lbs. gross, assembling to be done by airplane manufacturers. You are asked to consider not only pieces, but subassemblies for this quantity of planes. It should be remembered that planes to date have been more or less handmade and that, in order to transfer the operation to press and die work, production studies will have to be made.

It is therefore proposed to secure floor space in Detroit, in charge of Air Corps officials from Wright Field, and to secure a set of parts for each plane as designed now with the corresponding drawings, and study such production changes as are necessary to tranfer manufacturing from bench to machine. To accomplish this we ask that a steering committee of four be appointed which, with two from the plane manufacturers, push this vigorously.

It is also proposed that while the parts and drawings are being secured, these six men visit the two airplane plants where the bombers are now being manufactured in order to get the proper picture of the method of jigging and manufacturing as now done in production.

It is proposed that a survey of equipment now in place be secured and as allocation of die work is made, the order for the required number of pieces follow the die order wherever possible so as to get immediate action after the try-out. Also a survey should be made of plant facilities available for jig assembly of minor assemblies such as wings, ailerons, tail surfaces, rudders, etc.

It is also desired that the steering committee investigate the forging situation, both aluminum and steel, plus the machining facilities available for such forgings—there being a serious shortage at the moment of facilities of this order. In other words, we are trying to get from the industry a coordinated branch of our Washington set-up to deal with sub-assemblies and pieces rather than the complete assembly as dealt with by us in Washington.[44]

The result of Knudsen's appeal was the formation of the Automotive Committee for Air Defense in order to coordinate the industry's activities. Its task at first was purely educational, since the automotive production men were being asked to make things most of them had never seen before. One of the Committee's most useful functions was to sponsor an exhibition in Detroit of aircraft parts and components, as suggested by Knudsen. As technical adviser for this exhibition, and for the preliminary steps in the conversion of automotive facilities, the Air Force designated an officer named James H. Doolittle, who at that time held the rank of major.[45]

While this process was going on, the allocation of work on the bomber program was being planned. Some of it has already been described in connection with the expansion of the aircraft companies. The government undertook to build four assembly plants, to be operated by aircraft firms and supplied with parts and subassemblies by the automobile industry. It was anticipated that the main assembly plants would expend 22 per cent of the man-hours required to build a bomber, leaving the rest to come from the automotive firms.[46] The locations chosen, after careful investigation of the availability of labor, housing, power, transportation, and good flying weather, plus consideration of security from attack, were Fort Worth, Kansas City, Omaha, and Tulsa.[47] The Kansas City plant was assigned to North American Aviation to build B-25's in cooperation with the Fisher Body Division of General Motors, a sensible arrangement in view of the close relationship between North American and General Motors. Martin was to assemble B-26's at Omaha with components supplied by Chrysler, Hudson, and the Goodyear Aircraft Corporation.

The intention was that the fabrication of the subassemblies should be done in existing factories, with such modification and enlargement as might be needed but without major new construction, and this policy was workable for the medium bombers. The Consolidated-Douglas-Ford combination for building B-24's worked out rather differently. Since the manufacturing complexities in building airplanes increase with plane size by a geometrical rather than an arithmetic factor, and since Ford had already made a substantial addition at the River Rouge plant in order to make Pratt and Whitney engines, there was some reason for requiring a new plant if the company was to go into the airframe business.

However, the fundamental cause for the construction of what was later sardonically termed "Will It Run?" was simply the Ford Motor Company's insistence on doing things its own way. This attitude stemmed principally from Henry Ford's deep-seated antiwar feelings, plus his lifelong aversion to sharing the conduct of his business with anyone else, but it is clear that both Edsel Ford and Charles E. Sorensen concurred in the basic policy, although both were far more eager than Henry to get the company into the production of military aircraft. In July 1940 Ford rejected a proposal from Douglas to participate in the building of 2,500 planes.[48] However, when the government brought up the B-24 plan in December, Ford consented to look into it, partly because Edsel and Sorensen were enthusiastic,[49] and partly because the idea was presented to him by Dr. George J. Mead. Mead was a distinguished aeronautical engineer who had gone with F. B. Rentschler from Wright Aeronautical to found Pratt and Whitney and was the designer of the original Wasp engine. At this time he was director of procurement for the aeronautical section of the NDAC, and he was one man in the government whom Henry Ford respected and was willing to trust. Ford may also have been influenced by the belief he expressed to Sorensen: "Those planes will never be used for fighting. Before you can build them, the war will be over." [50] He was almost right.

The result was that in January 1941 Edsel Ford, his sons Henry and Benson, and Sorensen went to San Diego to discuss and study the construction of B-24's. Sorensen reports, "I liked neither what I saw nor what I heard," a reaction that can hardly have astonished "Cast-Iron Charlie's" acquaintances. Yet he had a case, best described in his own words: [51]

The work of putting together a four-engine bomber was many times more complicated than assembling a four-cylinder automobile, but what I saw reminded me of nearly thirty-five years previously when we were making Model N Fords at the Piquette Avenue plant. . . . The nearer a B-24 came to its final assembly the fewer principles of mass production there were as we at Ford had developed and applied over the years. Here was a custom-made plane, put together as a tailor would cut and fit a suit of clothes.

The B-24's final assembly was made out-of-doors under the bright California sun and on a structural steel fixture. The heat and temperature changes so distorted this fixture that it was impossible to turn out two planes alike without further adjustment. The Consolidated and the Air Force people talked about an order from Ford Motor Company for center and outer wing sections; but it was obvious that if the wing sections had uniform measurements, the way we made parts for automobiles, they would not fit properly under out-of-doors assembly conditions.

To employ Ford manufacturing techniques, Sorensen drafted a plan for a giant factory where there would be the automobile industry's accustomed orderly progression from minor to major units, and an estimated output of a bomber an hour in comparison with Consolidated's projected but still unrealized schedule of a bomber a day. He and Edsel then submitted the idea to Mead and Fleet, proposing that the Air Force back the Ford Motor Company to the extent of $200 million.[52] Fleet countered with a suggestion that Ford make components for Consolidated to assemble, to which Sorensen replied, "We'll make the complete plane or nothing." The final arrangement was a compromise, weighted in favor of Ford. Consolidated licensed the Ford Motor Company to build Liberators, and the Air Force underwrote the new Willow Run plant, but the output was divided between complete "fly-away" planes and "knock-down" assemblies for Consolidated and Douglas to complete. It took time to arrive at this solution. The Air Force was dubious about Ford's ability to make complete planes, and the first authorization for Willow Run provided only for a schedule of 100 subassemblies a month for Consolidated and Douglas. By mid-1941 the need for bombers caused an upward revision to a projected output of 200 "fly-aways" and 150 "knock-downs" a month.[53]

Experience would teach the Ford people that mass-producing a big bomber was even more difficult than they had thought. At the same time they were quite right in their feeling that Consolidated's production methods were inadequate for the needs of the situation. It is of no particular significance that Consolidated and Ford engineers bickered constantly while Willow Run was under construction.[54] This just reflected a disagreement that was chronic during the preliminary phase of cooperation between two industries with diametrically opposite approaches to production. It did not take very long for each group to discover that it could, and indeed must, learn from the other.

Consolidated, as has been indicated before, was something of a special case. The government was worried about its lagging production, and Reuben Fleet was feeling the pressure. According to Sorensen, Fleet invited him to take on the management of Consolidated, largely because he thought Sorensen could handle Knudsen.[55] When Sorensen said that Edsel would have to be consulted, Fleet then proposed that Ford buy Consolidated, but Sorensen dismissed this idea on the ground that the government would never permit it even if Ford was willing. Then Knudsen proposed a combination of Consolidated, Douglas, and Ford, but this idea got no further, and Consolidated was left to be taken over by AVCO.

The outstanding example of divergence in production techniques also comes from Sorensen. For Willow Run it was decided that the fuselage would be assembled in two longitudinal halves, which made for easy installation of wiring and piping. At the end of the line the two sections would be riveted together. At Consolidated the technique was to complete the fuselage and then pull the wiring and piping through the door for installation, a process described by Sorensen as "like a bird building his own nest while sitting in it."[56]

The Achievement

These production goals were impressive, but in 1941 they were still paper estimates. Construction of the four assembly plants and the Willow Run factory was started in the spring of 1941, so that under the most favorable circumstances they could make no appreciable contribution to aircraft production until some time in 1942. Meanwhile the manufacture of civilian automobiles continued unchecked until August 1941 when the government and the automobile industry agreed on a program for the curtailment of passenger-car production during the following year.[57] This agreement did not come in time to affect 1941 output, which was somewhat larger than in 1940.

There was understandably a good deal of dissatisfaction with what appeared to be a lack of drive in the mobilization program and some demand for more positive steps to compel conversion from civilian to military production. Yet as long as the nation was not formally at war and a large segment of the public saw no reason why it should be, the progress made was probably as much as could be achieved. As I. B. Holley has pointed out, "although they (government officials, both civilian and military) legally held authority to take the necessary steps and provide for the nation's defense, they could not exercise that authority until it was politically feasible to do so." [58]

There was in fact more achievement than the critics were willing to concede. It was easy to overlook the automobile industry's contribution to the total defense program; for example, 187,000 military vehicles were produced by mid-1941.[59] And the aircraft program, at which most of the criticism was directed, was definitely moving ahead. The output of military aircraft rose from 3,807 in 1940 to 19,433 in 1941, almost as many as were produced in completely mobilized Britain and 8,000 *more* than in Germany.[60] This increase was achieved through the expansion of facilities in the aircraft industry itself during the previous two years. The automobile industry's contribution at this point consisted of some valuable assistance in breaking production bottlenecks by filling about a million dollars worth of orders for machine-shop and die work.[61]

Could more have been accomplished? The answer is certainly "yes" if we postulate a situation in which the government had strong public support for a program drastically limiting nonmilitary production and rigorously controlling the allocation of scarce and strategic materials. Before Pearl Harbor such a program was considered to be unacceptable. Perhaps the necessary support could have been generated, but this is doubtful in view of the deep division of public opinion on the question of policy towards the war, and also in view of the fact that such a program would have created temporary but severe economic dislocations.

It therefore is more realistic to consider whether what was actually achieved could have been done better under the conditions that then existed. No conclusive answer can be given. Where aircraft production was concerned the choice between new construction, expansion of existing plant, or conversion of other facilities involved too many variables for any general policy to be applicable. For airframe assembly conversion was impractical because factories designed for other purposes could not readily be adapted for this one, with the conspicuous exception of the distillery in Burbank where Lockheed built P-38's.

Subsequent studies showed that it took an average of 31 months to get a new airframe plant from "green grass to full production," with a range of 24 months for fighter planes to 40 for B-29's.[62] Additions to existing plants took an average of 21 months. Conversion was possible for the manufacture of aircraft engines, but it was found that it took as long to convert as to put up a new factory, because the governing element was the time required for tooling.[63] In addition, decisions could seldom be made on a simple time calculation. The availability of labor, transportation, housing, and other factors had to be taken into account, and the preference of management for concentration about existing facilities had to be balanced against the government's desire to disperse aircraft production as much as possible into the Defense Zone.

The fundamental difficulty was that the program had to be improvised for the most part. The pre-1939 planning for industrial mobilization had never envisioned a need for the production of aircraft on this scale. It would have been much easier if there had been a consistent policy such as the aircraft industry kept pleading for but got only during the five years of the Morrow Board program: that is, a planned and regular system of procurement aimed at maintaining productive capacity that could be readily expanded in an emergency. Alternatively, if the automobile industry was to provide the aircraft industry's reserve facilities, there should have been more educational orders at an earlier date.[64] It would have been better still if the educational orders had been accompanied by something in the nature of shadow factories.

However, it has to be recognized that any such preparations for war were politically impossible in the atmosphere of the 1930's. When the emergency came there was no option but to improvise. It was fortunate first that time was available for improvising, and second, that the industrial skill and resources were there to make the improvisation work.

8. The Aircraft Industry in the Second World War

The story of American aviation in the Second World War has been recorded thoroughly and competently, including the organization of aircraft production. Detailed and scholarly studies have been made of the formulation of procurement policies and programs, the functioning of the military services and other government agencies, procedures for the negotiation of contracts, control of supplies of materials and labor: in general, the wartime management of production by the government. It is quite unnecessary for this volume to go over the same ground and repeat information which is both readily available and thoroughly authoritative. It seems more useful to focus on what went on within the industry, where the programs formulated by the government had to be translated into actual aircraft. It should be emphasized that this is not an opposing side of the story, but merely its obverse.

Full Mobilization

With the attack on Pearl Harbor, the hesitancies and uncertainties of the preceding two years came to an end. The United States was at war. Military requirements henceforth had a clear precedence over production for the civilian market, and the government had all the public support it needed to impose priorities and restrictions as it deemed best. To this extent the aircraft industry's position was improved, since it was at the top of the priority list. At the same time, however, a declaration of war did not by itself provide aluminum or machine tools or skilled labor, and it did increase the burden on the industry by sharply raising production goals. In January 1942 the President called for 60,000 airplanes that year and 125,000 in 1943.

These goals were not met.[1] They had in fact little relationship to existing or potential productive capacity, and it is open to question whether it was sound policy to formulate them at all. The objectives were impressive and glamorous, and it may be that they stimulated a degree of energy that would not have been forthcoming otherwise. The argument on the other side is that there were serious drawbacks to setting production quotas in terms of an arbitrary set of figures rather than on the basis of a reasoned calculation of requirements. The increase of emphasis on big bombers meant that production measured by airframe weight rather than numbers of units did actually increase at the desired ratio,[2] but there was an inevitable tendency to judge the aircraft industry's performance by the President's stated goals, and therefore some risk of exaggerating quantity at the expense of quality. This particular risk did not in fact materialize in any serious proportions, but the "numbers racket" had a definitely unfortunate effect in that military planners insisted on taking the President's statement as an order.[3] Production schedules were prepared accordingly, so that some resources were wasted to provide for planes that were never built. However, such wastage does not appear to have been on a damaging scale, and it undoubtedly has to be written off as the kind of error inevitable in wartime.

The first post-Pearl Harbor reaction to the problem of aircraft production was for the government to sponsor a vast new increase in plant facilities. In exactly a week (December 14, 1941) Bell Aircraft was brought into the heavy bomber picture by being asked to take charge of a new assembly plant for B-29's to be built at Marietta, Georgia.[4] Fisher Body was to do the same thing in Cleveland, but in practice this operation was limited to subassemblies. Boeing itself added a vast new factory (government-owned) to its existing Wichita property in order to accelerate the output of B-29's. The other major new facilities and operators were Douglas, at Oklahoma City and Chicago for transport planes; Curtiss-Wright, at Kenmore, New York, also for transports, and at Wood Ridge, New Jersey, for engines; Republic, at Evansville, Indiana, for P-47's; Dodge Division, Chrysler Corporation, at Chicago for Wright engines. (When it was completed, this plant was the biggest single facility constructed for the aircraft program. Its 6.5 million square feet was equal to the entire floor space occupied by the aircraft engine industry early in 1941.) [5] The smaller aircraft companies were also provided with increased capacity for the manufacture of such types as trainers and artillery-spotting planes.

In fact, more new plant construction was authorized in the four months after Pearl Harbor than during the whole previous year.[6] It has been suggested that there was undue, almost hysterical, haste in this process, and that the desired production would have been achieved more expeditiously and economically by converting and adding to existing facilities. This point of view is reinforced by the fact that when the War Production Board was created in 1942 with, for the first time, really effective power to enforce industrial mobilization, it curtailed new construction in favor of conversion. The question, however, has to remain open, since the considerations discussed in the previous chapter continued to apply. The only way to get new airframe capacity was to erect new buildings, because airframe assembly had specialized requirements that could seldom be met in a factory designed for something else. Even if the parts and subassemblies were fabricated elsewhere, as most of them were, the final assembly called for big buildings with plenty of floor space. Earlier and more thorough planning might have provided the needed engine capacity by conversion, but the Ford experience with Pratt and Whitney can be cited as evidence that automobile engine plants were not suited to the manufacture of aircraft engines, and it must be remembered that the automotive industry was making engines for many other military purposes besides airplanes. It can be reasonably argued that the slackening of new construction for aircraft manufacturing after mid-1942 meant that the necessary capacity had been provided rather than that the policy had been a mistake.

The allocation of facilities among types indicates some reconsideration of requirements. Nothing then or later shook the devotion of the AAF to the big bomber, but the distribution of these projected new plants shows recognition of other needs, principally transports and better fighters. At the time of the attack on Pearl Harbor the country's entire inventory of four-engined transport planes was 27, including 8 Boeing Clippers and 11 converted B-24's,[7] and the war situation made it clear that planes capable of carrying troops and supplies over long distances would be invaluable. The inclusion of the smaller companies (Aeronca, Beech, Bellanca, Piper) in the facilities program was designed to relieve the pressure on the big producers for the supply of training planes; it was also recognition of an Air Force failure to develop an effective liaison plane for artillery spotting.[8]

The aircraft companies were not involved in these policy questions. Their task, as before, was to implement the decisions, and whether these are measured by the stated objective or the actual output, it was a formidable prospect. There were already acute shortages of machine tools, such essential material for aircraft manufacture as aluminum, and skilled labor. The new plant facilities projected in 1941 were still under construction, so that it would be quite a while before any appreciable assistance came from this source. If the immediate goals were to be met, it would have to be done by optimum use of existing capacity.

This part of the aircraft industry's performance is probably the most creditable feature of its wartime achievements. Until the new resources of plant and equipment could be brought into play the industry had to do the best it could with what it had and its best turned out to be superlative. Companies that had been vigorous competitors in peace now pooled their resources. Douglas was associated with Consolidated in making B-24's; it was also teamed with Boeing and Lockheed to build Flying Fortresses. This partnership was formed in April 1941 at the request of the Air Force. It attracted less attention than the B-24 combination, because it did not include anything as spectacular as the

Willow Run project, but it had rather happier results. Douglas used its new Long Beach plant for B-17's, while Lockheed used its Vega subsidiary in Burbank—and inevitably the Boeing-Vega-Douglas grouping became known as BVD.[9] This process was repeated throughout the industry so thoroughly that every major firm was making someone else's planes in addition to its own. Coordination was facilitated by the organization of the Aircraft War Production Council, with a membership consisting of Consolidated, Douglas, Lockheed, Vega, North American, Ryan, Vultee, Northrop, and eventually Boeing.[10] The members shared aerodynamic and engineering data, exchanged information on tooling and equipment, and allocated a $250 million stockpile of material wherever it was needed most. The eastern aircraft firms followed this example by creating the Aircraft War Production Council, East Coast, with a membership of AVCO, Bell, Brewster, Curtiss-Wright, Fairchild, Martin, Republic, and the Eastern Aircraft Division of General Motors, which built naval aircraft under license from Grumman.[11]

More directly, each company worked to improve its production techniques. Perhaps the most striking transformation occurred at Consolidated, where the new management put an end to the floundering of 1941 and moved ahead so fast that by mid-1942 the potential capacity of the San Diego plants was ahead of the supply of parts and materials. This result was achieved by introducing a straight-line production system and pushing more of the assembly work back to the subassemblies, along with worker-training programs and decentralization of authority.[12] These techniques can be properly credited to the talents of Tom Girdler, but there is also a clear-cut indication that the association with Ford had taught Consolidated-Vultee some things about large-scale production. A very interesting Consolidated (hereafter referred to as Convair) innovation was the system of feeder plants introduced in December 1942. These can best be described directly from the company history: [13]

By 1943 Convair-San Diego was building B-24's with parts received from nearly 100 subcontractors, fabricating such normally factory-made items as horizontal and vertical stabilizers and bomb bay doors. At Convair-Fort Worth, it was estimated that 40 per cent of fabrication on bombers and transports was performed by subcontractors, who shipped a million pounds of parts to the plant monthly.

Feeder shops, another means of taking the work to the laborer, came into widespread use. The system was inaugurated at Convair-San Diego in December, 1942. By early 1944, the plant had a network of eleven feeder shops in California cities up to 130 miles distant, employing 1,700 workers (of whom 90 per cent were women).

Headquarters of the system was in Santa Ana, where three shops were situated. Raw materials were distributed from there, and finished parts collected for delivery to San Diego. Typical feeder shop products included bulkheads, electrical harnesses, sheet metal subassemblies, plexiglass moldings, and most of the upholstery going into B-24's. At Coronado, one shop specialized in sorting rivets swept up from plant floors.

The feeder-shop system was adopted generally throughout the aircraft industry. Lockheed was close on Convair's heels with a program establishing ten such plants, located in Bakersfield, Fresno, East Los Angeles, Pomona, Santa Barbara, and Taft, and eventually employing some 4,000 people.[14] North American moved entire subassembly departments into leased buildings in Pasadena and Los Angeles, the purchasing department and warehouse facilities being lodged near the main plant in the Hollywood Park race track.[15] It was a useful method of relieving some of the pressures on the major producing centers, plagued by shortage of labor, housing, and transportation, but the feeder shops were a minor part of the total production pattern. Next to direct plant expansion, the principal reliance of the industry for greater output was straightforward subcontracting. Lockheed, for example, increased its volume of subcontracting by 250 per cent in the first half of 1942, and, in all, subcontracting contributed between 30 and 40 per cent of the airframe weight produced during the war.[16]

Quantity and Quality

If the sole purpose of the aircraft program had been to produce the largest possible number of airplanes, the problem of organizing production would have been much simpler than it actually was. The latent resources of American industry could in a measurable length of time have met any quantitative require-

DOUGLAS AIRCRAFT, 1920

This is the first Douglas Aircraft factory. Aircraft, as can be seen, were built by hand; the picture shows most of the work force.

M-4

Built in 1927 to carry mail, this was a modification of the Douglas O-2 Army observation plane.

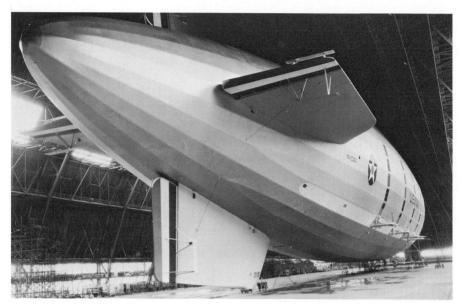

U.S.S. MACON

The enormous size of this last American dirigible can be judged by the people standing on the ground.

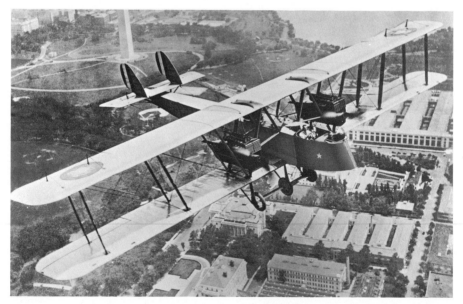

MARTIN MB

One of these first American-designed Army bombers is shown over Washington, D. C. The MB demonstrated its qualities in the Virginia Capes bombing tests.

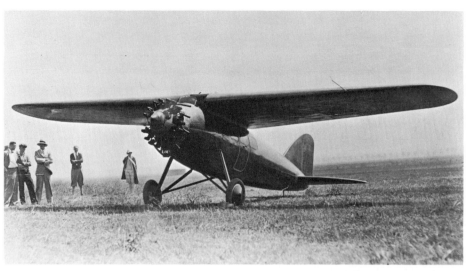

VEGA

The Lockheed transport of the late 1920's with many record flights. A Vega was used by Capt. George H. Wilkins in 1928 to fly over the North Pole, and later over Antarctica. Amelia Earhart's flight in 1931 from Newfoundland to Ireland, the first solo transatlantic flight by a woman, was made in a Vega.

THE "LONE EAGLE" AND HIS PLANE

Charles A. Lindbergh with the Ryan monoplane, "Spirit of St. Louis," in which he made his New York–Paris flight.

NORTHROP ALPHA

One of the pioneering designs by John K. Northrop, which contributed significantly to the phenomenal aeronautical advances of the 1930's.

MODEL 200 MONOMAIL

This Boeing design saw little actual service, but was an important step in the development of air transport.

Courtesy The Boeing Company

BOEING 247

The first of the twin-engined, all-metal monoplane airliners. Although outmatched by the DC-2 and DC-3, a number of 247's remained in service through the Second World War and for some time after. As a military transport it was designated C-73.

Courtesy McDonnell Douglas Corporation

DC-3

One of the most successful transport designs in aviation history. About 13,000 were built. Most served in the Second World War as military transports, designated C-47 Skytrain by the U.S. Air Force and Dakota by the British.

CESSNA, 1911

This is Clyde Cessna's first plane, an experimental model built while he was still a garage mechanic in Oklahoma.

D55 BARON

This is a good example of the modern "executive" plane, an increasingly important aid to business operations, especially for companies whose operations are widely scattered or in localities that are difficult to reach by other methods of transportation.

PIPER CUB
The J-3 model of one of the best-known American light planes.

CATALINA
The workhorse Navy patrol plane of the Second World War. The PBY was invaluable for long-range reconnaissance and antisubmarine patrol.

MARS

One of the giant Martin flying boats built during the Second World War
and used as Navy transports.

VOUGHT CORSAIR

One of a series of carrier-based fighters first produced in 1942. This one,
the F4U-4, went into service in 1944. The Corsair had a speed of over 400
m.p.h. It remained in operation through the Korean War, in which it was
used for ground-support missions.

P-38

The Lightning was one of the best American fighters of the Second World War. It also served as a light bomber, torpedo carrier, photoreconnaissance plane, and in many other ways.

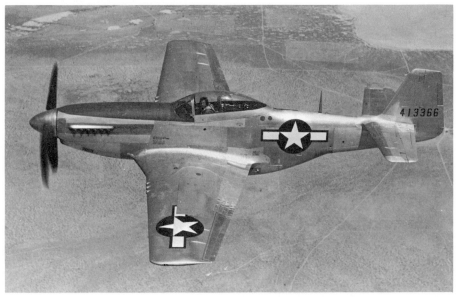

The Mustang

The P-51, evolved by North American Aviation from the Curtis P-40, was one of the best long-range fighters of the Second World War.

THUNDERBOLT
The Republic P-47N, a first-class fighter developed during the Second
World War.

FLYING FORTRESS
This is a B-17G, the final production model built during the Second World
War, incorporating modifications based on combat experience.

Courtesy General Dynamics Corporation

LIBERATOR

This is the B-24, Convair's counterpart to the B-17. It was the longest-ranged of the Second World War bombers until the B-29 came into production.

Courtesy General Dynamics Corporation

B-36

The first intercontinental bomber. This picture shows its unique arrangement of six pusher propeller engines and four jets.

Courtesy Ryan Aeronautical Company

EARLY DAYS AT RYAN
The B-1 Brougham in front of the shed marked "Ryan Flying Co."
illustrates the physical facilities used for aviation in the early 1920's.

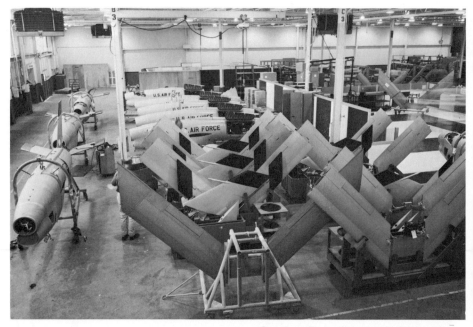

Courtesy Ryan Aeronautical Company

RYAN FIREBEE PRODUCTION
This picture of the production of Ryan's pilotless jet-propelled target plane
offers a contrast to the picture of Ryan operations when the company was
founded.

XP-59
The first American-built jet plane, test-flown at Muroc Dry Lake, California, October 2, 1942.

McDONNELL F4E
One of the Phantom series, Navy jet fighters, flying over St. Louis.

GRUMMAN INTRUDER

This is the A6A, a modern jet-powered attack plane designed to operate from carriers on advanced land bases.

EARLY HELICOPTER

This is the test rig with which Charles H. Kaman began to experiment with helicopters. It is mounted on the chassis of a 1933 automobile.

Courtesy Lockheed Aircraft Corporation

HERCULES
This picture is a striking illustration of the C-130's size and capacity. The plane appears to be swallowing the tank truck.

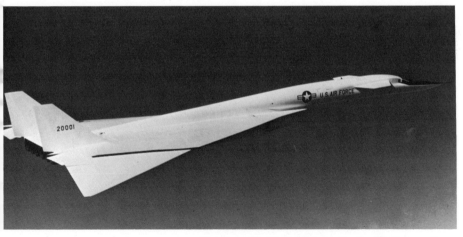

Courtesy North American Rockwell Corporation

XB-70
Intended as a supersonic jet bomber, North American's B-70 reached the prototype stage, but production was halted by a decision that intercontinental bombardment should become the function of missiles rather than manned aircraft.

"STRAIGHT UP"
Lockheed's experimental XFV-1, Vertical Riser, gives some indication of what may lie in the future.

WINGLESS FLIGHT
The Northrop M2-F2, an experimental design of the 1960's.

ment within reason. But in modern war, planning for production has to maintain a delicate balance between the need for immediate output and the need to keep one's own weapons at least equal in quality to the enemy's; there will seldom be agreement about the proper point of balance. It is a generally valid premise that today's war cannot be won with yesterday's weapons, but it will normally be better to have yesterday's weapons than none at all, and tomorrow's weapons are not much help if they exist only as blueprints. On the other hand, if the enemy has tomorrow's weapons and we have yesterday's, quantity will not help much.

All the belligerents of the Second World War had to wrestle with this problem, which was particularly acute in the field of aviation, where technical advance was rapid and unceasing. By the time any airplane leaves the factory, there is already a better one on the drawing board, and any good aeronautical engineer will always have ideas for improving the model that is currently being built. At some point designs must be frozen in order to get production, but if designs are frozen too early or remain so too long, the result may be a disastrous lag in quality.

For some months after Pearl Harbor the emphasis was overwhelmingly and understandably on quantity. The whole course of the war so far had been one of almost uninterrupted Axis success, with aerial superiority as apparently the decisive factor. Actually the early German and Japanese victories were due as much to skillful coordination of air and ground forces as to superiority in numbers of airplanes, but this point was not generally appreciated and could not have been in the absence of information that became available only after the war was over. What was painfully evident was the Axis advantage in the air, and this manifestly had to be overcome before victory could be won. The pressure for quantity was accentuated by the President's dramatic appeal for 50,000 planes and the proposals of Ford and Reuther for mass production of airplanes in automobile factories.

During the first hectic rush of rearmament in 1940 the government ordered the deferment of any research and development projects that might interfere with the production of existing airplane types, and an effort was made, with qualified success, to prohibit design modifications that would retard production.[17] The British, in a much more acute crisis at this time, followed the same policy, with the advantage that Lord Beaverbrook as Minister of Aircraft Production had effective authority to enforce it.[18] By the late fall of 1940, however, Britain was relaxing its restrictions, convinced by its own experience that some sacrifice of quantity was worthwhile in order to maintain quality. American military opinion swung the same way early in 1941, but after Pearl Harbor the demand for quantity again took precedence.

There was never any final resolution of this issue. In time the expansion of output and the favorable progress of the war relaxed the pressure for quantity, but before then the demands of quality had to be provided for. Not only was it essential to develop new and better planes in order to keep up with technical advance, but there was a constant stream of demands from the combat zones for specific improvements in existing types.

The most effective solution to this problem was the establishment of modification centers where desired changes could be made *after* the planes had come off the regular production lines. The system originated in Britain, where it was necessary to adapt American aircraft to British equipment and it was easier to do the modifying on arrival than to delay production by attempting to incorporate specialized features on American assembly lines.[19] When the decision was made early in 1942 to establish such centers in the United States, the aircraft manufacturers were too heavily burdened to take on this extra responsibility, and the government consequently turned to the maintenance shops of the airlines. Ten of these were operating as modification centers by May 1942. Subsequently twenty more such centers were established at a cost of $75 million and operated by aircraft manufacturers, who by then were getting clear of the teething troubles of their own expansion. Most of these establishments were adjacent to assembly plants of the operating companies, but some were in entirely new locations. Convair operated modification centers in Elizabeth City, North Carolina, Louisville, Kentucky, and Tucson, Arizona; Douglas at Daggett, California; Lockheed at Dallas (an unusual situation for Lockheed, whose only other major operation outside California was its service and modification center in Northern Ireland); Goodyear Aircraft in Phoenix, Arizona; and Rohr Aircraft (a parts manufacturer) in Chula Vista, California.[20] In addition, two companies from outside the field of aviation altogether operated modification centers: the Matson Navigation Company in San Francisco, California, and the Bechtel-McCone Corporation, a Los Angeles construction company, in Birmingham, Alabama.

The modification centers reached their peak in June 1944, with a total employment of 43,400.[21] The system was an improvisation and on the whole must be adjudged successful. It had flaws, as could have been expected. The work done at the centers was necessarily high-cost, since it was predominantly a mass of individual, handicraft operations; because most of it was done on rush order, accurate accounting was difficult. Moreover, under the urgency of demand for greater output, there was little effort to differentiate between the changes that should properly be made at the modification centers and those that should have been incorporated into the production process. Nevertheless, the modification centers materially assisted aircraft production by reducing the number of changes that would otherwise have had to be made on the assembly lines. Thus a manufacturer could concentrate on turning out a basic model and leave the centers to adapt individual planes to specific tactical purposes or theaters of war. It was never possible, or even desirable, to eliminate factory changes altogether, and by the end of the war the solution to the balancing of quantity with quality was found in improved techniques for the control of production.[22]

Labor and Finance

The physical expansion of the aircraft industry to its peak capacity was substantially achieved by the end of 1943, but completing the construction of new plant or the conversion of other factories did not by themselves mean that the industry had surmounted its problems. The factories had to be staffed. Employment in the manufacture of airframes and engines rose from 63,200 in 1939 to a maximum of 1,345,600 in 1943 (these are monthly averages).[23] This was a drastic enough change in terms of numbers alone, but there was a qualitative factor also to accentuate the labor problem. In 1939 about nine-tenths of the labor force in the aircraft industry was skilled or semiskilled, the highest proportion in the country. It was out of the question to maintain this ratio when close to a million and a half workers had to be recruited, with every other industry also clamoring for the limited supply of skilled labor, and having to compete with the military services into the bargain.

Some of the expedients adopted by aircraft companies to recruit and train labor have previously been described. Broadly speaking, the industry had to get its work force wherever it could and make the most of an astonishing assortment of human material. Lockheed's experience has been told in some detail and it may be taken as reasonably typical of what the other major companies were doing also:

Three weeks after Pearl Harbor, Lockheed-Vega was the U.S. aircraft industry's biggest employer with 54,000 men and women. . . . But these weren't enough. . . . The work force grew to a peak of 93,000. About 250,000 people, old and young, skilled and unskilled, at one time or another during the war forsook peaceful pursuits and joined production lines. . . . Recruiting efforts turned up unexpected talent. Violinists and paperhangers, morticians and midgets, schoolboys and housewives, Hollywood experts and shoe clerks worked side by side.

To aircraft manufacturers the draft was a constant problem. Bright young men who in peacetime learned the knowhow of building airplanes were just the kind Uncle Sam needed in uniform. Altogether almost 24,000 Lockheed and Vega employees entered military service before V-J Day. 394 of them died for their flag.

It took at least two untrained persons to replace each one who left for service. Despite every effort to keep skilled workers at their posts as long as possible, men still donned uniforms faster than substitutes could be found and trained.

Recruiting sources included the visually handicapped, the elderly, and disabled veterans. Lockheed pioneered in hiring them. And it found their employment stability high, accident frequency rate low, and morale and efficiency surprisingly good. One man with no hands was a tool dispatcher—and a capable one—although he had to keep track of things in his head. Numerous "seeing eye" dogs guided their masters through the maze of corridors to their work benches.

At the height of the manpower shortage employment interviewers used a somewhat grim jest. "If the applicants are warm," they said, "we'll hire them. We've even come close to hiring a few that were cold."

One answer to the problem was youth. Lockheed initiated a plan whereby more than 4000 high school boys came to work in shifts— four hours of school, four in the factory, or four weeks of normal schooling, four full-time weeks on the job.

But by far the greatest source was women.

"Big airplanes are made up of small parts," Courtlandt Gross declared when Vega was achieving its record production of B-17s. "And women build small parts to perfection."

They did much more than build small parts. Lockheed hired them by the thousands—when employment reached its 94,000 maximum in June 1943, nearly 35,000 were women, about 40 per cent of the total. It was the era of "Rosie the Riveter."

But handling riveting guns was only one of the hundreds of jobs the "weaker" sex did—and did well. Housewives, war widows, grandmothers became stress analysts, expediters, production engineers, tool planners, inspectors, turret lathe operators, and office workers.[24]

North American found by 1942 that its normal annual labor turnover rate of 30 per cent had shot up to more than 100 per cent, where it remained through 1944.[25] The company first employed women on production lines in its Dallas plant in November 1941, and just a year later women constituted 30 per cent of its total production force. Subsequently, like Lockheed, it hired 16- and 17-year old boys, and also instituted a shift for professional men from 6:30 P.M. to 11:30 P.M. It even hired service men on leave on a daily basis. One of the problems encountered by all aircraft companies was absenteeism, a consequence of having to absorb in a limited time vast numbers of inexperienced workers at high wages, secure in the knowledge that they could not readily be replaced. North American found that it frequently had to hire two or even three people to make a net gain of one in the working force. It also tried to conserve labor by instituting a system for shifting workers from operations that were temporarily slack to those that needed help—a recurring situation when model changes were coming along constantly.

Labor relations on the whole were good throughout the war. Union leadership had its own problems in dealing with this enormous and constantly changing mass of new workers, and in these conditions some friction had to be expected. But the no-strike pledge given when the United States entered the war was taken seriously, and such disputes as occurred were settled with a minimum of work stoppage either through labor relations structures within the industry or by government agencies such as the War Labor Board.

The labor situation had a profound influence on the wartime history of the aircraft industry, more than appears at first glance. It was probably the most important single factor determining the location of new plant. When the large-scale expansion of facilities began, the military authorities wanted as much of the industry as possible to be moved away from the coasts, but this policy involved no preference for one inland location over another. The specific choice of sites was made on considerations of labor supply, availability of housing, and resources in power and transportation, and of these labor easily ranked first—a contrast to prewar conditions, when the modest supply of skilled labor needed in aircraft manufacturing could be found in almost any city and was negligible as a locational factor.

Now, however, it was not a question of getting skilled labor (that would have been too much to expect) but of finding sites where there was a labor force not already preempted by another major industry. For this reason some dispersal of aircraft production would have occurred anyway, even without the pressure to move to "safe" locations. This pressure for military security, in fact, was never fully decisive, and it declined in importance as the war progressed. Without it there might have been more expansion into adjacent communities and less into the center of the country than there actually was, so that it did affect the locational shift, but there can be no doubt that in the eyes of management the recruitment of labor was a more urgent problem than protection from enemy attack.

The change in the composition of the labor force also influenced production techniques. While the aircraft men worked in close association with the automobile companies and adopted many of their methods, they were never fully convinced that these were really suitable for the manufacture of aircraft. There is eloquent testimony to this attitude in the fact that North

American, closely associated as it was with General Motors, still felt obligated to point out that an average automobile had perhaps 5,000 parts, while a B-25 bomber had some 165,000, not including engines, instruments, propellers, or 150,000 rivets.[26] And in spite of the vast increase in output, the aircraft industry even in wartime was not engaged in mass production by the standards of its automotive cousin. It produced about 300,000 airplanes during the war years (beginning in 1940), with a peak of 96,000 in 1944, divided among some twenty airframe manufacturers.[27]

If the requisite skilled labor had been available, this task might have been accomplished without any serious modification of manufacturing techniques. But because quantity production had to be achieved with a labor force that was largely unskilled and untrained, it was necessary to place greater reliance on mechanized processes and on breaking jobs down into the simplest possible components, so that each operation could be learned in a minimum of time.

The financing of this massive volume of production presented its own unique features, for which there was little precedent either in the aircraft or any other industry. What was done about plant expansion has been described. Practically all the necessary funds came from the government, which retained ownership of the new facilities and leased them to the aircraft companies for operation. Fundamentally the same solution was applied to the financing of production. None of the aircraft companies possessed anything like the amount of working capital needed for their expanded scale of activity—to meet their enlarged payrolls, for instance, or pay their suppliers and subcontractors. By 1943 the six largest airframe manufacturers had obligations amounting to ten times their working capital.[28] They relied on progress payments on their contracts and on V-loans, which were raised from private bankers but guaranteed by the government.

North American's summary of its wartime financing illustrates this general pattern nicely. The company's net worth on December 31, 1940, was $12,366,591, to which was added $66 million contributed by the government for added plant—or 74 per cent of the floor space in use by North American on September 30, 1944.[29] The company's inventory was partly financed by the government through fixed-fee contracts and progress payments on standard Air Forces procurement contracts. Operating funds were secured by V-loans raised through J. P. Morgan and Company, which on September 30, 1944, came to $30 million.

There was some risk in this procedure. Disputes over contract terms or delays in settlement could put the aircraft companies in difficulty. Yet there was no satisfactory alternative. The ordinary capital markets could not possibly have financed the wartime aircraft program; in any event the industry preferred to avoid methods of financing that might leave it overcapitalized when the war ended.

The risk of dependence on the government was minimal while the demand for aircraft was rising. The acute danger would develop when the war was coming to an end and military requirements were cut back. This hazard was recognized early; there was enough awareness of the consequences of abrupt contract termination at the end of the First World War to stimulate efforts to prevent a repetition. It was a problem, moreover, that concerned every industry engaged in war production. Late in 1943 the principal governmental contracting agencies formed the Joint Contract Termination Board for the purpose of working out uniform and equitable principles for the termination of war contracts and for assisting in reconversion to peacetime production.[30] The Board's work was given legislative sanction by the Contract Settlement Act of July 1944.

On the whole the process of contract termination worked reasonably well. For the aircraft industry the transition to a peacetime basis was not easy, but at least it was spared the additional burden of completely abrupt cancellations, with unused inventory and disputed claims.

There was an obverse to the problem of providing funds for the large-scale production of aircraft; namely, the question of earnings and profits far beyond any peacetime level. For every industry concerned with military production this was a touchy matter. Memories of profiteering during the First World War were still strong, and neither the public nor the government was disposed to have any repetition. Neither, for that matter, was industry. Apart from a normal patriotic aversion to taking advantage of their country's needs, responsible businessmen were quite aware that profiteering would certainly be penalized after if not during the war, and that all industry was likely to suffer for the sins of a few. Nevertheless it was a difficult question for both government and industry to handle, because there was considerably more involved than just establishing an acceptable rate of profit and taxing the rest as excess.

In aircraft production, once the program moved into dimensions of 50,000 planes a year and more, contract negotiations had to be largely guesswork. There was no previous experience by which to calculate what economies of scale might be realized, and if there had been, there was a still larger area of uncertainty about costs. Controls on prices and wages were not imposed until 1942, and even then they fell short of complete effectiveness. Consequently it was difficult to estimate costs of materials, and still more difficult to estimate costs of labor, since the necessary recourse to masses of unskilled workers and the rapid turnover in the labor force made it virtually impossible to calculate what could be expected in terms of productivity. In addition, the frequency and cost of design changes could not be accurately forecast.

The initiative in meeting this problem was taken within the aircraft industry. United Aircraft encountered the difficulty early in its contract negotiations with the Navy Bureau of Aeronautics for Pratt and Whitney engines. The Bureau pointed out that on the large volume under consideration a lower unit price could be expected.[31] E. E. Wilson, then president of United Aircraft, and J. F. McCarthy, the company's financial expert, concurred on the principle but had to point out that during the period of plant expansion, tooling, and recruitment of additional labor, costs would be high. Ultimately it was agreed that the first contract prices would be based on previous experience, and that the company would voluntarily adjust prices as cost reductions materialized. Since it was established procedure to have government cost inspectors stationed in the plant, there was an adequate check on performance.

United then calculated that in 1940 it had earned $12 million in plant provided by its own capital and decided to freeze its annual net earnings at that figure. The result was a reduction of prices within a few months amounting to a saving for the government of $10 million. The profit margin at first worked out at 3 per cent on sales after taxes and later dropped to 2 per cent.[32] Simultaneously North American, following the same policy, reduced its prices by a total of $14 million in 1941 and $60 million a year later.[33]

The procedures worked out between the aircraft firms and the government became the basis for the Renegotiation Act of 1942 and its subsequent revisions. By these acts Congress provided for compulsory renegotiation of war contracts in which there appeared to be excessive profits. It was unfortunate that in the enactment of the initial law an undue emphasis was given to its punitive aspects, thereby giving a strong impression that there was widespread profiteering and ignoring the extent to which industry was undertaking voluntary price adjustment. However, the agencies that had to administer renegotiation chose to operate as much as possible through voluntary compliance.

Since there had to be some standard of what constituted excessive profits, these agencies arrived at a rule-of-thumb figure of 10 per cent on sales before taxes as an equitable level.[34] This was above the average for the aircraft industry. In 1940 the twelve largest airframe manufacturers had net profits after taxes of 12.7 per cent of sales and 7.4 per cent in 1941. Subsequently this figure dropped to 2.2 per cent and even 1 per cent in 1944.[35] It is impossible to determine whether this decline was chiefly due to the Renegotiation Acts or to the policies of price adjustment adopted by the industry before the acts were passed.

These companies had aggregate net profits of over $350,000,000 from 1940 to 1945. They were not the whole aircraft industry (the engine and propeller manufacturers are excluded), but nevertheless in terms of the approximately $45 billion that the total aircraft program cost,[36] this figure does not suggest an excessive margin of profit. Moreover, while they were earning this amount, these companies were paying $1,171,300,000 in federal taxes.[37] It is possible to get a picture of swollen profits by shifting the base to investment or net worth.

Douglas, for instance, had profits after taxes amounting to 51 per cent of net worth in 1941 and 15 per cent in 1944.[38] But this is a meaningless calculation because of the very high proportion of production in government-financed facilities, and these were not a cost-free bonus to the industry. The government paid for the plant, but the manufacturer still had to meet the payroll and the bills from suppliers and subcontractors.

The aircraft industry's record in the matter of renegotiation of prices, whether voluntary or under the Renegotiation Acts, is quite impressive. A few subcontracting firms came under unfavorable publicity, but these were exceptional. The established aircraft companies, along with the great majority of their licensees and subcontractors, remained free, during and after the war, from accusations of profiteering. This was a substantial feat, considering that they were operating under constant pressure for more and faster production, with hastily trained clerical staffs to take care of a greatly enlarged volume of records. This situation could, of course, have been used to conceal malpractice, but such concealment could have been only temporary. The scrutiny of bodies like the Truman Committee would have led to exposure sooner or later.

The Role of the Automobile Industry

In view of all the discussion regarding the potential contribution of the automobile industry to aircraft production, some attention needs to be given to the actual performance. In general, it was excellent. As subcontractors or licensees, the automobile firms were the largest single group of suppliers to the aircraft manufacturers. They produced over $11 billion worth of aircraft, subassemblies, and parts, or 38.7 per cent of the dollar value of all military production by the automotive industry.[39] They built 455,522 aircraft engines out of a total of 812,615 and 255,518 propellers out of 713,717.[40]

Automobile companies also made some 27,000 complete aircraft (including helicopters and gliders). Taken in conjunction with the figures on aircraft components, this also represented a substantial contribution, but at the time it was a source of disappointment and criticism, and some of this attitude has held over. Exaggerated claims and estimates regarding the feasibility of converting automobile facilities to aircraft production had created in the public mind unreasonable expectations of what could be achieved.

After Pearl Harbor the heart of the difficulty was in the over-publicized project at Willow Run. The story of "Will It Run?" has been told several times, and the arguments have been beaten to exhaustion,[41] so that no useful purpose can be served by attempting to review all the details again. However, several salient points emerge from the record as essential to an evaluation of the over-all Willow Run performance.

The project was adversely affected from the start by the internal stresses of the Ford Motor Company at the time. The aged and ailing head of the company was determined to do things his own way, regardless of whether it was the most effective method of contributing to the war effort, and his intransigence was completely shared by Charles E. Sorensen. Sorensen was also engaged in a bitter rivalry with Harry Bennett, which did nothing to facilitate the venture into aircraft manufacturing. Edsel Ford was a sick man (he died in 1943) unable to pull the organization together. Part of the long delay in getting Willow Run up to its scheduled production was the insistence of Ford officials and engineers on using their own mass-production techniques without due consideration of their applicability. Admittedly they introduced improvements that expedited the production of B-24's in Convair plants, but they refused to acknowledge that they could learn anything from the aircraft manufacturers. Their effort to process aluminum with the type of steel die used on sheet steel for automobiles is an illuminating case in point: steel dies scar aluminum and scarred surfaces are aerodynamically undesirable.[42]

They also encountered the problem of design modification, a major cause of delay. But, as we have seen, this was a universal problem in aircraft production. The aircraft manufacturers had to wrestle with it, they warned their automotive subcontractors that they too would encounter it, and most of the automobile companies in due course adapted their procedures to it. The modification centers helped, of course, but they were not intended to handle major changes. Sorensen's comment on this problem is unintentionally self-revealing. He says:

The most annoying feature of our bomber operation was change in design during production. We would agree on freezing a design, then be ready to go ahead. Back from the fighting fronts would come complaints or suggestions regarding certain features; and the plane designers came through with alterations in design with no consideration for the production program.[43]

Doubtless some of the changes should have gone to modification centers rather than the factory; nevertheless Sorensen never seems to have considered that the purpose of making B-24's was to help win the war, not to establish production records or demonstrate the virtues of a particular method of manufacture.

There is, furthermore, no convincing explanation anywhere of why the company picked the Willow Run site, other than that Henry Ford owned part of it, or why the government permitted it to be selected. Its one obvious asset was that there was plenty of room for an enormous factory and an adjoining airfield; beyond that it had little to offer. It was assumed that Ypsilanti and Ann Arbor would provide the necessary labor, but apparently no one tried to find out in advance if this was so. Actually most of the labor force had to come from labor-scarce Detroit to a community with no housing facilities and wholly inadequate transportation; in the middle of the war, with all the other demands on labor and materials, the government had to build an express highway from Detroit to Ypsilanti.[44] Even so, it was never possible to recruit more than 42,000 workers out of the 70,000 needed for full production.[45] Apart from the housing and transport problems, there was discontent on other grounds, notably Harry Bennett's efforts to keep the UAW out of Willow Run.

One source of delay was definitely not attributable to the Ford organization. The mass of drawings and other data turned over by Convair (they occupied two freight cars) proved to be largely unusable. It was not just that there were differences in technical terminology or that the aircraft company's system assumed that the drawings were going to be interpreted by skilled craftsmen on the plant floor. There were also discrepancies in the plans which made it impossible to use them to prepare the elaborate tooling that the automobile men required.[46]

Dissatisfaction with Willow Run's failure to produce became so intense in mid-1943 that there was serious talk of the government taking over the operation. This solution was eagerly championed by the elements in the government who had been maneuvering for nationalization of the aircraft industry since the early days of the New Deal. Government operation would have pleased the UAW, and to that extent might have improved the labor situation. Beyond that it is difficult to see how government operation could have improved matters. As it turned out, by late 1943 some of the difficulties had been ironed out and Willow Run began to come up to expectations. In 1944 it delivered the greatest airframe weight produced by a single plant in one year, almost 100 million pounds.[47] Its total output in units was 6,791 B-24's, with the significant commentary on the plant's prolonged teething troubles that 5,476 of these were built in 1944 and 1945.[48] Willow Run also delivered 1,893 "knock-down" units for assembly elsewhere. It began turning out subassemblies, in fact, late in 1942, although in small quantity.

Since Willow Run did eventually demonstrate that B-24's could be built by mass-production methods, it has to be accounted a partial success. But it was an expensive demonstration in time, resources, and labor, and it was characteristic of the misfortunes that haunted the enterprise that it never reached its full capacity. By 1944 the plant had a potential output of 650 planes a month,[49] but it never turned out more than two-thirds of that number in any one month because there was no longer a need for that many B-24's. The plane was obsolescent in 1944. Its outstanding assets were its long range and its large capacity, both somewhat greater than those of the competing B-17, but on both points the B-24 was now superseded by the B-29.

Ford had much better but far less publicized success as a manufacturer of the GC-4A glider. The company received its first order (actually a letter of intent) [50] in April 1942 and was in production by the end of the year. For this purpose (and here the contrast to Willow Run is striking) Ford converted a plant it owned in Iron Mountain, on Michigan's Northern Peninsula, for making wooden bodies for station wagons. It had a sawmill, wood-working equipment, and an adequate labor force.[51] The total Ford glider production was 4,291. The only flaw in the product was a nose opening for unloading cargo, an ingenious piece of design in which the Ford engineers took justifiable pride. What they had overlooked was that, as General James A. Gavin of the 82nd Airborne Division pointed out, four out of five gliders ended up with their noses against fences, houses, stone walls, or trees.[52]

The only other automobile company to be extensively involved in manufacturing complete airplanes was General Motors through its Eastern Aircraft Division. This was a completely different operation from Willow Run. It was put together as a temporary organization by converting five existing General Motors plants. Three were in New Jersey—an assembly plant at Linden, a Delco-Remy branch at Bloomfield, and an automobile hardware factory at Trenton—and the other two were Fisher Body properties at Tarrytown, New York, and Baltimore, Maryland.[53] As was stated earlier, the Division made planes under license from Grumman: TBF Avengers, and F4F Wildcat fighters. The final assembly was done at Linden and Trenton.

Eastern's record for the war was 5,927 fighters and 7,522 torpedo bombers, about twice Willow Run's number of units but only 40 per cent of its airframe weight (123 million pounds for Willow Run to 48 million for Eastern).[54] Eastern's problem was simpler than Ford's; torpedo bombers and fighters were far less complicated than B-24's. Nevertheless this phase of the automobile industry's participation in the aircraft program appears to have received less credit than it deserves.

New Developments

Just as the incorporation of technical improvements without unduly retarding production was one of the major problems of aircraft manufacture, the same consideration applied to the introduction of novel types or designs. The risk of interfering with the production of tested models for something that might prove a failure had to be weighed against the risk of letting the enemy gain a technical advantage. This balancing of forces can be seen in three of the principal aeronautical innovations undertaken during the war: gliders, helicopters, and jet engines.

None of these was a product of the Second World War itself. The glider, indeed, is the oldest form of heavier-than-air flying machine, going back probably to the English monk Eilmer of Malmesbury in about 1010 A.D.[55] and certainly to Sir George Cayley and a number of distinguished successors in the nineteenth century, including the Wright brothers. However, the military potential of the glider was ignored in the United States until the Germans showed what airborne forces could accomplish, especially in the spectacular if costly conquest of Crete in May 1941. Fortunately gliders present no great difficulties in design or manufacture. Some 15,700 gliders were built for military use, either by the aircraft firms specializing in light planes, by companies organized specifically to make gliders, or by outsiders like Ford that had convertible facilities.[56] The gliders were urgently needed and would have had to be built even if it had meant interrupting other production. There was no need to make such a choice, however. The aircraft companies involved were not equipped to manufacture combat planes, and the rest of the glider manufacturers were facilities that were not engaged in other military production.

The helicopter, although also old in concept, was a much more recent arrival on the aeronautical scene than the glider. The idea of an aircraft capable of taking off and landing vertically had a strong appeal for designers and inventors. A partial solution was offered by the autogiro invented by the Spanish aeronautical engineer, Juan de la Cierva, in the 1920's.[57] A few were built in the United States between 1929 and 1932 by the Pitcairn Autogiro Company, founded by Harold H. Pitcairn, who was operating the progenitor of Eastern Airlines. The autogiro was actually an airplane with rotor blades rotating freely instead of wings. For its forward motion it had a conventional engine and propeller. It was not capable of vertical takeoff or landing; it simply required considerably less distance for either than the winged plane.

The critical step in making the helicopter possible was the introduction of the controllable-pitch propeller, which permitted designing a powered rotor capable of both lifting and propelling by changing the blade settings. Some experimental helicopters were flown in Europe in the middle 1930's, but it is generally agreed that the first practical design was Igor Sikorsky's VS-300, which made its initial test flight on April 20, 1939.[58]

The variety of potential uses for a workable helicopter attracted the military and led to an attempt at production. The results, however, were not very satisfactory. Fewer than 400 helicopters were built, with output about equally divided between Sikorsky Aviation and the Nash-Kelvinator Corporation in Detroit.[59] E. E. Wilson, who became president of United Aircraft in 1940, has maintained that this effort at production was premature and was undertaken only on orders from the government.[60] Whoever made the decision, it was certainly premature. A device as complicated as a helicopter was bound to require a long period of testing and development before it was ready for regular service, particularly in war. One historian of vertical flight has commented that "his [Sikorsky's] first authentic helicopter, the Vought-Sikorsky 300, was tinkered so unmercifully in its four years of existence that only six items—the seat, landing wheels, transmission box, central fuselage, and gas tank—remained unchanged." [61] After the developmental problems were solved, manufacturing difficulties were to be expected, especially if quantity was desired. The helicopter that would come into its own in later years was simply not ready for the Second World War. It warranted no greater production effort than was actually made.

The jet engine was certainly a more important innovation of the Second World War than the glider and probably than the helicopter. Like the glider, its development was pushed under the pressure of military necessity; like the helicopter, it did not come into effective operational use until after the war. Reference has been made previously to the studies of jet engines made by the NACA, which indicated that at existing aircraft speeds the jet offered no advantage over the piston engine. It has to be remembered that the fighter planes of the Second World War were the first to achieve speeds as high as 400 m.p.h., and the propeller engine is more efficient than the jet up to about 500 m.p.h. This limitation affected studies of gas turbine engines for airplanes made during the 1930's by the Army and Navy and by some private companies, in directing them toward engines to drive propellers.[62] Apparently there was no knowledge of the work of Frank (later Sir Frank) Whittle in Great Britain or Hans von Ohain in Germany. The one place where the United States could be considered ahead in the development and use of the gas turbine for aviation was the turbosupercharger, whose development yielded valuable experience in some of the problems of gas turbines as well as useful metallurgical information.[63]

About the time war broke out three American aircraft companies initiated the first really productive studies of gas turbines for airplanes. Two were airframe firms, Northrop and Lockheed. The Northrop project began in 1939, contemplating a turboprop engine.[64] A development contract for $483,600 was finally awarded on June 31, 1941, but since J. K. Northrop estimated that it would take over a million dollars to get an operational engine, progress on what was termed the Turbodyne was very slow. The second airframe concern was Lockheed, which began work shortly after Northrop. The Lockheed design was done by Nathan Price, who during the early 1930's had worked on a steam turbine for aircraft but had to drop it for lack of support. Price decided in 1940 that the only feasible approach was to aim for jet propulsion and to design both an engine and an airplane accordingly. These became the L-1000 engine and L-133 plane, with a planned performance of 625 m.p.h. at 50,000 feet.[65] Lockheed submitted its plans to the Air Force in 1942, only to be told that the company's job was to concentrate on building P-38's and B-17's.[66] So Lockheed's early development work was done at its own expense.

The third entry was Pratt and Whitney, where experimental work on a gas turbine was begun in 1940 under the supervision of L. S. Hobbs.[67] The initial design, PT-1, was based on the ideas of an engineer at M.I.T., Andrew Kalitinsky. The engine had a two-stroke diesel operating a free-piston compressor, while the exhaust drove the turbine. It was still to be a propeller engine, but smoother functioning and greater fuel economy were hoped for. Experimental work on the PT-1 went on all through the war, with some support from the Navy for a short time, but at a cost to Pratt and Whitney of over $3 million of its own money.

Curtiss-Wright (specifically the Wright Aeronautical Division) did no work of its own in this field, but it seems to have been the first American company to realize the importance of what was going on in Britain, because in 1941 it began to negotiate with Power Jets (Whittle's company) for a license to make the Whittle engine.[68] These negotiations, however, had to be dropped when the Air Force came into the picture and took charge of jet-engine development.

By this time (1941) the military authorities were getting worried about reports of German work on jet propulsion. The immediate concern was with rocket engines; whether information on turbojets was lacking or whether these were confused with the rockets is not clear. At any rate, the NACA established a Committee on Jet Propulsion in March 1941, recalling W. F. Durand from retirement at the age of 82 to be its chairman.[69] The Durand Committee promptly initiated research and development programs by the nation's principal manufacturers of turbines, General Electric, Westinghouse, and Allis-Chalmers. Meanwhile, General H. H. Arnold of the Air Force visited Britain, also in the spring of 1941, and discovered that the British were far ahead of the United States in jet-engine development; that, indeed, the Whittle engine was almost ready for a test flight.[70] As a result, arrangements were made for a Whittle engine to be sent to the United States, and in October the General Electric plant at Lynn, Massachusetts, where most superchargers were manufactured, received a contract to build engines based on the Whittle design. The airframes for the first experimental jet planes were assigned to Bell.[71]

The omission of the aircraft engine manufacturers from this program stands out conspicuously. There is an obvious and probably adequate explanation: they were already fully extended in trying to meet the demand for piston engines and the government did not want to jeopardize production by imposing on them the immensely difficult task of jet-engine development. The engine firms were in fact ordered to concentrate on the production of their existing types and not to allocate any resources or engineering talent to research and development on jets.[72] Pratt and Whitney, however, kept its PT-1 program going on a limited scale. Apart from this question of production, there was the compelling consideration that the major problem in jet-engine development was the turbine, and the companies that were brought into the program had the country's largest reservoir of experience and talent in this field. As a matter of fact, because of its previous work with turbosuperchargers, General Electric was able to improve the Whittle engine and overcome some difficulties that had baffled the British engineers.[73]

The first American-built jet plane, the XP-59A, with the Bell airframe and two General Electric engines, made its trial flight at Muroc Dry Lake, California, (now Edwards Air Force Base) on October 2, 1942, piloted first by Robert M. Stanley, the test pilot for Bell, and then by Colonel (later Lieutenant General) Laurence C. Craigie, who has given the following description of this historic event:

On October 1, 1942, Bob Stanley (Robert M. Stanley, currently President of Stanley Aviation Corporation) conducted taxi tests on the XP-59A on Muroc Dry Lake. He taxied back and forth several times, gradually increasing speed and feeling out the controls as he did so. Eventually, he got the airplane up to such a speed that he was able to lift it off the ground. He had several miles of smooth lake bed on which to conduct these tests so the situation was similar to that which would exist when testing a sea plane. Bob and I were discussing this test the other day and he recalls that he probably got the airplane about 10 feet above the lake bed. On the following day, October 2, 1942, the official first flight took place. This was performed by Bob. I then flew the airplane. The flight lasted between 20 and 30 minutes.

As I told the group at Edwards Air Force Base at the 25th Anniversary ceremony which took place there on October 2, I sort of backed into the distinction of being the first military pilot to pilot a jet airplane. Both Colonel Ralph Swofford, who was project officer on the airplane, and Colonel Don Keirn, who was project officer on the jet engine, were out of the country at the time the airplane was ready to make its first flight. I was Chief of Experimental Aircraft projects at that time and had, therefore, been following this particular project very closely. I, therefore, went out to Muroc from Dayton and spent several days there while we made the final preparations for the test program and got it underway.

As a matter of fact, it is rather unusual for the company pilot to release an experimental airplane to one of the customer's pilots quite this early in the program and there is a rather interesting story in that connection. As you can appreciate, General Electric Company's I-A engine was really much more experimental than the airplane. After all, an airplane doesn't really care whether it is being pulled by a propeller or being pushed by a jet. It is only interested in receiving thrust. The General Electric Company imposed rather severe restrictions on our early operation of these engines. We were permitted to accumulate only three hours of running time on them (and this included ground running time as well as taxiing and flight time) before they were to be removed from the airplane, partially disassembled and inspected. When Bob finished his flight on October 2, there was approximately 20 minutes of time remaining before the required inspection. Bob didn't consider this amount of time long enough to permit him to conduct a very meaningful test and the idea occurred to him that it might be a nice gesture to offer me the opportunity to fly the airplane. He did so and, naturally, I jumped at it.[74]

The XP-59A flew well enough, but its performance fell short of expectations, and the production P-59's, of which 66 were built, were used only as trainers. The Air Force then turned to Lockheed, which up to this time had been left in complete ignorance of what was going on, and in mid-1943 asked for an airframe to be used with a jet engine.[75] Lockheed produced the desired prototype, XP-80, in 143 days. It was successfully test-flown on January 8, 1944, with a De Havilland Goblin engine. Subsequently the plane was redesigned for a more powerful General Electric engine, the J-33, with 4,000 pounds of thrust compared to the 1,600 of the engine used in the XP-59A. The P-80, known as the Shooting Star, went into production and 243 were completed before the end of the war, although none flew in combat. Most of the engines used for P-59's came from General Electric; production of the J-33 was about equally divided between General Electric and the Allison Division of General Motors.[76] The Navy, meanwhile, contracted with McDonnell Aircraft for a carrier-based jet fighter, the FD-1, with Westinghouse-built engines, but it was just at the prototype stage when the war ended.[77] It subsequently went into service as the Phantom.

The Record

The details of the wartime production record are set forth in Tables 8 and 9 and in the Appendixes. In round figures

Table 8. Major Producers of Airplanes, 1940–1945

A. By numbers of planes, July 1, 1940–August 31, 1945

Company	Number of Units
North American	41,188
Convair	30,903
Douglas	30,696
Curtiss-Wright	26,154
Lockheed	18,926
Boeing	18,381
Grumman	17,428
Republic	15,603
Bell	13,575
Eastern Aircraft Division, General Motors	13,449
Martin	8,810
Chance Vought	7,890
Ford	6,791
Goodyear	3,940

B. By airframe weight, January 1, 1940–December 31, 1944
(in thousands of pounds)

Company	Total	Per Cent of 5-Year Grand Total
Douglas	306,573	15.3
Convair	291,073	14.6
Boeing	226,477	11.3
North American	210,913	10.5
Lockheed	180,118	9.0
Curtiss-Wright	136,091	6.9
Martin	126,970	6.3
Ford	123,076	6.2
Republic	75,893	3.9
Grumman	73,767	3.7
Bell	53,037	2.7
Eastern	47,869	2.4
Chance Vought	28,952	1.4
Goodyear	13,668	0.7
All other plants	101,136	5.1
Grand total—all plants	1,995,613	100.0

Source: W. F. Craven and J. L. Cate, Men and Planes (Chicago, 1955) pp. 354–355.

Table 9. Engine and Propeller Production, 1940–1945

ENGINE PRODUCTION BY TYPE: 1940–1945

Year	Procuring Agency		Type		
	AAF	Navy	Air-Cooled (Radial)	Liquid-Cooled (In-line)	Jets
Total 812,615	660,950	151,665	685,964	125,321	1,330
1940	22,667	15,346	7,321	21,524	1,143	0
1941	58,181	39,502	18,679	51,684	6,497	0
1942	138,089	103,809	34,280	115,933	22,156	0
1943	227,116	188,803	38,313	193,728	33,388	0
1944	256,911	223,861	33,050	213,495	43,294	122
1945	109,651	89,629	20,022	89,600	18,843	1,208

ENGINE PRODUCTION BY HORSEPOWER: 1940–1945

Year	Under 300 h.p.	300–999 h.p.	1000–1599 h.p.	1600 h.p. and up
1940	9,138	4,422	7,149	1,958
1941	18,652	12,841	17,526	9,162
1942	23,724	23,098	61,265	30,002
1943	29,741	23,871	127,011	46,493
1944	11,101	13,267	146,585	85,836
1945	3,366	857	46,169	58,050

PROPELLER PRODUCTION: 1940–1945

Year	Units Accepted
	Total 713,717
1940	14,290
1941	39,123
1942	106,136
1943	213,937
1944	243,741
1945	96,490

Source: I. B. Holley, *Buying Aircraft: Material Procurement for the Army Air Forces* (Washington, D. C., 1964), p. 549.

the aircraft industry during the war years built 300,000 airplanes with an aggregate airframe weight of over 2 billion pounds, 800,000 engines, and 700,000 propellers. In the process the industry rose from 44th in dollar value of output in 1939 to first in 1944.[78] Of the total airframe weight over half was accounted for by aircraft factories that existed before the war but were expanded during it, and most of the rest by new plants managed by aircraft companies.[79] In fact, the only important manufacturers of airplanes who were not in the business before the war were Ford, General Motors, and the Goodyear Aircraft Corporation. The last-named built close to 4,000 Vought F4U Corsairs for the Navy, plus subassemblies and components for other planes, while the parent company, Goodyear Tire & Rubber, had its five commercial blimps taken over by the Navy and made 154 more for antisubmarine work.[80] The engine situation was different, with about half the output contributed by automobile companies, although for the most part from new facilities rather than from existing automobile engine plants.

The quantitative record of aircraft production is so staggering that it is easy to overlook the qualitative accomplishments. Throughout the war the aircraft industry was called on both to produce more planes and to keep making them bigger and more complex. For example, the B-17G of 1944 was 9,000 pounds heavier than the B-17C of 1939, had 300 miles more range, about three times as much bomb load, heavier armament, and an assortment of electronic equipment that did not even exist when the earlier Flying Fortress was designed.[81] Simultaneously, Boeing was bringing the much bigger B-29 into production.

The heavy bomber continued to hold first place in Air Force thinking; it is significant that the total of B-29's, B-17's, and B-24's procured by the AAF exceeded the combined total of all medium and light bombers.[82] Consequently the heavy bomber remained the type in which the United States excelled. The only foreign counterpart that could be considered in the same class was the British Lancaster. At the same time there were marked advances in the area where American development had previously lagged most conspicuously, that is, in fighters. The P-40 had to carry most of the load for the Air Force through 1942; then the newer types (P-38, P-39, P-47, P-51) began to come into service and proved to be qualitatively comparable to their competitors. The P-40 was out of production by 1945, as was the P-39 Airacobra. The latter was replaced by the bigger and faster P-63 Kingcobra. In the last half of the war the Air Force also had the Northrop P-61 Black Widow, designed specifically for night fighting.[83]

One important feature of the production record was the construction of almost 23,000 transport planes. Most were adaptations of existing commercial types; some 10,000 were DC-3's, renamed C-54. The conversion of projected new airliners to military use has been described in Chapter 5. In addition, several light planes were redesigned for utility transport service, the largest number being contributed by Beech, Cessna, and Fairchild.[84] These were improvisations, but they turned out well. Fairchild's C-61, the Forwarder, was a remodeling of the F-24, originally introduced in 1931 as a two-place, high-wing cabin monoplane.[85]

There were, of course, the inevitable disappointments and false starts. The demand for transport aircraft was going to be solved by bringing into the picture Andrew J. Higgins of New Orleans, who had performed apparent miracles of shipbuilding and had the additional asset of being a staunch political adherent of the administration. So Higgins Aircraft was launched with much fanfare and succeeded in building just two C-46's at a cost to the government for plant and equipment of $23 million.[86] The Hughes Aircraft Company of Culver City, California, proposed a reconnaissance plane, the F-11 (*not* F-111) with a speed of 400 m.p.h., a range of 3,000 miles, and a ceiling of 60,000 feet. The Material Command of the Air Force was convinced that these specifications could not be met, but Hughes had the backing of Colonel Elliott Roosevelt and the project was approved.[87] The F-11 was not finished until some time after the war ended, and it did not achieve its planned performance.

These, however, were minor failures and have to be written off as the kind of error of judgment that must be expected in the stress of war. A more serious question might be raised about the commitment of such vast resources to the construction of heavy bombers, in view of the subsequent findings of the United States Strategic Bombing Survey that both the high-level "precision" bombing of industrial targets in Europe and the bombardment of Japanese cities were less effective than had been assumed in weakening the resistance of either country. This was a policy decision that had to be made at the top level of government, and to a considerable extent the decision was based on quite honest miscalculations of the accuracy that could be achieved in aerial bombardment.

In any case, the issue concerned the use to which the planes were put, and not the way in which they were built. The task of the aircraft industry was to meet the requirements of the government, and it did so superlatively.

By way of comparison, the production of military aircraft by the four major belligerents (figures for the U.S.S.R. are not available) for the years 1939 and 1944 was as follows.[88]

Year	Germany	Great Britain	Japan	United States
1939	8,295	7,940	4,467	2,141
1944	39,807	24,461	28,180	96,318

Airframe weights would show a still more striking American expansion, but they are not really relevant here, because in the latter part of the war both Germany and Japan concentrated on fighter production. In other respects the comparison has some inequities; the United States started with a higher potential in industrial capacity, and its mainland, where the aircraft manufacturing was conducted, was never subject to hostile attack. Nevertheless, with all due allowance for these qualifications, the wartime record of the American aircraft industry remains an outstanding achievement of industrial production. The following statement may perhaps summarize it as effectively as it can be done:

The statistical record of aircraft production shows a remarkable growth between 1940 and the peak year of 1944: an increase of about 1600 per cent in the number of military planes, of about 4500 per cent in total airframe weight, and about 2700 per cent in total horsepower of the engines built. That these records were made with an increase in factory floor space of only 1200 per cent and of manpower by about 1600 per cent indicates an appreciable gain in efficiency of operations.[89]

9. Reconversion and Readjustment

At the end of the Second World War a casual survey of the American aircraft industry would probably have left a strong impression that history was repeating itself. By the end of 1945 contracts amounting to well over $21 billion had been canceled, and sixteen airframe plants remained in operation out of 66 that had been functioning a year earlier.[1] It was unquestionably a difficult time; between 1944 and 1947 the industry's sales dropped by over 90 per cent, with corresponding effects on earnings and employment. Nevertheless the clock had not been turned back; 1946 was not 1919. To begin with, while some abrupt and fairly large-scale cancellation of military contracts was unavoidable, this contingency had been anticipated by both government and industry. Procedures for orderly contract termination were adopted in 1943 and were incorporated into the Contract Settlement Act of 1944.[2] In order to avoid needless disruption of industry when military requirements changed or disappeared, the contract termination process attempted to: (1) phase out war contracts as gradually as conditions permitted, (2) prevent manufacturers and their subcontractors from being left with vast quantities of unusable inventory, and (3) provide some assistance in reconverting to peacetime production. The normal pattern was for the subcontractors to be cut back first, so that the industry gradually resumed its prewar structure. In addition, this time the government did not flood the civilian market with surplus planes and engines.

There were other factors of greater long-range significance. First of all, the Second World War left both the American government and public convinced of the importance of air power (almost oversold, indeed, because there was a strong tendency to accept uncritically the Mitchell doctrine that air power could replace all other kinds of military force). Second, air transport was now well established and held the promise of substantial growth. Among other reasons, the war had accustomed a great many Americans to flying. Third, the possibilities of new technologies, such as the jet engine and the helicopter, were still unrealized. And finally, there were hopes that perhaps the dream of a great expansion of private flying was at last going to come true.

Postwar Survey

The experiences of the member firms of the aircraft industry in returning to a peacetime status varied widely. All had to review their position and decide what the most promising course would be: whether to continue exclusively as airframe or engine manufacturers or to seek diversification into nonaeronautical fields; whether to aim for military or commercial markets for aircraft; what to do about prospective new developments such as guided missiles, jet propulsion, VTOL (Vertical Take-Off and Landing) aircraft, and high-altitude, supersonic flight. The only generalization that can be made concerning the choices is that no two firms followed exactly the same policies. To understand what was happening in the industry during the immediate postwar years requires virtually a company-by-company survey.

Four of the five large companies on the West Coast, Boeing, Douglas, Lockheed, and North American, emerged from the war in reasonably strong positions, even though this point might not have been immediately apparent to harassed managements wrestling with contract cancellations, shortages of materials, dubious market prospects, uncertain new technologies, and the postwar upsurge of labor unrest. Their mood undoubtedly matched the uncertainty reflected in a statement emanating from the engineering department of the fifth major West Coast producer, Convair, in April 1945:

"Work has just started on possible airplanes for supersonic speeds. A turbo-rocket power plant seems to be the most promising at the present time. Practically no aerodynamic data are available in this speed range, and what there is isn't consistent." [3]

The leaders of the industry would have been considerably more relaxed if the only confusing prospects had been in aerodynamics.

At Boeing there was a change of management. Philip Johnson died in 1944, and after a year's delay he was succeeded by William Allen, who had been the company's legal adviser for twenty years.[4] Allen's reluctance to accept the job was understandable. By the end of 1945 employment in the Seattle plants was down from its wartime peak of 45,000 to 15,000 and was likely to go lower. Future military orders were guesswork, and a return to the commercial transport market faced stiff competition with existing Douglas and Lockheed types. But there was a bright side to the Boeing picture also. At the end of the war the B-29 was the Air Force's first-line heavy bomber and it continued to be built, although in reduced quantity, until 1947.[5] It was then replaced by the B-50, essentially an enlarged B-29, and some 370 of these were built before the type was discontinued in 1952.[6] Moreover, in the customary Boeing fashion the B-29, B-50 design was adapted for transport purposes, in a highly successful military version designated the C-97 and a commercial transport named the Stratocruiser. The C-97 remained in production until 1956 and almost 900 were built.[7] The Stratocruiser was also a good plane, but it had hard going against its Douglas and Lockheed rivals, and after making 56, Boeing discontinued it in 1950. This was a new era; where Boeing's history-making 247 had sold for $50,000 in 1932, just fifteen years later the 377 Stratocruiser had to be held down to $1,250,000 to be competitive, and the result was a loss of $15 million.[8] Finally, Boeing was getting a start on jet planes. In 1943 it began to design at Air Force instigation a jet-propelled, medium-range bomber, XB-47, one of the first planes to have a distinctive sweep-back to the wings; in 1946 it won a design competition for a long-range bomber, XB-52.[9] Initially this plane was to have six turboprop engines, but after two years of study Boeing's engineers opted for jet propulsion.

The jet planes were a prospect for the future; in fact their development cost added to the company's burdens. However, the first B-47 production order came in 1948, and for the first time since the end of the war Boeing was able to show a profit. Two years earlier there had been a loss of $5 million, although tax carry-overs of wartime profits under the Contract Settlement Act made up over $3 million.[10] Therefore, when despite a prolonged strike in Seattle by the Aero Mechanics Union, which the company eventually won, Boeing could show a profit, it felt that reconversion had been satisfactorily accomplished.

Douglas' descent from its wartime peak was no less painful but shorter-lived than Boeing's. Essentially Douglas Aircraft picked up where it had left off in 1939 as the world's largest manufacturer of commercial aircraft. The DC-4 remained in production for a short time after the war, but in 1946 its design was "stretched" to become the DC-6.[11] The DC-6 went through several modifications and then in turn was stretched into the DC-7 series, the last of the great American piston-engined transports. These planes had pressurized cabins, wing loadings of 55–64 pounds, and cruising speeds over 300 m.p.h.[12] The DC-7 series, using the Curtiss-Wright turbo-compound 3350 engine, was capable of nonstop transcontinental flight in either direction —against the prevailing wind as well as with it—and the final version, DC-7C (Seven Seas) permitted similar nonstop translantic service. Prices ranged from about $600,000 for the original DC-6's to $2.5 million for the DC-7C.

Douglas was also still in the military aircraft business. It was building a few large transports, C-74 Globemasters, and from these developed the C-124, beginning in 1948. It was also making the AD (Skyraider) series of Navy attack bombers, which would eventually go through 28 configurations.[13] Consequently, although Douglas Aircraft lost over $2 million in 1947, it turned the corner in the next year and reached a position where as late as 1958 over half of all the commercial aircraft in the world were Douglas-built.[14]

Douglas' most effective competitor in the transport field at this time was Lockheed, whose management anticipated the problems of reconversion as thoroughly and competently as anyone in the business. In 1944 Robert E. Gross considered and rejected proposals for moving into automobile manufacturing, either by merging with the Crosley Corporation or joining Goodyear in working on an experimental car.[15] It was a sound decision; in view of the experience of Henry J. Kaiser in attempting to break into automobile manufacturing, it is clear that this was no field for even a well-financed amateur.

Lockheed occupied a strong position in what was left of the military market. The P-80 Shooting Star continued in production, and the Navy picked up a design it had been interested in in 1941 and had to suspend during the war. This was the P2V Neptune, a patrol bomber intended for antisubmarine work. Eventually Lockheed built 900 of them, in seven major versions.[16]

For the transport market Lockheed, like Douglas, returned to the plans it had made in 1939 and as rapidly as possible reconverted the C-69 military transport to the L-049 Constellation— rapidly enough so that deliveries to the airlines began in November 1945, a full year ahead of the DC-6. Lockheed had orders for 103 Constellations for $75.5 million at the end of 1945.[17] This was a bright prospect, certainly brighter than most aircraft companies faced at that point, but trouble came in very short order because the L-049 turned out to have a propensity for catching fire in midair. After several such incidents, culminating in a crash near Reading, Pennsylvania, on July 11, 1946, the Civil Aeronautics Administration ordered all Constellations grounded.[18] However, after six weeks of hard work, the defects were remedied and the Constellations were allowed to fly again.

The fires had been caused by malfunctioning of the engine air induction systems and short circuits in electrical connections that set fire to cabin insulating material. For what comfort it might have been to Lockheed, the DC-6 in its turn had similar difficulties. With it, the intake for the cabin heater was so located that fuel from the fuel vent could be drawn into it and start a fire.[19] Fundamentally, designers were learning that the greater complexity of airplanes built for high-altitude, high-speed flight required close attention to the most minute details. The lesson was learned, and subsequent models had no comparable deficiencies. Eventually the Constellation developed through six improved designs, matching the DC-6 and -7 progression, and 850 were manufactured, including the Super Constellation, before they were superseded by the jet airliners; but it took until 1950 for Lockheed to begin to recover the approximately $25 million it put into the plane.[20]

For some time, therefore, the Constellation looked like more of a threat than a promise. Shortly after the grounding, a strike of TWA pilots resulted in cancellation of orders, and the combination of misfortunes left Lockheed at the end of 1946 in an operating loss of $21.9 million, of which half was recovered in tax carry-over, and a bank debt of $40 million.[21] Yet Lockheed's place in the industry was strong enough that there was some discussion of relieving Convair's continuing corporate distresses by having Lockheed take over the aviation divisions from AVCO. The negotiations were never pressed with any great vigor, and the grounding of the Constellations seems to have frightened the Convair people away.

Lockheed had also created during the war an elaborate service and maintenance organization, beginning with the bases in Britain established by Henry H. Ogden and given corporate structure as the Lockheed Overseas Corporation. There was also a worldwide field service operation for Lockheed planes, run by the parent company. At the end of the war Lockheed reorganized its service structure, with discouraging results until at the end of 1946 it returned to the policy that had worked so successfully for Lockheed Overseas Corporation in its military work: namely, to provide service, repair, and modification for airplanes of all makes. This policy was implemented by the formation of Lockheed Aircraft Service, Inc., as a wholly owned subsidiary.[22] Its first president was Cyril Chappellet, one of the founding group in

1932. He was succeeded in 1949 by J. Kenneth Hull, who had been Ogden's chief assistant in Britain.

North American shared with Lockheed a change of status from being a minor producer before the war to being one of the leading firms in the aircraft industry. Unlike its competitors, however, North American continued to concentrate on military aircraft. Its one venture into nonmilitary planes was an effort to reach the private-plane market through a model called the Navion. It was a four-place "executive sedan," which cost $10,000 to make and sold for $7,000, with the result that after losing $8 million North American decided to leave light planes to the companies specializing in them and sold the design to Ryan Aeronautical in 1947.[23] North American achieved more satisfactory results by getting an early start in the development of missiles and undertaking studies of nuclear technology for the Atomic Energy Commission.[24] From these activities several new divisions subsequently emerged: Atomics International, for nuclear technology; Autonetics, for electronic products, especially inertial guidance systems; and Rocketdyne, for liquid fuel rocket engines.

However, military aircraft were still the heart of the North American operation. At the end of 1945 the company was in the discouraging position of seeing its backlog of orders drop from 8,000 to 24, and its employment from a wartime high of 90,000 to 5,000; in 1947 it had its first year of deficit.[25] This situation was remedied by an energetic development of jet planes. During this reconversion period North American came up with the B-45 bomber, the first four-engined jet to be test-flown in the United States, although it did not progress beyond the experimental stage; the FJ-1 Fury jet fighter for the Navy; a new training plane; and, above all, the F-86 Sabrejet, the first-line fighter of the Korean War.[26] The F-86 was begun in 1945, but in its initial version could go no faster than 0.8 Mach ("Mach" denotes speed of sound, or 761 m.p.h. at sea level). The F-86 was redesigned with swept-back wings, and when a test flight reached a speed of 671 m.p.h., it became the first operational American fighter plane with this configuration.

Finally, North American's reconversion included the termination of the General Motors interest in the company. This occurred on June 3, 1948, when General Motors sold its 1,000,100 shares of North American for $12.75 a share.[27] This action resulted from a study of postwar policy made by General Motors, which indicated that the airframe market was unlikely to offer sufficient volume to make it attractive, and furthermore that as a producer of aircraft engines and accessories for the entire aviation industry, a field that did have a potential for volume production, General Motors stood to lose rather than gain by attempting to compete with its own customers. This consideration applied to partial as well as complete ownership of an airframe manufacturing company, and so General Motors withdrew from North American. The summing up of this policy decision is very interesting in comparison with the discussions in 1940 and 1941 regarding mass production of airplanes by the automobile industry: "It became increasingly clear that General Motors could not employ its mass-production techniques effectively in the airframe industry." [28]

The move had very little effect on the management of North American. Henry M. Hogan of General Motors retired as board chairman and was replaced by J. H. Kindelberger, who was succeeded as president by J. L. Atwood.[29] These two had worked together for a long time and would continue to do so until Kindelberger's death in 1962. James H. "Dutch" Kindelberger was a molder's son from Wheeling, West Virginia, who became a factory apprentice at sixteen, studied drafting at night, and spent one year at the Carnegie Institute of Technology before enlisting in the Army in 1917.[30] He became a pilot in the Signal Corps and at the end of the war went to Cleveland as designer and chief draftsman for Glenn L. Martin. In 1925 he joined his former Martin associate, Donald Douglas, as chief engineer and remained with Douglas until Ernest R. Breech of General Motors offered him the presidency of North American.[31] John Leland Atwood was a Texan with a degree in civil engineering who got into aviation because Wright Field needed an engineer to do stress analysis.[32] He left the Air Corps to work with a small aircraft company in Wichita, moved to Los Angeles when this company failed after the 1929 crash, and eventually joined Douglas Aircraft, where he met Kindelberger.

The American Institute of Management had this to say about the Kindelberger-Atwood combination:

> The growth and success of North American Aviation refutes the statements of some commentators that engineers are seldom good managers—Messrs. Kindelberger and Atwood deserve special compliment on the manner in which they have kept the company healthy through hectic wartime growth and drastic retrenchment.[33]

Convair was in a less happy situation. To meet the problems of reconversion the company launched what now looks like an overambitious and poorly thought-out program of diversification. To quote the company history:

> One Vultee Field project was the development of a prototype plastic-and-aluminum packaged home. Experimental flying autos were given a whirl at San Diego. In January, 1946 a controlling interest was purchased in ACF-Brill Motors Co. of Philadelphia (transit buses) and its wholly owned subsidiary, Hall-Scott Motor Car Co. of Berkeley, California (auto and marine engines). At an outlay of $2.5 million, the Nashville plant was equipped to manufacture kitchen ranges and freezer cabinets for Crosley Corp. (an AVCO affiliate) and buses for ACF-Brill.[34]

The stated purpose was to hold the technical force together and keep working capital profitably employed. The first may have been achieved but hardly the second.

For its airframe business Convair had highly promising prospects. At San Diego the Convair-Liner, a twin-engined medium-range transport, was under development, and at Fort Worth the B-36, the first intercontinental bomber. The Vultee Division was working on prototype missiles and designs for a delta-wing fighter. The only division actually making planes for the market was Stinson, which was producing a four-place light plane called the Voyager and apparently doing well. The retention of the Fort Worth plant deserves attention; Convair was almost alone in retaining a wartime government-built factory at a distance from its main plant.

Convair officials were aware that they would lose money for a while, but with a $25 million "carry-forward" of war profits the risk seemed acceptable.[35] Unfortunately everything went wrong that possibly could. Development costs on the Convair-Liner ran well above estimates, and there were delays in getting into production, including a 101-day strike in 1946.[36] Consequently, while the original estimate fixed the break-even point at 158 planes, by early 1948 it had risen to 300, and the company had had to write off $14 million in costs.[37] In addition, keen competition for a limited market led to frequent underpricing in order to make sales. Stinson sold 5,000 planes in 1946 and 1947, but then the demand for light planes declined and a year later the assets of the Stinson Division were sold to the Piper Aircraft Corporation.[38] For the year 1947 Convair showed a loss of $36 million, reduced to $16.7 million by tax recovery.[39]

Under these conditions Convair should not have appeared an attractive investment. AVCO, with 26 per cent of stock, agreed, but Floyd B. Odlum, president of the Atlas Corporation, an investment company, saw in Convair's financial distresses a favorable opportunity to buy into a company that had potential for the future; during the summer of 1947 Atlas bought 117,000 shares of Convair, about 7 per cent of the total. Then an agreement was reached whereby AVCO's holdings in Convair were retired, leaving Atlas with 10 per cent of the remaining outstanding stock, and AVCO bought from Convair its interest in the Nashville and ACF-Brill properties.[40] From this transaction Convair received $5 million to help meet bank loans of $15 million.

Management changes followed. Odlum brought in La Motte T. Cohu, then president of TWA and formerly general manager of Northrop, to replace Woodhead, and I. M. Laddon resigned as vice-president but remained a director. Girdler had already gone; he returned to the steel industry as soon as the war ended. An issue of over 1,100,000 shares of new stock, sold to the existing stockholders, brought in $10.3 million of additional cash, and dividends were passed in 1948 and 1949. These measures restored financial stability, and after losing $11.9 million in 1948 Convair managed to make a profit of $3.7 million a year later.[41]

By this time the Convair-Liner was in production, and the company eventually produced over 1,000, ranging in series from the 110, the prototype, to the 440 of 1955.[42] More important in terms of earnings, the B-36 was also coming into production by this time. It had its problems too, but they were technical and political rather than financial.

The first design studies for an intercontinental bomber were instituted by the Air Force in 1941,[43] and development contracts were subsequently awarded to Northrop and Convair for the XB-35 and XB-36, respectively. The former was a six-engined, flying-wing design which was test-flown in 1946 but never went into service. The XB-36 was initially designed to weigh 256,000 pounds, with a range of 10,000 miles with 5 tons of bombs. Power was provided by six Pratt and Whitney R-4360 Wasp Majors, 28-cylinder engines developing 3,000 h.p. each. These were placed on the trailing edge of the wing, making the plane a "pusher," because it was thought that this arrangement would work better with the NACA laminar-flow airfoil that was being used.[44]

A production contract for 100 B-36's was awarded in 1944 ($154,250,000 plus a fee of $6,170,000), but the prototype did not make its first flight until August 8, 1946. As could be expected, design and engineering problems cropped up. The pusher arrangement gave the plane good climbing capability, but it also created turbulence effects at the trailing edge of the wing, which caused intense vibration and metal fatigue. Consequently it was August 1948 before the first production models were delivered. Eventually 350 were built, the last in 1954. By then the B-36 had grown in size by 100,000 pounds and had become a 10-engined monster through the addition of four jets.[45] Its speed was somewhat above 435 m.p.h. and its ceiling about 45,000 feet. The political entanglement of the B-36 will be discussed later.

Since Atlas was an investment company it can be taken for granted that Odlum had never planned to stay in the aircraft business, but merely intended to rehabilitate the company and sell out at a profit. It is, however, somewhat surprising to find him seeking a buyer as early as 1949. There was definitely a second attempt to combine Convair and Lockheed and apparently an approach to Curtiss-Wright.[46] Nothing came of these moves. Robert E. Gross felt that Odlum's price was too high, and Curtiss-Wright was not interested at all. Atlas remained the controlling interest in Convair until 1953, when the General Dynamics Corporation bought Atlas' 400,000 shares of Convair. In that year Convair's sales exceeded $370,000,000, of which 83 per cent was for military aircraft, missiles, and other services to the armed forces, making Convair the country's eighth largest defense contractor in dollar volume.[47]

On the other side of the country, the Glenn L. Martin Company was having even worse difficulties. Like everyone else in the industry Martin tried to plan its postwar future. An engineering report in 1944 suggested exploration of products other than aircraft, such as airplane parts or plastics that had been developed during the war, and Martin did in fact build a factory in Painesville, Ohio, to make a plastic resin, polyvinil chloride, used in flexible fuel tanks.[48] The eventual choice, however, was to rely on a twin-engined, medium-range transport, the 2-0-2 (later revised with a pressurized cabin as the 3-0-3) plus such military aircraft business as was available.

This decision was based on an elaborate survey made early in 1946, which forecast a large market for twin-engined planes on the ground that the average journey for an air traveler was about 400 miles. It was calculated that twin-engined planes had direct operating costs of 40–45 cents per mile against 70–85 cents for four-engined planes. The survey estimated that 360–400 of the 2-0-2 and 3-0-3 types would have to be produced to break even but claimed orders in hand for 200 and predicted a sale of 500.[49] Both types were to have Pratt and Whitney R-2800 engines, and the report pointed out that 3,000 of these were available as war surplus.

This was a reasonable enough appraisal under the circumstances, but the 2-0-2/3-0-3 series ran into greater trouble than its rival Convair-Liner. In order to get ahead of the competition the 2-0-2 was put into production without a prototype, with the result that expensive flaws appeared after it went into service. The worst blow occurred when a Northwest Airlines 2-0-2 crashed on August 29, 1948, and the Martin Company was held liable for the fatigue failure in the wing that caused the accident.[50] Only 31 2-0-2's were built. They gave good service when modified, but this figure was far short of expectations. Moreover, with its transports Martin ran into precisely the same difficulty as Convair; development costs persistently exceeded estimates, and competition, chiefly from Convair, kept prices down.

The Martin situation at the end of 1947—before the Northwest Airlines crash—was spelled out in an application for an RFC loan.[51] When the program was begun, airline inquiries indicated a sale of 152 2-0-2's and 159 3-0-3's for a potential $83 million. By March 31, 1947, Martin had invested $25.5 million in the 2-0-2 plus $8.5 million for materials. Production of the 3-0-3 was abandoned in December 1947 for a loss of $36 million. The company had a short-term loan from the Guaranty Trust Company for $3 million and was asking the RFC for $25 million. There was further RFC borrowing, because in 1949 Glenn Martin reported RFC loans of $28 and $16 million.[52]

The losses and disappointments in Martin's commercial-plane venture were not, or at any rate should not have been, any worse than those Convair and Lockheed were suffering, but Martin had no compensating military business like the F-80 or the B-36. The company was still making naval flying boats, but the last PBM Mariner was delivered in 1949 and the P5M-1 Marlin was still in the design stage. A six-engined jet bomber, XB-48, was unsuccessful in competition with Boeing's B-47. By 1949 Glenn Martin himself was desperately pleading for Air Force orders to stave off impending receivership, even proposing that his company be allowed to manufacture the B-47.[53] As it worked out, the company survived this crisis without going through receivership again, but at the cost of a complete overhauling of its management. A management survey firm examined the company in 1948 and its report pointed to a need for reorganization that led to the retirement of Glenn Martin himself a year later.[54] He had been a great pioneer in American aviation, but he could not delegate authority effectively, and his company became too big for his methods. He died in 1955.

Under the new management, headed by C. C. Pearson, conditions slowly improved. The outbreak of the Korean War helped, but there were other factors as well. Financial assistance was provided by another RFC loan of $13 million and credits from the Mellon National Bank and Trust Company of Pittsburgh beginning with $5 million and rising to a total of $32.5 million.[55] In 1950 the Marlin flying boat and a revised transport, the 4-0-4, were in production, with an initial Navy contract for 95 Marlins and orders for 76 4-0-4's from Eastern Airlines and TWA. In addition, Martin negotiated with English Electric to build the Canberra Intruder bomber, which was adopted by the Air Force as the B-57, and got started in missiles with the Navy's Viking and the Air Force's Matador.[56] In March 1951 the company's backlog was $400 million.

The Martin picture, however, remained clouded. The 4-0-4, like its predecessors, was a satisfactory airplane except in the matter of earning profits for its builder. Rising costs of labor and materials could not be offset by volume sales. In seeking additional orders Martin quoted a price of $535,000 a plane, $40,000 less than the company's original estimate of the selling price, only to find that Convair was quoting $495,000. At the end of 1951 Martin showed an operating loss of $22 million, attributable predominantly to fixed-price contracts for transports negotiated before the Korean War.[57] There was another change of management in 1952. George M. Bunker, a graduate of M.I.T. in mechanical engineering and former president of the Trailmobile Corporation, became president and chief executive officer.[58] The unprofitable transport venture was discontinued after 103 4-0-4's had been built, military business increased, and in the last half of 1952 the company was able to show a profit. Early in 1953 the RFC loans were paid off, and a year later the company was completely free of debt. But it was essentially a different company. Except for the Marlin and the B-57, whose production continued through the 1950's, the Glenn L. Martin Company was out of the airframe industry. Instead, it became a diversified operation in missiles, electronics, and nuclear reactors.

Elsewhere in the airframe industry experiences with reconversion were equally varied. Some firms disappeared, mostly "war babies" but also a few prewar producers like Brewster Aeronautical, whose wartime record had been marred by poor management, bad labor relations, and finally a takeover by the government.[59] The Naval Aircraft Factory in Philadelphia was closed also. The others adapted themselves in one way or another. Bell Aircraft saw its employment drop from 90,000 to 1,400 but successfully recovered by diversifying into helicopters, missiles, rocket engines, and experimental aircraft, plus a "prime mover" wheelbarrow that permitted loads of 1,000 pounds to be carried.[60] The Bell-built X-1 was the first plane in the world to break the so-called "sound barrier"; it did so on October 14, 1947, at Muroc, California, piloted by Major Charles Yeager, USAF. Grumman developed a profitable sideline of aluminum canoes and fiber glass boats, and gradually recovered its market for military aircraft, plus a few nonmilitary utility types.[61] It also built up a substantial volume of subcontracts. Neighboring Republic tried to market a four-engined transport, the Rainbow, redesigned from a bomber, but soon gave it up and concentrated on a very successful series of high-speed fighters, beginning with the prototype YF-84 in 1946 and continuing through several F-84 models, swept-wing and jet-powered, to the F-105, which first flew in October 1955 and was credited with Mach 2 speed.[62] Northrop Aircraft, Inc., was well established as a designer and builder of experimental aircraft; it also produced the first of the F-89 Scorpion jet interceptors in 1946 and received an initial order for 48, at a contract price for the airframes of over $52 million.[63] Ryan Aeronautical, as we have seen, took over the Navion executive plane from North American, but production of this model was terminated in 1950 and Ryan devoted itself to military production.[64] Although the governing factor in this decision was undoubtedly the Korean War, it still suggests that the light-plane market was disappointing, because Ryan did not return to it. During the late 1940's the company was making the FR-1 Fireball for the Navy, a fighter with a piston engine in front and a jet in the rear, followed by the F2R-1, which used a turboprop in place of its predecessors' piston engine.[65] This was very much an interim design. Ryan soon afterward turned to diversified aerospace activities, and remained in airframes chiefly as a subcontractor.

Two important newcomers got themselves established at this time. One, McDonnell, was not, strictly speaking, a postwar arrival, but the company lived through the Second World War by subcontracting rather than as a full-fledged aircraft manufacturer. Its carrier-based jet fighter, the Phantom, was designed during the war but did not go into production until afterward. The Phantom series was continued into the 1960's, and McDonnell also designed and built for the Air Force the F-101 two-place interceptor.[66] The other company was the Texas Engineering and Manufacturing Company (Temco), founded in 1945 by Robert McCulloch and H. L. Howard, who had been officials in North American's Dallas plant and saw an opportunity to use the building when North American gave it up at the end of the war.[67] They leased part of the plant from the RFC and went into business with about $250,000 of local capital. They became subcontractors for Fairchild and made their way, after some anxious moments, into manufacturing private planes, including Fairchild F-24's.

Fairchild itself was comfortably situated not only as a manufacturer of light utility planes but more important as the builder of the C-82 Packet, a twin-engined military cargo carrier with clam-shell doors at the rear of the fuselage for end-loading of bulky items.[68] Production of the C-82, dubbed the Flying Boxcar, began in January 1945 and continued, without reduction or cancellation of orders, through 1948 to a total of 222 planes. It was then replaced by the larger C-119.[69] While this was going on there was a contest for control between Sherman Fairchild and J. Carlton Ward, who had succeeded Fairchild in the presidency. Fairchild won the proxy fight and his candidate, Richard S. Boutelle, replaced Ward in 1949.[70]

Temco required only part of the war-built Dallas factory. In 1948 it was announced that the rest would be occupied by Chance Vought. This was a unique step. The Department of Defense still wanted the aircraft industry dispersed and moved as much as possible away from the coastal areas, but the manufacturers preferred to stay at their established locations. The Navy was able to persuade Vought to move because its Connecticut facilities had become uneconomical to operate, and Texas offered better flying conditions for testing high-speed planes. The move, completed on July 1, 1949, involved 1,300 key employees and their families, and 1,006 freight cars carrying 27 million pounds of machinery and equipment.[71] While the move was in progress, Vought continued to make carrier-borne fighters, including the twin-jet F7U Cutlass, tested in 1948 and put into production in 1950. Subsequently (1954) Chance Vought was separated from United Aircraft, because United, as a supplier of engines and components to aircraft industry, concluded, as General Motors had done, that having an airframe manufacturer in the organization was a liability.[72] Later Vought and its Dallas neighbors became part of a diversified corporation, Ling-Temco-Vought, Inc. (1961).

A conspectus of the aircraft industry in 1947, the middle of the period of peacetime reconversion, appears in Tables 10 and 11. Its interesting feature is that one new entrant (McDonnell) and one manufacturer of light planes (Beech) appear among the sixteen leaders. The plethora of personal plane manufacturers represents the chronic expectation of a mass market in private flying. When the war ended, the accumulated demand and sanguine hopes resulted in a production of 35,000 nonmilitary planes (including transports) in 1946.[73] Three years later the figure was 3,545. The output of private planes rose steadily thereafter, but it did not reach five figures again during the whole decade of the 1950's.

The inclusion of Curtiss-Wright and Pratt and Whitney in the table gives only a partial picture of what was happening in this part of the industry. The effect of the wartime arrangements for developing the jet engine was to give General Electric and to a lesser degree Westinghouse and the Allison Division of General Motors an advantageous position in the aircraft engine field after the war, when it was evident that the piston engine was on the way out. The regular engine firms had some continuing business in piston engines for commercial transports and military planes like the B-36, but they were faced with the urgent necessity of switching to gas-turbine engines if they were to survive. Pratt and Whitney was materially aided by the research it had done during the war in defiance of governmental fiat, and when in 1946 it was awarded a Navy contract to build an American version of the Rolls-Royce Nene, for installation in the Grum-

Table 10. U.S. Aircraft Industry *

Company	Location	Plant Area (sq. ft.)	Plant Employment	1947 Sales	1947 Profit or Loss	Backlog (10/30/47)
Beech Aircraft Corporation	Wichita, Kans.	966,447	2,500	$26,211,000 [1]	-$1,816,000	$20,000,000
Bell Aircraft Corporation	Niagara Falls, N.Y.	1,200,000	2,000	10,645,000 [1]	-381,000 [1]	13,092,313
Boeing Airplane Company	Seattle, Wash.	1,700,000	17,000	14,345,000 [1]	-357,000 [1]	227,659,436 [8]
	Wichita, Kans.	306,207	1,700			
Consolidated Vultee Aircraft Corporation	San Diego, Calif.	2,370,373	10,785	31,465,000 [2]	6,265,000 [2]	211,632,429
	Fort Worth, Tex.	4,106,108	11,529			
	Wayne, Mich.	231,100	933			
Curtiss-Wright Corporation	Columbus, Ohio	1,408,693	3,000	58,828,000 [1]	-465,000	130,000,000 [8]
	Caldwell, N.J.	750,000	3,900			
	Wood-Ridge, N.J.	2,289,784	6,025			
Douglas Aircraft Company	Santa Monica, Calif.	6,005,645	13,300	92,563,000 [2]	-1,170,000 [2]	182,600,000
	El Segundo, Calif.	113,055				
	Long Beach, Calif.	347,275				
Fairchild Engine and Airplane Corporation	Farmingdale, N.Y.	204,750	1,175	NA	NA	27,700,000
	Hagerstown, Md.	882,450	3,550			
	Winfield, Kans.	91,175	76			
Grumman Aircraft Engine Corporation	Bethpage, N.Y.	—	3,500	NA	1,238,000 [8]	NA
Lockheed Aircraft Corporation	Burbank, Calif.	1,520,000	12,684	133,000,000	NA	126,000,000 [8]
The Glenn L. Martin Company	Middle River, Md.	2,800,000	10,500	NA	-15,500,000 [4]	122,000,000
McDonnell Aircraft Corporation	St. Louis, Mo.	1,343,793	3,465	11,172,000 [5]	541,000 [6]	NA
North American Aviation, Inc.	Los Angeles, Calif.	3,787,288	18,522	20,509,000 [6]	-28,000 [4]	269,148,114 [3]
Northrop Aircraft, Inc.	Hawthorne, Calif.	1,148,000	4,900	28,819,000 [7]	241,000 [1]	19,900,000
Republic Aviation Corporation	Farmingdale, N.Y.	650,000	5,800	20,181,000 [1]	-944,000 [1]	60,266,578
Ryan Aeronautical Company	San Diego, Calif.	640,197	1,200	NA	NA	3,000,000
United Aircraft and Transport Corporation	East Hartford, Conn. (Pratt & Whitney)	3 000,000	14,000	144,084,000 [1]	6,088,000 [1]	280,000,000
	East Hartford, Conn. (Pratt & Whitney)	300,000	2,100			
	Bridgeport, Conn.	180,000	1,200			
	Stratford, Conn.	900,000	8,000			
Totals		39,242,340	163,344			

Source: Aviation Week, 48, No. 8, p. 21.
* Sixteen Leading companies listed by President's Air Policy Commission.
NA—Not available.
[1] Nine months to Sept. 30, 1947.
[2] Nine months to Aug. 31, 1947.
[3] Six months to June 30, 1947.
[4] Predicated on winning tax suit.
[5] Year ended June 30, 1947.
[6] Year ended Sept. 30, 1947.
[7] Year ended July 31, 1947.
[8] As of Dec. 31, 1947.

Table 11. Shipments of Leading Personal-Plane Manufacturers, 1947

	Numbers Jan.–Dec.	Value (All Models) Jan.–Dec.
Aeronca		
Super Chief 85 h.p.	333	$ 2,329,000
Champion 65 h.p.	487	
Chief 65 h.p.	295	
Scout	89	
Champion 85 h.p.	14	
All American-10A	1 *	3,000 *
Beech-Bonanza	1,209	7,945,000 †
Bellanca-Cruisair	214	1,070,000
Cessna		
120	1,009	5,976,000
140	1,312	
190	8	
195	61	
Engineering & Research		
Ercoupe	805	2,084,000
Fairchild-F-24	16	71,000
Funk-Bee	41	155,000
Luscombe-Silvaire	1,401	3,413,000
North American Aviation-Navion	853	5,021,000
Piper		
Cub Special	950	7,697,000
Supercruiser	2,158	
Cub Trainer	356	
Republic-Seabee	818	3,902,000
Ryan-Navion	18	125,000
Stinson-Voyager	2,662	11,525,000
Taylorcraft		
Taylorcraft	196	366,000
Texas Engineering		
Fairchild F-24	66	787,000
Swift	143	
Total Personal	15,515	$52,469,000
Aeronca-L-16	508	737,000 ‡
Total	16,023	$53,206,000

Source: *Aviation Week, 48*, No. 8, p. 25.
* Incomplete figures for the year.
† Excludes January, February, and March.
‡ Payments from military customers.

man F9F fighter, its future could be considered reasonably secure.[74] This engine, the J-42, became operational in 1948 and was followed two years later by the J-48 (Rolls-Royce Tay), with 6,250 pounds of thrust.

Curtiss-Wright was somewhat slower to move and had managerial difficulties also. The reconversion period found the company overextended. Where Pratt and Whitney abandoned its Kansas City operation as soon as the war ended, Curtiss-Wright was still using the Columbus, Ohio, plant two years later. There was enough dissatisfaction so that Guy Vaughan retired in 1949 from what he called a "troublesome business," and in 1950 policy changes at Curtiss-Wright were announced, including emphasis on "manufacturing engineering" rather than "academic design," improved planning and scheduling, and product diversification.[75] The changes evidently achieved their purpose. In the process Curtiss-Wright moved its headquarters to the plant in Wood Ridge, New Jersey, that it had operated for the government during the war.

Finally some reference should be made to the completion of what was then and remained for some years thereafter the largest airplane in the world. This was an eight-engined flying boat built in the Aircraft Division of the Hughes Tool Company in Los Angeles. It began in 1942 as a joint project of Henry J. Kaiser and Howard Hughes for large cargo planes to circumvent U-boats, but the first and only model was not ready to fly until November 1947.[76] It provided some useful design information, at a cost to Hughes of $17 million and the RFC of $18 million, but as built it was not suitable for any practical use.

Reformulation of Air Policy

The condition of the aircraft industry at any given time is, as its members well know, a function of the government's policy toward aviation. At the end of the Second World War there was a clear need for a policy reappraisal, not only because of the confused condition of the aircraft industry but still more because of the introduction of the atomic bomb and the development of aircraft of greater size, longer range, and higher speeds and altitudes. In response to this need President Truman on July 18, 1947, appointed an Air Policy Commission composed of Thomas K. Finletter, a prominent attorney who had been connected with the State Department, as chairman, and four other members: Professor George P. Baker, internationally known authority on transportation; Palmer Hoyt, publisher of the *Denver Post;* John A. McCone, engineer and executive of construction companies and steamship lines; and Arthur D. Whiteside, president of Dun and Bradstreet. The commission submitted its report, *Survival in the Air Age,* at the end of December 1947.

The Finletter Commission stated emphatically that the defense of the United States must be based on air power and for this purpose recommended an Air Force of 70 groups and 22 special squadrons, with a total of 12,400 modern planes, compared with the existing establishment of 55 groups with 10,800 active planes.[77] An expansion of naval aviation was also considered, but the commission confined itself to urging a program for the replacement of obsolescent planes, pending a review of overall strategy by the Joint Chiefs of Staff.

To maintain an adequate air strength it was essential to maintain a healthy aircraft industry, capable of expansion in an emergency. The Finletter Commission, noting in passing that expectations of a postwar market for nonmilitary aircraft sufficient to tide the industry over the readjustment period had not materialized, then analyzed succinctly the special problems of the aircraft industry. These were as follows:

1. A product that was both a weapon and a carrier of commerce.
2. A market with one major customer, the government, which normally took 80 to 90 per cent of the total output.
3. Violently fluctuating demand, due to the uncertainty of the government's requirements.
4. Lack of the production continuity needed to keep a trained work force together and hold down costs.

5. A rapidly changing technology, resulting in a high rate of design obsolescence and abnormally high engineering costs.
6. An extremely long design-manufacturing cycle.
7. Organization in excess of present requirements.[78]

This was certainly an accurate summation not only of the situation in 1947 but of the conditions under which the aircraft industry normally functioned. In addition, the report stated

In a freely competitive economy the number of companies manufacturing a particular product levels off at a point determined by the ordinary laws of economics. In the case of the aircraft industry, however, it would be dangerous to rely on the operation of these laws. The demand factor fluctuates too violently from peace to war. If a reasonable degree of expansibility is to be maintained for periods of emergency, it is necessary to exercise some industry-wide control in the interests of national security. It may even be desirable to keep a few marginal manufacturers in business who might be forced out if the normal laws of supply and demand were allowed to operate.[79]

The commission believed that a military program calling for the procurement of 30 to 40 million pounds of airframe weight annually would, in conjunction with nonmilitary demand, meet the needs of the aircraft industry.

The work of the Finletter Commission invites comparison with that of the Morrow Board of 22 years before. There were quite fundamental differences between the two. The members of the Finletter Commission were, like their predecessors, able and public-spirited individuals; unlike the Morrow Board, however, there was no representation from the aeronautical engineers, the military services, or the Congress. Moreover, since the most publicized of the Finletter Commission's recommendations was the 70-group Air Force, it was somewhat unfortunate that the chairman should have become Secretary of the Air Force in the following year. The suspicion of special pleading was unwarranted, but it was bound to arise.

A more vital difference was the atmosphere in which the two reports were formulated. The Morrow Board's proposals were made at a time of international calm and could be considered at some leisure; the Finletter Commission had to work in the heightening tensions of the Cold War. Consequently, *Fortune* magazine erred when it equated the Finletter and Morrow Reports and termed the former "a modern substitute for the charter American aviation lost." [80] The recommendations of the Finletter Commission were never implemented along the lines of *Survival in the Air Age*. Shortly after they appeared the Berlin blockade produced a crisis, helpful in that it dramatized air power but not conducive to orderly programming.

The Finletter program had the greater misfortune of becoming entangled in internal disputes. Congress voted the funds to begin the implementation of the commission's recommendations in fiscal 1949, but in the fall of 1948 the Truman administration cut the budgets for the armed forces drastically. The Air Force had to cancel about $300 million in contracts, but orders for the B-36 were increased. [81] At the same time Secretary of Defense Louis A. Johnson stopped the construction of a large new aircraft carrier, the "United States," which the Navy had planned for operating planes capable of carrying atomic bombs. The consequence was the so-called "revolt of the admirals."

This incident began with charges by Congressman Charles A. Van Zandt, a former Navy man and onetime president of the Veterans of Foreign Wars, claiming collusion in the award of the B-36 contract on the ground that Johnson had been a director of the Atlas Corporation, and also alleging that the plane itself would be an easy target for jet fighters and could not carry out its assigned mission. [82] Van Zandt's information came from Cedric Worth, assistant to Undersecretary of the Navy Dan A. Kimball. A somewhat unedifying argument then dragged on for several months before the public and the House Armed Services Committee. Admiral Arthur W. Radford called the B-36 a "billion-dollar blunder"; Secretary of the Air Force Stuart A. Symington and a host of Air Force generals understandably came to its defense. In the end, Worth's charges were withdrawn and both Johnson and Convair were cleared of any suspicion of impropriety. The B-36 received a half-hearted endorsement as the only intercontinental bomber then available to carry atomic weapons on strategic missions.

It is regrettable that the argument over the technical qualities of the B-36 served to obscure the underlying and unresolved issue. The B-36 was merely a symbol; what was at stake and should have been discussed more lucidly was a fundamental question of American military policy. The Navy was not really condemning a specific airplane. It was protesting what it considered an excessive commitment of the nation's military resources to a strategic concept which assumed that "all modern war is total war" and relied on long-range aerial bombardment with nuclear weapons, at the expense not only of surface forces but of the tactical employment of air power.[83] The case was weakened because the "United States" was manifestly intended to give the Navy a share in strategic bombing, so that the basic policy problem was never clearly presented or resolved.

Concurrent with this dispute there was a less publicized but equally hard fought controversy over the location of aircraft and engine plants. The return of aircraft production in general to its prewar locations, in spite of pressure from the Defense Department, had been noted. The Finletter Commission expressed regret that the wartime dispersal had not been maintained and recommended that future expansion take this situation into account.[84] The only action taken by the government, however, was to provide for maintaining a number of the government-owned war-built plants on a stand-by basis.[85] In 1949 six airframe companies on the Pacific Coast (Boeing, Convair, Douglas, Lockheed, North American, and Northrop) had 69 per cent of the dollar total of military orders.[86] The proportion of actual airframe production on the West Coast was somewhat less than this percentage figure because Convair was building one of its largest dollar items, the B-36, at Fort Worth, and some Boeing work was done in Wichita. The second largest concentration of airframe manufacturers, plus the bulk of the engine production, was on the eastern seaboard.

A campaign for greater dispersal of the aircraft industry was energetically conducted by the Mid-Continent Industrial Council, composed of business and political leaders in Texas, Oklahoma, Kansas, Nebraska, South Dakota, Iowa, Missouri, and Arkansas. It was opposed by the All-America Defense Association, representing the Pacific Coast, the Rocky Mountain states, the Great

Lakes area, New England, and New York.[87] This agitation had very little effect. The Mid-Continent Industrial Council claimed credit for Chance Vought's move to Dallas and for Boeing's switching some production to Wichita. There were other factors in the Vought move, and even if the Council's claim is accepted at face value, the move was well short of a major relocation of the aircraft industry. Aircraft manufacturers, like any others, were reluctant to abandon existing plant facilities and uproot their trained staffs unless there was compelling reason to do so. There was some shifting in that Texas emerged as an important center of airframe assembly. Beyond that, the whole argument disappeared when the Korean War came along.

The Korean War

The process of adjusting to peacetime production ended abruptly for the aircraft industry when the Korean War broke out in June 1950. At that time the larger firms were in reasonably sound condition although a continuation of the sharp cutback in military expenditures would have hurt them. The smaller ones were contending with the shrinkage of the market for private planes. Beech was surviving largely by manufacturing spare parts and rebuilding and overhauling Beechcraft for the Navy, and Cessna was making furniture and hydraulic cylinders for farm machinery[88]—and these were the two leaders in the light-plane field.

The unexpected outbreak of war changed the situation rapidly. For example, by July 10, 1950, Cessna had a $5 million Army contract for 400 liaison planes, and Lockheed's backlog doubled in six weeks, from $200 to $400 million.[89] There was not, however, an exact duplication of the experience of the Second World War. The Korean conflict was on a smaller scale and did not require the same full mobilization of industry. The production of military aircraft in 1952, the last full year of the Korean War, was just over 7,000 compared with the 96,000 of 1944.[90]

The figures themselves tell an incomplete story, because there was a qualitative factor also. As J. H. Kindelberger pointed out, building a plane in 1950 was about four times as complicated as building one in 1940.[91] To put it in other terms, the 6,000 military planes produced in 1940 represented an airframe weight of 23.1 million pounds for an average of 3,850 pounds per plane, whereas the 5,500 military planes of 1951, just eleven years later, totaled 50.2 million pounds, or about 9,000 pounds per plane. Thus the aircraft program for the Korean War could not, even if it had been larger, have employed the same quantitative methods as were employed in the Second World War. This was a contributory factor to the reluctance of the manufacturers to expand again into the government-owned plants. It was just not feasible to make 1950 planes with managerial and technical talent spread thin and with makeshift labor, especially on the limited scale being called for.

Consequently such expansion of facilities as was needed was financed primarily by the industry, which invested $805 million in plant between 1950 and 1953 compared with $280 million by the government.[92] Equipment was more of a problem than plant, because the tooling for aircraft construction was becoming increasingly elaborate and expensive. Here the relationship was reversed; the government put up $2 billion for equipment compared with $400 million from the industry. A survey of aircraft manufacturers at the midpoint of the Korean War showed that the principal companies were operating on an average working capital of $20–$25 million. Bell had a $25 million loan from ten commercial banks, Boeing had arranged credits of $30 million and Convair of $20 million, Douglas was backed by a consortium of five banks, Martin had $18 million from the RFC, and Republic could borrow up to $5 million at Chase National.[93] The value of aircraft production increased from almost $2 billion in 1949 to $8.5 billion in 1953, and employment from 281,800 to 779,100.[94]

Lockheed's experience in the Korean War deserves some special attention, because it was the one large airframe manufacturer to reopen and remain in one of the government-built stand-by plants, whereas in the Second World War it had been distinctive in keeping its production facilities closely concentrated. In 1949 Lockheed had reached a satisfactory position.

The Constellation was at last showing a profit, with earnings of $5.5 million on sales of $117.7 million.[95] Military sales were even more encouraging. Besides the F-80, Lockheed had produced a jet trainer, the T-33, which was later modified to become the two-place F-94 when the Air Force decided it needed a fast-climbing interceptor. Lockheed was able to pay off its bank loans in 1949 and early in the next year to launch a program for modernizing its plant and equipment at a cost of $6.5 million. Just before the war started Robert E. Gross and Hall Hibbard, vice-president of engineering, calculated that the company would have one more round of military planes and then go into missiles.[96]

The one more round became several. In addition, because of the urgent need for planes in Korea, the Air Force asked Lockheed to reactivate the factory in Marietta, Georgia, where Bell had made B-29's during the Second World War. Lockheed's first assignment there, in fact, was to recondition 120 B-29's for service in Korea.[97] Then it once again combined with Boeing and Douglas, this time to make B-47's. After the war Lockheed retained the Marietta plant as its Georgia Division. This step was taken because the company's facilities at Burbank and Van Nuys were overcrowded; for the same reason Lockheed Aircraft Service moved to Ontario, California, in 1952.

The automobile industry was not drawn into airframe manufacturing during the Korean War except for subcontracting of parts and components, and this was on a lesser scale than in the Second World War. The smaller volume of production made it less necessary to use automotive facilities for airframe subassemblies. On the other hand, with practically all military planes multi-engined, the automobile companies could and did provide needed help in this field. Their participation in manufacturing aircraft engines was as follows: [98]

Ford	Westinghouse J-40 and Pratt and Whitney R-4360
Buick	Curtiss-Wright J-65
Chevrolet	Allison J-85
Chrysler	Pratt and Whitney J-48
Packard	General Electric J-48

Studebaker	General Electric J-48
Hudson	Wright R-3350
Kaiser-Frazer	Wright R-1300

Finally, the Korean War provided a convincing demonstration of the need to keep pace with the accelerating advance of aeronautics. Two relatively new technologies, the helicopter and the jet plane, played very important roles, and neither could have been provided on short notice. The war in the air was fought with the weapons in hand when it began. No new designs could be made operational before the war ended. Jet fighters, for instance, were in existence in time to be used in combat; jet bombers were still under development and took no part in the war. The lesson was well known to those who were involved in aviation; it remained to be seen if it had also been learned by others.

10. Aeronautics to Aerospace

The mid-1950's were a landmark period for the American aircraft industry. Not only were helicopters and jet planes brought into practical operation, but the development of missiles absorbed an increasing proportion of the technical skills and productive capacity of the industry, and the second half of the decade witnessed the start of the penetration of space. The missile and space programs were responsible for transforming the aircraft into the aerospace industry, to the extent that by the late 1950's airplanes had ceased to be its principal product.[1]

It does not follow that aircraft manufacturing became unimportant. An examination of Table 12 will show that whatever change occurred was relative rather than absolute. The high point of the decade was 1953, when the expansion of output for the Korean War became effective. Then, contrary to what happened previously, there was a gradual rather than an abrupt decline in the production of military planes, and this was almost exactly offset by increases in the output of civil aircraft. Airframe weight also went down gradually. The significant feature is the increase in the average weight of nonmilitary planes; 8,000 civil aircraft in 1960 weighed almost three times as much as 7,000 in 1948 or 4,000 in 1953. The decrease in the number of military planes produced in 1959 and 1960 reflected a belief that

Table 12. Aircraft Production, 1946–1960

Year	Number of Aircraft			Airframe Weight (millions of pounds)		
	Military	Civil	Total	Military	Civil	Total
1946	1,417	35,001	36,418	12.9	25.5	38.4
1947	2,122	15,617	17,739	11.4	17.9	29.3
1948	2,536	7,302	9,838	25.1	10.1	35.2
1949	2,592	3,545	6,137	30.3	6.7	37.0
1950	2,680	3,520	6,200	35.9	6.0	41.9
1951	5,055	2,477	7,532	50.2	5.0	55.2
1952	7,131	3,509	10,640	107.3	9.3	116.6
1953	8,978	4,134	13,112	138.0	10.4	148.4
1954	8,089	3,389	11,478	130.4	10.5	140.9
1955	6,664	4,820	11,484	114.3	10.2	124.5
1956	5,203	7,205	12,408	90.0	16.2	106.2
1957	5,198	6,745	11,493	79.4	21.8	101.2
1958	4,078	6,860	10,938	66.1	16.7	82.8
1959	2,834	8,242	11,076	51.8	23.1	74.9
1960	2,056	8,181	10,237	35.8	28.2	64.0

Source: *Aerospace Facts and Figures, 1964*, pp. 25–26.

strategic bombardment was more and more the function of the missile than of the manned bomber.

Helicopters

The advance of the helicopter beyond the experimental stage reached during the 1930's began effectively after the Second World War. The Sikorsky helicopters built during the war did not come into service until 1944, so that they provided little more than a sample of the kind of useful work they could do. But the sample indicated such a promising future for the helicopter that when the war ended Sikorsky found himself with active competition.

The next firm to become a substantial producer was Bell Aircraft, which began design work in 1941 but because of the pressures imposed by the war was unable to manufacture until 1946. Bell spent $10 million on helicopter development before it made a single sale.[2] Progress was rapid after that. In 1951 Bell's helicopter business had grown enough so that the company found it necessary to establish a separate plant in Fort Worth.

Bell and Sikorsky were the principal helicopter manufacturers i the 1950's, but there were others with an important share. The history of helicopter manufacturing, indeed, is similar to the history of aircraft manufacturing in general: a story of men with ideas beginning on a small scale and gradually getting a foothold. The technical complexity of the helicopter lent itself to this process. To cite two obvious problems, the speed of the rotor blades in relation to the motion of the vehicle varies according to whether the blade is in the forward or rearward phase of its spin, and the revolving rotor has a torque effect that tends to make the fuselage spin in the opposite direction unless it is offset. There are several methods of keeping the helicopter stable, each with its advantages and drawbacks, so that there has been ample room for new ideas and experimentation.

After Sikorsky and Bell the next important producer was Frank Piasecki, an engineer who had worked for a small firm in Philadelphia, the Kellett Autogiro Company, in the 1930's.[3] Like Bell, Piasecki experimented with helicopters during the war, and then in 1946 founded the Piasecki Aircraft Corporation to develop his ideas on tandem-rotor design (Sikorsky and Bell both used a single main rotor with a small tail rotor to offset torque). This company became the Vertol Aircraft Corporation of Morton, Pennsylvania, in 1956 and in 1960 was absorbed by Boeing as the Vertol Division.[4] The Kellett firm became the Kellett Aircraft Corporation in 1943 and switched from autogiros to helicopters. Piasecki worked during the war with two other engineers, Havilland H. Platt and W. Laurence Le Page, whose associations traced back to the Pitcairn Autogiro Company of the early 1930's.[5] The Platt–Le Page designs were taken over by McDonnell Aircraft, which made its entry into the field with the Whirlaway in 1945, the world's first twin engined helicopter.[6] McDonnell also worked on a ram-jet helicopter, a design with the jets at the tips of the rotor blades. This arrangement has the advantage of eliminating vibration and fuselage torque. An experimental model was tested in 1951.

Two other helicopter designs produced important commercial development. Stanley Hiller, a California engineer, joined with Henry J. Kaiser during the war to design a coaxial helicopter, with contrarotating blades. This arrangement counters fuselage torque effectively, but there is risk of shaft vibration and loss of lift.[7] At the end of the war Kaiser withdrew, whereupon Hiller founded his own company, the Hiller Aircraft Company, in Menlo Park, California, in 1945. The company remained independent until 1960, when it became a division of Electric Autolite; in 1964 it was bought by Fairchild for $12 million, and the two merged as the Fairchild Hiller Corporation.[8]

Another approach to helicopter design was made by Charles H. Kaman, an engineer of Hartford, Connecticut. He began in 1945 with a capital of $2,000 to develop a design using intermeshing rotors, or synchropters, and "servo flaps," which were aileron-type devices on the rotor foils to provide more sensitive control.[9] Kaman got a contract for $15,000 from the Navy Bureau of Aeronautics for an experimental rotor and in 1946 secured further financial backing from a group of investors in Boston called New Enterprises. The Kaman Aircraft Corporation was established in Bloomfield, Connecticut, and its first production helicopters went into operation in 1949. Eleven were built and were used chiefly for crop-dusting.[10] Contracts from the Navy followed, with the result that Kaman grew to be principally a manufacturer for the military services. Kaman Aircraft built the world's first helicopter with a gas turbine engine in 1951.

One other independent producer, Glidden Doman, began in 1945 to design helicopters intended for passenger travel.[11] Doman Helicopters was located in Danbury, Connecticut. In addition, several aircraft companies entered the helicopter field in the 1950's: Cessna, Chance Vought, Grumman, Hughes, Lockheed, and Republic. Much of their work extended beyond the helicopter to VTOL or STOL aircraft generally,[12] that is, to designs incorporating the advantages of both the helicopter and the standard airplane. These were still in development when the decade ended. (Table 13.)

This branch of the aircraft industry was attractive because the demand for helicopters was rising. Military sales rose from 44 in 1946 to 983 in 1952 at the height of the Korean War.[13] They then tapered off but the decrease was offset by an enlarged nonmilitary demand. Besides rescue operations, helicopters found a

Table 13. Helicopter Production, 1953–1960

Year	Military	Commer- cial	Total
1953	943	111	1054
1954	431	131	562
1955	444	146	590
1956	647	268	915
1957	689	311	1000
1958	668	196	864
1959	451	291	742
1960	494	294	788

Source: Aerospace Industries Association.
This table covers the eight years after the Korean War. The high figure for 1953 is accounted for by the completion of military orders placed during the war. The time span is too short to show a clear trend, and both military and civilian demand fluctuate irregularly. Nevertheless, there is evidence of a substantial market for helicopters.

number of military uses. During the Korean War some 25,000 wounded were evacuated from combat areas by helicopter, and troops and supplies were moved in by the same method to places that would otherwise have been inaccessible. In the civil sphere, Los Angeles Airways began to carry mail by helicopter between the Los Angeles Airport and outlying communities in 1947, and started to carry passengers seven years later.[14] During the same period helicopter interairport service was instituted in New York and Chicago.

The Arrival of the Jet Era

In spite of the use of jet fighters in the Korean War, the jet plane was still a novelty when the decade of the 1950's began. Except for the first models of the B-47, which were just coming off the production line, the United States had no jet-propelled bombers or transports, and it was not yet completely clear whether in the immediate future such types should be powered with jet or turboprop engines. The jet engines of the 1940's were lavish consumers of fuel; they were acceptable for fighters, where speed was more important than range, but they needed refinement to be completely satisfactory for bombers or transports. Furthermore, the design problems of large aircraft intended for high altitudes and near-sonic or trans-sonic speeds required elaborate study and experimentation. The first jet transport, the British De Havilland Comet, was well ahead of its competitors in going into service, because of Britain's lead in jet engine development, but it demonstrated the familiar fact that pioneering has its hazards when structural defects caused disastrous accidents.[15]

In the United States four airframe companies had the necessary combination of technical and financial resources to contemplate the manufacture of large turbine-engined aircraft: Boeing, Convair, Douglas, and Lockheed. North American could have been on this list, except that its emphasis in the 1950's was on jet fighters. The B-70 bomber was very much in the experimental stage. In the pure jet field Boeing secured a commanding position because of its work with the B-47 and B-52. Through them Boeing engineers gained valuable experience—for example, the B-47, which borrowed from German designs, showed the advantages of mounting the engines in pods—and for the military types the cost of research and development was absorbed by the Air Force. The prototype 707 (for development purposes designated 367–80) was begun in 1952 and first flew in 1954.[16] This design went into production in two versions: the KC-135 Stratotanker for the Air Force, and the 707-120, the first American jet transport, put into service in October 1958. It was the third jet transport to go into regular operation, being preceded by both the Comet and the twin-engined Russian Tu-104.[17]

Douglas was a little slower to move, partly because it did not get the same early experience as Boeing with jet bombers. There was some consideration of jet propulsion at Douglas Aircraft as early as 1945 and of a jet transport in 1950, but serious study was first undertaken in 1952.[18] The initial report states

Operational experience and cost data on the use and maintenance of engines of the size required for jet transports of the future are meager or non-existent. These cost figures will play a deciding part in the desire or ability of the airlines to absorb the jet transport into the existing traffic patterns of their individual operations and earn sufficient additional income to pay for the new equipment.[19]

Other major factors requiring study were the costs of development and construction of prototypes and of production airplanes, the number that any one manufacturer could expect to sell over a reasonable period of time, and the cost per unit to the operators.

The airlines were fully aware that the gas turbine was replacing the piston engine and they were watching the situation closely, but in 1952 the superiority of the pure jet for commercial purposes was by no means evident. C. R. Smith, president of American Airlines, predicted at about this time that the piston engine would be replaced by the turboprop rather than the jet and later explained why he had been wrong:

I don't think anybody could have anticipated, at the time I made all the speeches about fuel consumption, that we'd get the problem cured as readily as we did. And we would not have gotten it cured had it not been a military necessity, because the military necessity brought about a tremendous expenditure of funds for that purpose.[20]

When American Airlines decided to introduce jet planes in 1955, with an order for 30 707's, it had to borrow $200 million for the purpose, and it committed itself to a total outlay of twice that amount.[21] This was manifestly not a step to be taken without complete assurance that the jet engine had become suitable for commercial operation. The caution of the Douglas engineers in 1952 was therefore justifiable. Boeing could decide in that year to proceed with the prototype 707, not only because of its experience with jet bombers but because the plane had an alternative market as a military tanker. The boldness of the decision is not in question, but for Boeing the risk was more calculable than it was for Douglas.

Was Douglas too cautious? There is a somewhat defensive quality about a statement made by Donald Douglas, Sr., in 1953 to the effect that his company would not compete with Boeing for the early jet transport market: "There may be some distinction in being the first to build a jet transport. It is our ambition at Douglas to build the best and most successful."[22]

The hesitation was quite understandable. In the first half of the 1950's Douglas Aircraft was in as enviable a position as any airplane manufacturer has ever occupied. It had a solid foundation of military production. For the Navy, the AD series continued to the mid-1950's and was carried on in the A3D and A4D jet-powered Skywarrior and Skyhawk attack bombers; Douglas was also making two Navy fighters, the F3D Skynight, a night interceptor, and the F4D Skyray, a supersonic interceptor.[23] For the Air Force, Douglas built the C-124 transport until 1955 (about 250 altogether) and followed with the C-133, a giant with four Pratt and Whitney T-34 turboprop engines, capable of lifting almost 100 tons into the air.[24]

In the transport field Douglas' position was even stronger. In 1954, out of 164 million passenger-miles flown daily on regularly scheduled air routes all over the world, 81 million were flown in Douglas-built planes.[25] It was therefore only natural that Douglas should have wanted to keep things as they were as long as possible before launching into the expensive and technically uncertain field of jet airliners.

The period of grace ended in 1955. When American Airlines, a Douglas customer of long standing, placed its order for Boeing 707's, it was time for Douglas Aircraft to act. The historian of the DC-8 quotes Donald Douglas as saying in 1958, "Our hand had been forced. We had to go into the building of the DC-8 as a jet transport or else give up building airplanes." [26] So the decision to proceed with the DC-8 was announced in 1955, and such was the Douglas reputation that ten major airlines immediately placed orders, led by United with an order for 30 at a price of $175 million.[27] This much was encouraging, but Douglas nevertheless assumed an enormous risk, summed up by Arthur E. Raymond, who was vice-president of engineering at the time:

It was built without any assistance from the government on tooling costs or buying airplanes for military use. It represented a stupendous task for any private company to finance, and probably it would be about the biggest project ever taken on by any company in the United States. It almost broke the company, but not quite.[28]

The financing was done by using the profits of the DC-6 and -7 series, borrowing, and requiring a 25 per cent advance payment on orders (50 per cent from foreign purchasers). To catch up on Boeing, the DC-8 went into production without a prototype. The first test flight was made in 1958, and the plane went into airline service a year later. It was a magnificent effort by Douglas Aircraft, but not quite good enough to overtake Boeing.

Convair's experience differed from that of its competitors and in some ways repeated the performance of the immediate postwar years: satisfactory results with military planes but not with commercial transports. The delta-wing experiments begun by the Vultee Division in the 1940's blossomed into the F-102 fighter, one of the first aircraft to be developed under the "weapons system" concept. The design had to incorporate an airframe and power plant capable of supersonic speed, and elaborate electronic fire-control equipment for homing missiles and rockets.[29] The fire-control system, which was made by Hughes Aircraft, was ordered first and the plane was designed around it.

Construction began in 1951. The first flight was made two years later, but in the meantime wind-tunnel tests had shown that as designed the F-102 would not pass Mach 0.9. Fortunately the cause of the difficulty and its solution were found by Richard T. Whitcomb at the NACA in 1952. This was the "area rule," which demonstrated that in short-winged planes the rise in drag near the speed of sound was proportional to the distribution of cross-sectional areas measured along the longitudinal axis.[30] The remedy was to indent the fuselage where the wings were largest so as to avoid rapid change in the total cross-sectional area. A redesigned F-102 (it became the F-102A) easily attained supersonic speed in a test flight late in 1954, and full-scale production began in the following year.

The delta-wing design was carried over into Convair's B-58, a four-engined bomber intended to operate at supersonic speeds and altitudes over 54,000 feet. Convair was given the contract in 1951, production began in 1954, the first flight was made in December 1956.[31] According to its builders, the B-58 reached speeds in excess of Mach 2. Among its unusual features was a detachable pod slung underneath the fuselage where extra fuel and other materials could be carried for long-distance flights.[32]

The B-58 went into service in limited quantity, but it was primarily an experimental design. Convair officials hoped that it would provide experience and data for future transport aircraft. If it did, the lessons were not immediately applicable, because

Convair's entries in the transport field, the Astrojet 880 and 990, were designed on the same general lines as the 707 and the DC-8. The 880 first went into service in 1960, a little too late to penetrate a market already pretty well preempted by Boeing and Douglas. There is not much elasticity of demand for airplanes costing over $5 million each. High development costs and insufficient sales resulted in monumental losses and abandonment of the program.

The designing of this first group of jet-powered transports was one of the outstanding achievements of the American aircraft industry, even with allowance for the fact that the Americans were able to learn from the British experience with the Comet. An airplane intended for regular passenger service must be constructed with more rigorous safety factors than would be acceptable in a military plane or a cargo carrier. The great advantage of jet propulsion, once the matter of fuel consumption had been brought under control, was the high speeds made feasible. However, as had happened with the all-metal, cantilevered-wing monoplane in the 1930's, the entire airframe had to be designed for these speeds. In some military planes excellent results were achieved with very thin wings to reduce drag, but this method was undesirable for passenger or cargo carriers because it required the fuel to be stored in the fuselage.[33] The alternative was the swept-back wing, which functions well at high speeds but creates stability problems at low speeds; a great deal of ingenuity had to be expended on working out flaps and tail and rudder configurations that would permit safe landing speeds. Boeing and Convair used a 35-degree sweep-back; Douglas used 30 degrees, which made the DC-8 somewhat slower than its competitors but also somewhat easier to handle at low speeds.

Lockheed, one of the "big four" in the manufacture of transport aircraft, chose to stay out of the jet competition. The company was well established as a builder of jet fighters. After the F-80 came the F-94 Starfire, first produced in 1949 and later modified as the F-94C; it was designed, like Convair's F-102, around the Hughes fire-control system.[34] This was followed by the F-104 Starfighter, started in 1952 and flown in 1956.[35] Lockheed also made the U-2, the very high altitude reconnaissance plane that figured in an international incident at the end of the Eisenhower administration.

For larger aircraft, however, Lockheed opted for designs using turboprop engines. The decision was made after careful study of the prospects, which concluded that Lockheed could undertake either long-range jets or medium-range turboprops, but not both.[36] Because of the British lead in jet transports, R. E. Gross believed the American industry would need help from the government to catch up,[37] and when Boeing secured its advantageous position in jet bombers and tankers, the Lockheed planners decided not to compete. As early as 1950 Lockheed considered redesigning the Constellation as a turboprop plane but eventually concluded that a completely new plane would be preferable to further stretching of a model whose basic design was fifteen years old.[38]

By the time this decision was made, Lockheed's Georgia Division was starting to produce the C-130 Hercules, a four-engined prop-jet military transport, with a capacity for 22 tons of cargo.[39] The C-130 first flew in 1954 and went into service two years later. Initial orders amounted to about $650 million. The design experience with the C-130 helped Lockheed to win an American Airlines competition for a turbine-engined transport to operate on medium and short-haul routes. The Lockheed entry was a new Electra, with four prop-jet engines, a cruising speed of 400 m.p.h., and intended to operate economically on trips between 100 and 2700 miles.[40] The Electra was test-flown late in 1957, by which time the company had $300 million in orders, representing 144 planes. Regular operation began early in 1959, but then Lockheed had to face several disasters that led to severe restrictions on the Electra until it could be modified. The source of the trouble was quite unique. The normal vibration of the engine nacelles happened to coincide in period with the equally normal vibration of the wings in such a way as to create abnormal stresses at high speeds and cause fatigue failure at the junction of the wing with the fuselage. The deficiency was identified and remedied and the Electras remained in operation.

Lockheed did build one jet transport late in the 1950's. This was the JetStar of 1957, a twin-engined transport-trainer for the

Air Force,[41] which had potential for nonmilitary use by business concerns.

By 1960, therefore, the American aircraft industry was leading the world in the design and manufacture of large turbine-engined airplanes—bombers, cargo carriers, and passenger transports—and their products dominated the world's airlines just as the planes of the DC-3 generation had done twenty years before. The earlier achievement, indeed, contributed to the later. In the 1960's the accumulated American experience in building all-metal, cantilevered-wing airliners more than offset the British lead in aircraft gas turbine engines.[42] It was not a question of basic design. The pioneering turboprop Vickers Viscount and the Comet were both well-designed, although the Comet lacked the swept-back wings of its American competitors, and the Comet's troubles were no worse than, for example, those Lockheed had to face with both the Constellation and the Electra. The difference was in multitudinous small details that made the American planes of the period more satisfactory for passenger service. Convair, for instance, in planning the 240-440 series made exhaustive studies and tests on such matters as acoustics for passenger cabins and fiber glass seats.[43]

Conclusion

The end of the 1950's makes a good point at which to close this account of the American aircraft industry. The launching of the space race and the increasing military reliance on missiles shifted the industry's emphasis. As a matter of fact the ability of the airframe manufacturers not only to shift to missile production but virtually to take over the field was a remarkable success story in itself, because there was no compelling reason for missiles to be made by aircraft firms.[44] However, while the industry adapted itself successfully, in the process its basic structure was changed. The aerospace industry is an outgrowth of the aircraft industry, but it is not just the aircraft industry under a more glamorous name.

The decisive change as the 1960's arrived was a decrease in orders for military planes, although predictions that manned

aircraft would disappear from military use altogether were
nitely exaggerated. There was some compensating increa
the output of civil aircraft, as air transport grew and private
flying increased, although still not to the mass-production levels
that the industry has periodically dreamed of. There were also
exciting prospects for the future: supersonic transports, "jumbo"
jets, variable-sweep wing designs, and V/STOL planes. Nevertheless, the fact remained that military aircraft had always
constituted the largest segment of the industry's business, and
when this dropped off the industry had to find an alternative.

The nature of the change is reflected in the composition of the
work force. Between 1954 and 1962 the percentage of hourly
wage workers dropped from 71.6 to 40, while the proportion of
scientific and engineering employees increased correspond-
ingly.[45] Total employment in this period rose from 782,900 in
1954 to 1,177,000 in 1962, making the aircraft industry the
largest employer among manufacturing industries in the United
States.[46]

Some alterations in corporate structure would also emerge in
response to these new conditions. Bell Aircraft became the Bell
Aerospace Corporation to indicate more accurately the nature of
the company's business, and in 1960 it was acquired in a diversification move by Textron, Inc., originally a holding company in
the textile industry. The Glenn L. Martin Company became simply The Martin Company in 1958 and three years later expanded
beyond the aerospace field by merging with the Marietta Corporation, a manufacturer of cement, lime, and rock products as
well as chemicals, as the Martin-Marietta Corporation. North
American, which had concentrated on military aircraft, not only
became a major participant in aerospace and nuclear technology
but in 1967 followed Martin's example and merged with the
Rockwell-Standard Corporation to become North American
Rockwell Corporation.[47] A similar combination, Ling-Temco-
Vought, Inc., has already been listed. Douglas ran into serious
financial difficulties. The company lost $34 million in 1959,[48]
largely because of the development cost of the DC-8, and conditions failed to improve. Although the DC-8 and the later medium-range DC-9 were technically successful, delays in production

and failure to reach estimated sales totals resulted in continuing deficits. There were managerial problems also, and the eventual solution was to unite with McDonnell Aircraft in 1967 under the name of the McDonnell Douglas Corporation. Boeing became simply The Boeing Company in 1961, and Northrop Aircraft, Inc., became the Northrop Corporation in 1958. Fairchild Hiller acquired Republic Aviation in 1965. In short, a new industry was growing out of the old.

To reach the position it attained at this landmark juncture in its history, the aircraft industry had had a long uneven climb from its negligible status of 40 years before. At the beginning of the period American aircraft production was almost nonexistent, and in both airframe and engine design the American industry, with a few exceptions, was below contemporary European standards. At the end, American production far outstripped the rest of the world in quantity, except possibly for the Soviet Union,[49] and qualitatively was generally superior in large aircraft types and at least equal in others. In 1960 80 per cent of the world's airliners were American-built (see Table 14).

The progress of the American aircraft industry was upward, but sporadically so. The term "feast or famine" is a reasonably good although not completely accurate description. The ups and downs are readily distinguishable. In the early 1920's the industry was struggling for a bare existence. Then came the Morrow Board program and a period of relative prosperity, swept up into the speculative boom of 1928–1929. The depression years were as bad for the aircraft manufacturers as for everyone else, perhaps worse because of the hostility of the New Deal administration and its adherents in Congress. The industry pulled itself up by brilliant achievement with commercial transports, and the worsening international situation created a stronger market for military planes in the late 1930's. The hot-house expansion of the Second World War followed, constituting a challenge that was successfully met. After the war came another slump, then an upsurge with the Korean conflict. The late 1950's was another difficult period, until the transition to aerospace activity opened a new phase in the industry's history.

Behind this record of upsurge and downswing was the aircraft

Table 14. U.S. Manufactured Aircraft in Operation on World Airlines 1958–1962

	1958	1959	1960	1961	1962
TOTAL MANUFACTURED IN U.S.	2,819	2,868	2,766	2,542	2,345
4 Engine	1,404	1,511	1,568	1,505	1,474
Turbojets	5	97	285	423	517
Boeing 707	5	76	143	150	209
Boeing 720	—	—	23	40	51
Boeing 720B	—	—	—	44	25
Douglas DC-8	—	21	110	149	167
Convair 880	—	—	9	40	44
Convair 990	—	—	—	—	21
Turboprops	9	108	127	137	137
Lockheed Electra	9	108	127	137	137
Piston Engine	1,390	1,306	1,156	945	820
Boeing Stratocruiser	44	26	—	—	—
Lockheed Constellation	426	412	362	261	206
Douglas DC-7	325	296	276	254	232
Douglas DC-6	420	418	372	316	277
Douglas DC-4	175	154	146	114	105
2 Engine	1,384	1,308	1,125	971	833
Turboprops	3	17	21	8	7
Fairchild F-27	3	17	21	8	7
Piston Engine	1,381	1,291	1,104	963	826
Convair 240, 340, 440	384	364	321	288	250
Martin 202, 404	99	91	75	40	4
Curtiss Commando C-46	68	60	48	36	36
Douglas DC-3	799	750	634	568	516
Other	31	26	26	31	20
1 Engine	—	11	37	34	12
Helicopters	31	38	36	32	26
ALL MANUFACTURERS GRAND TOTAL	3,402	3,479	3,376	3,319	3,162
Per Cent of Grand Total Manufactured in U.S.	82.9	82.4	81.9	76.6	74.2

Source: International Air Transport Association, "World Air Transport Statistics" (Annually). Based on reports by IATA members. Published by Aerospace Industries Association, *Aerospace Facts and Figures, 1964*, p. 104.

industry's distinctive near-monopsonic character; i.e., it had a single customer, the government, for 80 per cent of the dollar value of its products. It was, therefore, acutely dependent on the fluctuations of public policy with regard to aviation, and the record reveals the startling fact that the only time during this 40-year period when the United States had a consistent, planned policy in peacetime for maintaining a healthy level of aircraft production was the five years (1926–1931) in which the Morrow Board program was in effect.

In these conditions, although it was natural that the American aircraft industry should have become big, simply because of the sheer over-all size of the American economy in which it was growing, there was no deterministic reason for the industry's remarkable qualitative performance, or for the particular organizational pattern that evolved. A trend to oligopoly could have been expected, since a few large concerns would be better able to withstand the feast-and-famine cycle than a multitude of small ones. The industry did move in this direction. Boeing, Convair, Douglas, Lockheed, North American, and until about 1950, Martin, emerged as the dominant airframe manufacturers, while Curtiss-Wright and Pratt and Whitney occupied a similar position with engines, subject to the competition that developed from General Electric and General Motors, companies whose primary interests were outside the field of aviation. However, regardless of how many, or rather how few, firms constitute a true oligopoly, the aircraft industry cannot qualify. Smaller concerns remained vigorously competitive and occasionally moved up among the leaders.

Part of the reason for this situation was that the aircraft industry was not, except during the Second World War, a quantity producer. The largest number of units made in any one year, excluding the Second World War but including the Korean War, was 36,418 in 1946, and all but about 2,000 of these were small planes built in anticipation of a postwar boom in private flying.[50] The manufacturing operation was predominantly qualitative; the task was to manufacture a complex article to a very high standard of precision, so that each airplane was essentially a separate product rather than a replica of the initial design. The airplane, moreover, was a product in which a fairly minor technical superiority could confer a strong competitive advantage. There were no economies of scale sufficient to be of decisive benefit to the large companies. Consequently it was feasible for a small firm with good management and a high level of technical skill to establish, retain, and frequently expand a foothold.

Much of the credit for maintaining a vigorously competitive aircraft industry belongs to the military services, which were the principal purchasers of aircraft. Both the Air Force, in its various incarnations, and the Navy normally operated with limited funds and rigid procurement procedures, but both consciously used their resources as far as possible to maintain competitive producers of airframes, engines, and other components. It was manifestly desirable on grounds of military security to have more than one supplier available, but this was a secondary reason for the policy. A more important reason was that the service officials responsible for procurement (General H. H. Arnold and Admiral William A. Moffett are conspicuous examples) were committed to the concept of private enterprise and in addition had evidence from experience that competition made for better products and stimulated new ideas. Experience also confirmed the wisdom of the customary service policy of inviting bids on the basis of performance specifications and leaving the manufacturers free to submit whatever designs they believed would meet the requirements.

On the industry's side, active competition was sustained by a constant influx of able, aggressive entrepreneurs who were either technically competent themselves or had the ability to work in harmony with others who possessed this competence. The market for aircraft is not the conventional consumer's market. One does not sell airplanes to the military services or the airlines by having comely young females utter banalities and go through inane performances on television commercials. All that counts are rigorous standards of performance. The entrepreneurs and the companies that could meet these standards stayed in business and occasionally even prospered; the others did not.

As could be expected of an industry in which technology is the most vital element, most of the men who organized and managed aircraft companies were engineers, and academically trained engineers at that. Such engineers include Donald Douglas, Sr., Grover Loening, Chance Vought, Leroy Grumman, P. G. Johnson and Claire Egtvedt of Boeing, James McDonnell, and

J. L. Atwood of North American. William E. Boeing was primarily a businessman, but he was educated at Yale's Sheffield Scientific School. J. H. Kindelberger (North American) and Carl Squier (Lockheed) had some formal engineering education, followed by aviation training in the Army during the First World War. Igor Sikorsky was a brilliant engineer, a pupil of the great Russian aerodynamicist N. A. Zhukovsky, but he hardly qualifies as an entrepreneur.

Some outstanding leaders were self-trained, starting as mechanics: the Lockheed brothers, John K. Northrop, Lawrence Bell, Glenn L. Martin, and Clyde Cessna. The Lockheeds dropped out of aviation in the 1920's, and Northrop's genius was in originality of design rather than in management.

Walter Beech, Reuben Fleet (Consolidated), F. B. Rentschler (Pratt and Whitney), and T. Claude Ryan were all products of the Air Service in the First World War. Rentschler was a graduate of Princeton and had industrial experience in manufacturing machinery. They have to be classified as business rather than technical men, along with Robert E. and Courtlandt Gross, who entered aviation from the world of finance. Sherman Fairchild began as an inventor of photographic equipment.

These are some of the more prominent figures among the leaders of the aircraft industry. Except for the understandable preponderance of men with technical skill and training, there is no clearly marked pattern. A few, notably Boeing, came from wealthy families, but no great fortunes are represented. At the other end of the economic scale there was a rather larger group who had to support themselves, but there is no well-defined example of "rags to riches." In educational background they varied considerably, although a majority had completed college. The one thing they had in common was a complete and unwavering dedication to aviation.

Most of these men were still living when the aircraft industry became the aerospace industry; many of them, indeed, had a part in the transition. They therefore had the experience of rebuilding a nearly defunct industry at the end of the First World War and then reconstituting it when new technologies came along to demand change. Between these points was a dramatic process of growth: economically from the shoestring operations of the 1920's to an industry whose total sales in 1960 were over $17 billion, representing almost 5 per cent of all manufacturing industry and 3.4 per cent of the Gross National Product; [51] technologically from the wood-and-wire puddle-jumpers of the early days, with in-line piston engines, to jet-powered planes flying in the stratosphere at supersonic speeds. Along the way were the development of the all-metal, cantilevered-wing monoplane, the radial air-cooled engine, and the controllable-pitch propeller, all achievements attributable to the American aircraft industry in terms of putting them into practical operation. Along with these technological innovations the industry accomplished a stupendous production feat in the Second World War.

The government's contribution to both the technological and the economic progress of aircraft manufacturing has been considerable and should be acknowledged. The research work of the NACA and the military services was vitally important in the advance of aeronautical science and technology. Economically, beyond the support given through the purchase of military aircraft, the expenditure of public funds for airports, air traffic control and navigational aids, and the promotion of safety stimulated the expansion of aviation and therefore the demand for aircraft. On the other side, some public policies, such as legislative restrictions on profits on government contracts, have been a handicap to an industry that has been overwhelmingly dependent on government purchases of its products.

Consequently, although appropriate credit should be given to the support of governmental agencies, the American aircraft industry rose to greatness primarily by its own efforts. It had to face a fluctuating demand for its products; erratic, uncertain, and occasionally hostile policies on the part of its principal customer; and the need to keep pace with a complex and rapidly progressing technology. Surmounting the challenges presented by these conditions would have been a sufficient measure of success by itself. The American aircraft industry, however, went further. It not only met but surpassed the demands placed on it, so that its standards of performance became a model for others to emulate. This feat was accomplished with a product whose one constant characteristic was its inconstancy. There was always a better plane to be designed than was being built, and a better one being thought up than was being designed. The aircraft industry was forever, as John L. Atwood put it, "nibbling at the edge of the unknown"; [52] its fundamental problem was succinctly expressed by John K. Northrop when on a jet flight to Hawaii he wrote, "You know, I still don't know what keeps them up here." [53]

Appendix A

This list gives the actual achievement of the aircraft program of the First World War. The figures carry over for an extra year to include contracts completed after the Armistice, and the bulk of the production was too late for combat service. It is, however, useful to see how much was built and by whom, both to remove misconceptions about what was really accomplished and to give a survey of the American aircraft industry as it existed at that time.

Consolidated List of Aircraft Contracts and Deliveries in the United States, April 6, 1917–November 1, 1919 Airplanes, Engines, Airships, Balloons (Supply, Free, Toy, Observation, Target, Propaganda, Experimental)

AIRPLANES	
Number Received	Amount
Aeronautical Industry	
4014 Curtiss	$ 29,366,397.24
1033 Standard	15,589,694.63
1 Sturtevant	11,250.00
51 Wright	329,250.00
131 L. W. F.	1,649,377.50
10 Glenn Martin	822,575.27
599 Thomas-Morse	3,106,103.27
7 Lewis and Vought	61,676.00
2 Heinrich	11,328.00
4 Gallaudet	140,013.02
300 Breese	591,325.85

Aeronautical Industry—Continued

1	Burgess	26,009.50
0	Aeromarine	—
50	Fowler	323,166.90
3506	Dayton-Wright	31,446,575.88
25	Packard	1,084,670.12
8	Ordnance	144,742.98
9742		$ 84,704,155.16

Automobile and Kindred Industries

2000	Fisher	19,643,837.39
0	Brewster	200,000.00
2000		$ 19,843,837.39

Miscellaneous

(Emergency War Organizations, New Concerns,
Missions, etc.)

0	Empire	$ 15,000.00
3	Pigeon-Fraser	19,075.00
200	Liberty Iron Works	1,002,366.28
1	Italian War Mission	49,227.79
2	Equipment Holding	10,000.00
588	Springfield Aircraft Co.	3,457,229.52
450	St. Louis	2,137,500.00
50	U.S. Aircraft Co.	326,170.10
75	Howell and Lesser	394,121.41
1	Schiefer	11,720.00
100	Various mfrs. for Handley-Page Parts	—
680	Canadian Aero Co.	1,733,136.00
2	Pacific	17,504.74
2152		$ 9,173,050.84

Recapitulation of Airplanes

9742	Aeronautical Industry	$ 84,704,155.16
2000	Automobile and Kindred Industries	19,843,837.39
2152	Miscellaneous	9,173,050.84
13894		$113,721,043.39

ENGINES

Number Received	Amount

Aeronautical Industry

2	Ordnance	—	*
1	Lawrance	$ 21,000.00	
1255	Hall-Scott	2,944,631.03	
750	Curtiss	634,547.23	
41	Standard	215,093.14	
94	L. W. F.	—	*

Aeronautical Industry—Continued

73	Sturtevant	* 302,000.00
30	Burgess	133,500.00
5816	Wright	54,372,268.68
69	Thomas-Morse	321,990.08
4	Gallaudet	— *
6630	Packard	42,780,339.50
14765		$101,725,369.64

Automobile and Kindred Industries

4	Van Blerck	$ 8,913.04
4	Sterling	11,680.59
2	Wisconsin	2,878.00
40	Duesenberg	4,934,798.62
0	Pierce Arrow	1,584,164.81
2543	General Motors	9,766,499.68
8500	Willys-Overland	21,030,871.60
61	General Vehicle	43,700.00
451	Excelsior Motor	295,000.00
2000	Nordyke and Marmon	18,015,240.38
1	Winton	1,485.00
1	Trego	1,145,008.11
6500	Lincoln	45,859,985.18
3950	Ford	29,401,393.62
1	Willys-Morrow	400.00
24058		$132,102,018.63

Miscellaneous

400	Canadian Aero	$ 252,000.00
121	Aero Engineering	523,723.14
1	Schiefer	— *
4	Italian War Mission	— *
8	British War Mission	—
2585	Union Switch	10,131,298.89
6	Murray and Tregurtha	103,752.00
3	Equipment Holding	— *
2	Pacific	— *
3130		$ 11,010,774.03

Recapitulation of Engines

14765	Aeronautical Industry	$101,725,369.64
24058	Automobile and Kindred Industries	132,102,018.63
3130	Miscellaneous	11,010,774.03
41953		$244,838,162.30

BALLOONS AND AIRSHIPS

Number Received	Amount
Aeronautical Industry	
128 Connecticut	$ 393,464.10
28 Knabenshue	198,501.66
1 French-American	1,800.00
687 * Goodyear	4,160,588.19
844	$4,754,353.95
Automobile Industry	
249 Goodrich	$1,788,253.94
6437 U.S. Rubber	428,252.68
7 Firestone	76,223.56
2275 Revere	2,030.63
8968	$2,294,760.81
Miscellaneous	
3 Halsey	$ 1,185.24
161 Scott	18,579.71
1 Columbia	60.00
22,866 (pilot balloons) Faultless	1,608.30
44 Navy Dept.	70,000.00
8,500 (pilot balloons) Sterling	8,735.00
31,575	$ 100,168.25
Recapitulation of Balloons	
41,387 Total Balloons and Airships	
Total Expenditure	$7,149,283.01

Source: *Aircraft Yearbook, 1922*, pp. 186–189.
* Amounts wholly or partly included in the same contracts covering airplanes.

Appendix B

Wartime Producers of Aircraft * [*Second World War*]

Manufacturer	Plant Location	AAF Acceptances	Character of Major Items Produced
Aeronca Aircraft Corp.	Middleton, Ohio	2,439	PT-19, PT-23 (995), L-3, (1,439)
Beech Aircraft Corp.	Wichita, Kans.	7,430	C-45 (1,771), AT-7, AT-10, AT-11 (5,175), including 47 items bought for Navy in 1941 and 1942
Bell Aircraft Corp.	Atlanta, Ga.	652	B-29
	Buffalo, N.Y.	12,941	P-39 (9,588), P-63 (3,273), and 1 Navy fighter
Bellanca Aircraft	New Castle, Del.	42	C-50 (3), AT-21 (39)
Boeing Aircraft Corp.	Renton, Wash.	1,000	B-29 (998), C-97 (2)
	Seattle, Wash.	7,339	B-29 (3), B-17 (6,942), A-20 (380), and 1 Navy patrol bomber
	Vancouver, Canada	0	290 Navy patrol bombers
	Wichita, Kans.	9,890	B-29 (1,595), PT-13, PT-17 (7,839), including 600 trainers bought for Navy in 1940 and 1941
Brewster Aircraft Corp.	Johnsville, Pa.	0	1,997 Navy light bombers and fighters
Budd Mfg. Co.	Long Island City, N.Y.	2	A-32
Canadian Car Co.	Philadelphia, Pa.	0	17 Navy transports
Cessna Aircraft Co.	Fort Wilham, Canada	0	832 Navy light bombers
Cessna Aircraft Division of United Aircraft	Wichita, Kans.	5,359	C-78 (3,206), AT-8 (673), AT-17 (1,480)
	Stratford, Conn.	0	7,897 Navy light bombers, reconnaissance aircraft, fighters, and transports
Columbia Aircraft	Valley Stream, N.Y.	0	319 Navy transports

Wartime Producers of Aircraft *—Continued

Manufacturer	Plant Location	AAF Acceptances	Character of Major Items Produced
Consolidated-Vultee, Aircraft Corp. (2)	Allentown, Pa.	0	174 Navy light bombers
	Downey, Calif.	11,687	BT-13, BT-15, (11,537), A-31 (2)
	Fort Worth, Tex.	3,148	B-24, (2,743), B-32 (114), C-87 (291)
	Nashville, Tenn.	1,966	A-31, A-35 (1,529), B-38 (113), L-1
	New Orleans, La.	0	221 Navy patrol bombers
	San Diego, Calif.	6,729	B-24 (6,725), B-32 (4)
	Wayne, Mich.	4,104	AT-19 (500), L-5 (3,590)
Culver Aircraft Corp.	Wichita, Kans.	19	Liaison types
Curtiss-Wright Corp.	Buffalo, N.Y.	17,489	P-40 (17,738), P-47 (354), C-46 (2,674), and 86 new light bombers and fighters
	Columbus, Ohio	0	6,343 Navy light bombers, reconnaissance aircraft
	Louisville, Ky.	458	C-46 (438)
	St. Louis, Mo.	2,261	A-25 (900), C-46 (29), AT-9 (791), and 505 Navy trainers
De Havilland Aircraft of Canada	Toronto, Canada	200	PT-24
Douglas Aircraft Co., Inc.	Chicago, Illinois	629	C-54
	El Segundo, Calif.	3	A-26 and 5,411 Navy light bombers and transports
	Long Beach, Calif.	9,439	B-17 (3,000), A-26 (1,155), A-20 (999), C-47 (4,285)
	Oklahoma City, Okla.	5,319	C-47, C-117
	Santa Monica, Calif.	7,309	A-20 (6,006), P-70 (60), C-54 (460)
	Tulsa, Okla.	2,870	B-24 (964), A-26 (1,291), A-24 (615)
Eastern Aircraft Division of	Linden, N.J.	0	5,927 Navy fighters
General Motors	Trenton, N.J.	0	7,522 Navy light bombers

Manufacturer	Plant Location	AAF Acceptances	Character of Major Items Produced
Engineering and Research Corp.	Riverside, Md.	1	C-55
Fairchild Aircraft Division	Burlington, N.C.	105	AT-21
	Hagerstown, Md.	5,975	C-82 (2), C-61 (1,012, including 3 for Navy)
	Montreal, Canada	0	PT-19, PT-23, PT-26 (4,958), 300 Navy light bombers
Fisher Body Division of General Motors	Cleveland, Ohio	14	P-75
Fleet Aircraft Corp.	Fort Erie, Canada	1,150	PT-23, PT-26
Fleetwings, Inc.	Bristol, Pa.	25	BY-12
Ford Motor Co.	Willow Run, Mich.	6,792	B-24
G & A Aircraft Corp.	Willow Grove, Pa.	7	Rotary wing aircraft
Globe Aircraft Corp.	Fort Worth, Tex.	600	AT-10
Goodyear Aircraft Corp.	Akron, Ohio	0	3,940 Navy fighters
Grumman Aircraft Corp.	Bethpage, Long Island, N.Y.	0	17,478 fighters, light bombers, and transports for Navy
Higgins Aircraft, Inc.	New Orleans, La.	2	C-46
Howard Aircraft Corp.	Chicago, Ill.	349	PT-23 and 483 transports and trainers for Navy
Interstate Aircraft and Engineering Corp.	El Segundo, Calif.	259	L-6 (251), L-8 (8)
Kellett Autogiro Corp.	Philadelphia, Pa.	7	O-60 autogiro
Lockheed Aircraft Corp.	Burbank, Calif.		
	Plant A	3,764	B-17 (2,750) B-24 (1,014), and 1,929 Navy patrol bombers
	Plant B	13,384	A-28, A-29 (2,189), P-38 (9,423), P-80 (115), F-4, F-5 (500), C-69 (14), including 1 Navy transport in 1941

Wartime Producers of Aircraft *—Continued*

Manufacturer	Plant Location	AAF Acceptances	Character of Major Items Produced
Glenn L. Martin Co.	Baltimore, Md.	5,611	B-26 (3,572), A-30 (1,575), and 1,275 Navy patrol bombers
McDonnell Aircraft Corp.	Omaha, Neb.	2,100	B-29 (515), B-26 (1,585)
	Memphis, Tenn.	30	AT-21
	St. Louis, Mo.	1	P-67
Nash-Kelvinator Corp.	Detroit, Mich.	201	R-6 helicopter
Naval Aircraft Factory	Philadelphia, Pa.	0	1,302 Navy patrol bombers, reconnaissance aircraft, light bombers, and trainers
Noorduyn Aviation Co., Ltd.	Montreal, Canada	2,252	C-64 (752), AT-16 (1,500)
North American Aviation, Inc.	Dallas, Tex.	18,784	B-24 (966), P-51 (4,552), E-6 (299), AT-6 (12,967)
	Inglewood, Calif.	16,447	B-25 (3,208), A-36 (500), P-51 (9,949), AT-6 (2,163), including 36 trainers for Navy in 1940
	Kansas City, Kans.	6,608	B-25
Northrop Aircraft, Inc.	Hawthorne, Calif.	1,083	A-31 (400), P-62 (682), and 24 Navy light bombers
Piper Aircraft Corp.	Lockhaven, Pa.	5,611	L-4, L-14, and 330 Navy trainers and liaison
Platt-LePage Aircraft Co.	Eddystone, Pa.	2	R-1 helicopter
Rearwin Aircraft	Kansas City, Kans.	25	Liaison
Republic Aviation Corp.	Evansville, Ind.	6,225	P-47
	Farmingdale, N.Y.	9,438	P-43 (272), P-47 (9,006), etc.
Ryan Aeronautical Corp.	San Diego, Calif.	1,443	PT-20, PT-21, PT-25 (392), P-22 (1,048), and 42 Navy fighters
St. Louis Aircraft Corp.	St. Louis, Mo.	363	PT-19, PT-23 (350)
Sikorsky Aircraft Division of United Aircraft	Stratford, Conn.	151	R-4 (130), R-5 (16), R-6 (5) helicopters

*Wartime Producers of Aircraft * —Continued*

Manufacturer	Plant Location	AAF Acceptances	Character of Major Items Produced
Spartan Aircraft Corp.	Tulsa, Okla.	0	201 Navy trainers
Taylorcraft Aviation Corp.	Alliance, Ohio	1,940	L-2
Timm Aircraft Corp.	Van Nuys, Calif.	0	262 Navy trainers
Universal Aircraft	Bristol, Va.	19	L-7
Vickers Canadian, Ltd.	Montreal, Canada	0	230 Navy patrol bombers
Waco Aircraft Co.	Troy, Ohio	6	PT-14 (2)

Source: I. B. Holley, *Buying Aircraft: Material Procurement for the Army Air Forces. The United States Army in World War II*, Special Studies, No. 7 (Washington, D. C., 1964). Reproduced by courtesy of the Office of the Chief of Military History, Department of the Army.

* In those instances where a firm produced only for Navy cognizance or for the Navy as well as the AAF, the number of units so produced is indicated in the column on the right along with the description of the principal items turned out.

Note: Figures in parenthesis show the total production for each aircraft or group of similar aircraft.

Appendix C

Major Producers of Aircraft Engines: July 1940–August 1945 *

Manufacturer	Plant Location	Conventional Reciprocating Engines Produced	Description, Approximate Horsepower, and Use (Major Items Only)
Pratt & Whitney	East Hartford, Conn.	122,302	R-2800 R-1830 R-1340 R-985
	Kansas City, Mo.	7,815	R-2800
Licensees of Pratt & Whitney			
Ford	Dearborn, Mich.	57,178	R-2800
Buick	Melrose Park, Ill.	74,198	R-2800 (Flint) R-1830
Chevrolet	Tonowanda, N.Y.	60,766	R-2800 R-1830
Nash-Kelvinator	Kenosha, Wis.	17,012	R-2800
Jacobs	Pottstown, Pa.	11,614	R-1340 R-985
Continental	Muskegon, Mich.	5,100	R-1340
		355,985	

R-2800: Double Wasp 18 cylinder twin row, 2000 hp. used on B-26, C-54, etc.
R-1830: Twin Wasp 14 cylinder twin row, 1200 hp. used on B-24, C-47, etc.
R-1340: Wasp 9 cylinder 650 hp.
R-985: Wasp Junior 9 cylinder 450 hp.

Manufacturer	Plant Location	Conventional Reciprocating Engines Produced	Description, Approximate Horsepower, and Use (Major Items Only)
Wright Aeronautical	Patterson, N.J.	77,554	R-3350 R-2600 R-1820 R-975 R-760	R-3350: Cyclone 18, 18 cylinder twin row, 2200 hp. used on B-29
	Lockland, Ohio	61,940	R-3350 R-2600	R-2600: Cyclone 14, 14 cylinder twin row, 1600 hp. used on A-20, B-25, etc.
Licensees of Wright Aero				R-1820: Cyclone 9, 9 cylinder 1200 hp. used on B-17, etc.
Dodge (Division of Chrysler)	Chicago, Ill.	18,349	R-3350	R-975: Whirlwind 9 cylinder 450 hp.
Studebaker	South Bend, Ind.	63,789	R-1820	R-760: Whirlwind 7 cylinder 225 hp.
Continental	Muskegon, Mich.	19	R-975	
Naval Aircraft Factory	Philadelphia, Pa.	1,385	R-975 R-760	
		223,036		
Allison	Indianapolis, Ind.	69,305	V-1710:	12 cylinder 1500 hp., liquid cooled; P-38, P-39, P-40
			V-3420:	24 cylinder 2000 hp., liquid cooled
Rolls Royce license to:				
Packard	Detroit, Mich.	54,714	V-1650:	Merlin, 12 cylinder, 1800 hp., liquid cooled; P-51
Continental	Muskegon, Mich.	797		
		55,511		

*Major Producers of Aircraft Engines: July 1940–August 1945 *—Continued*

Manufacturer	Plant Location	Conventional Reciprocating Engines Produced	Description, Approximate Horsepower, and Use (Major Items Only)
Continental	Muskegon, Mich.	I-1430: 23	12 cylinder 1350 hp., inverted V, liquid cooled
		R-670: 11,828	7 cylinder 220 hp.; PT-13, etc., PT-19, etc.
		O-170: 16,977	4 cylinder 80 hp.; opposed; L-4, etc.
		28,828	
Lycoming	Williamsport, Pa.	R-680: 12,476	9 cylinder 295 hp.; AT-8, AT-10, etc.
		O-435 O-290 O-235 O-145: 12,395	4–6 cylinder 50–210 hp.; L-5, etc.
		24,871	
Jacobs	Pottstown, Pa.	R-915: 5,759	7 cylinder 330 hp.
		R-755: 14,746	7 cylinder 225 hp.; AT-17, etc.
		20,505	
Ranger	Farmingdale, N.Y.	V-770: 2,748	12 cylinder 520 hp., air cooled; AT-21, etc.
		L-440: 11,518	6 cylinder 200 hp., in line, air cooled; PT-19, etc.
		14,266	
Air Cooled Motors	Syracuse, N.Y.	O-805: 178	12 cylinder 500 hp.
		O-405; O-300; O-200; O-175: 6,044	4–6 cylinder 80 to 200 hp.; L-6, etc.
		6,222	

Major Producers of Aircraft Engines: July 1940–August 1945 *—Continued

Manufacturer	Plant Location	Conventional Reciprocating Engines Produced		Description, Approximate Horsepower, and Use (Major Items Only)
Kinner Motors	Glendale, Calif.	R-540:	2,356	5 cylinder 165 hp.; PT-22, PT-25
		R-440:	802	5 cylinder 135 hp.; PT-20, PT-24
			3,158	
Warner	Detroit, Mich.	R-550:	184	7 cylinder 200 hp.; R-4 helicopter
		R-500:	1,704	7 cylinder 175 hp.
		R-420:	127	7 cylinder 110 hp.
			2,015	
Menasco	Burbank, Calif.	L-365:	525	4 cylinder 125 hp., inverted in line, air cooled

Source: I. B. Holley, *Buying Aircraft: Material Procurement for the Army Air Forces. The United States Army in World War II*, Special Studies, No. 7 (Washington, D. C., 1964). Reproduced by courtesy of the Office of the Chief of Military History, Department of the Army.
* Because cross procurement played such an important role in engine production, total rather than AAF acceptances are shown.

Notes

Chapter 1

1. W. G. Cunningham, *The Aircraft Industry: A Study in Industrial Location* (Los Angeles, 1951), p. 33.
2. A refreshing and scholarly approach to this problem is I. B. Holley, Jr., *Ideas and Weapons* (New Haven, Conn., 1953), which points out that the heart of the difficulty was the absence of any clear strategic or tactical doctrine for the use of aircraft in war, accentuated by an unbelievable lack of information about British and French experience in aerial warfare. It is difficult to plan and organize aircraft production when no one is sure how the product is to be used.
3. C. F. Taylor, "Aircraft Propulsion: A Review of the Evolution of Aircraft Powerplants," *Smithsonian Report, 1962,* No. 4546 (Washington, D. C., 1963), p. 261. Edward A. Deeds, who was in charge of aircraft production, gave the following instructions to J. G. Vincent of Packard and E. J. Hall of the Hall-Scott Motor Company, who did the initial design of the Liberty: "The engine must be light in weight in proportion to power. It must embody no device that has not already been tested and proved in existing engines. You must avoid all experimentation. Finally, the engine must be adapted to quantity production." See I. F. Marcosson, *Colonel Deeds, Industrial Builder* (New York, 1948), p. 238.
4. W. F. Craven and J. L. Cate, *The Army Air Forces in World War II,* Vol. 6, *Men and Planes* (Chicago, 1955), p. 186.
5. J. S. Day, *Subcontracting in the Airframe Industry* (Cambridge, Mass., 1956), p. 17.
6. H. Mingos, *The Birth of an Industry* (New York, 1930), p. 49; C. L. Lawrance, *Our National Aviation Program* (New York, 1932), p. 4.
7. *Aerospace Facts and Figures, 1964,* p. 24.
8. Holley, *Ideas and Weapons,* p. 153.

9. W. A. Shrader, *Fifty Years of Flight: A Chronicle of the Aviation Industry in America, 1903–1953* (Cleveland, Ohio, 1953), p. 8.

10. The crux of the controversy was the Wrights' claim that their patent on the wing-warping device covered the use of ailerons. The issue was never settled. When the United States entered the war, government pressure resulted in a cross-licensing agreement administered by the Aircraft Manufacturers' Association. See Mingos, *Birth of an Industry,* p. 12.

11. *Aircraft Year Book, 1919,* p. 112.

12. Willys sold his interest in the company to its president, Clement M. Keys, for $650,000.

13. Three of these planes, NC-1, NC-3, and NC-4, started from Newfoundland, May 16, 1919. NC-4 reached Plymouth, England, via the Azores, on May 31st. The other two landed short of the Azores in fog and were unable to take off again. NC-1 sank, but NC-3 *sailed* 205 miles to Ponta Delgado. They had four Liberty engines, arranged as three tractors and one pusher. See Douglas Aircraft Co., Inc., *Fiftieth Anniversary of Naval Aviation,* Service Information Summary (El Segundo, Calif., 1962), p. 26. Conrad Westervelt, designer of the first Boeing plane, the B. and W. (for Boeing and Westervelt), took part in this flight.

14. The literature on the Wrights is naturally extensive. This account is based on Orville Wright, *How We Invented the Airplane* (New York, 1953), pp. 67–72; N. W. McFarland, *Papers of the Wright Brothers* (Washington, D. C., 1956), Vol. 2, p. 1112; "Wright Engines: The First Quarter Century," *Aero Digest,* 47 (Nov. 1, 1944), pp. 73–75.

15. President's Aircraft Board (Morrow Board), *Aircraft in National Defense,* Senate Document No. 18, 69th Congress, 1st Session (Washington, D. C.), Vol. 4, p. 1459; Statement by Glenn L. Martin, April 17, 1934, Martin Papers, Library of Congress, Box 77.

16. E. E. Wilson, *Air Power for Peace* (New York, 1945), p. 61.

17. *The Martin Company,* pamphlet (Baltimore, Md., 1960), p. 37.

18. H. Mansfield, *Vision* (New York, 1956), p. 9.

19. *Ibid.,* pp. 31 ff. British aircraft firms faced the same problems at this time as did American firms and tried similar remedies. Avro made billiard tables and Westland metal beer barrels.

20. "Boeing Aircraft Co., 25th Anniversary," *Aero Digest,* 39, No. 1 (July 1941), pp. 47 and 77.

21. E. E. Freudenthal, *The Aviation Business: From Kitty Hawk to Wall Street* (New York, 1940), p. 78.

22. J. Niven, C. Canby, and V. Welsh (eds.), *Dynamic America: A History of General Dynamics Corporation* (New York, 1958), p. 128; Convair Division, General Dynamics Corporation, "Convair History" (Ms. compiled by Howard O. Welty), IV-1, 3. The Morse in the title was Frank L. Morse of the Morse Chain Co. of Ithaca, which financed the expansion of the Thomas firm. The Herring-Curtiss Company was one of the early organizational phases through which the Curtiss firm passed. It was a short-lived partnership between Glenn Curtiss and Augustus Herring.

23. G. Loening, *Our Wings Grow Faster* (Garden City, N.Y., 1935), p. 78.
24. See *Naval Aviation News*, March 1957, p. 1, for the early history of Chance Vought.
25. There is considerable literature on the career of Donald W. Douglas. F. Cunningham, *Skymaster: The Story of Donald Douglas and Douglas Aircraft Co.* (Philadelphia, 1943), is the most complete account of Douglas' career until 1942. The sketch given here is based mainly on C. Maynard (ed.), *Flight Plan for Tomorrow: The Douglas Story. A Condensed History*, rev. ed. (Santa Monica, Calif., 1966), and a transcript of a recorded interview given by Mr. Douglas, March 1959, for the Aviation History Project, Oral History Research Office, Columbia University.
26. Douglas transcript.
27. R. G. Hubler, *Big Eight: The Biography of an Airplane* (New York, 1960), p. 22.
28. Maynard, *Flight Plan for Tomorrow*, pp. 8–9.
29. P. W. Litchfield, *Industrial Voyage* (Garden City, N.Y., 1954), p. 235.
30. Interview with Jerome C. Hunsaker, April 1960, Aviation History Project, Oral History Research Office, Columbia University.
31. F. Cunningham, *Skymaster*, p. 145.
32. Douglas Aircraft Co., Inc., *Fifty Years of Naval Aviation*, p. 7.
33. W. G. Cunningham, *Location of the Aircraft Industry*, p. 56.
34. K. M. Johnson, *Aerial California* (Los Angeles, 1961).
35. The biographical data on Fleet is from "Convair History," I-4.
36. Niven, Canby, and Welsh, *Dynamic America*, p. 123. Gallaudet's admirers credit him with having discovered the wing-warping principle a year before the Wrights. The evidence, a drawing published in 1920 of a Gallaudet model dated 1898, seems slender. There is better evidence that John J. Montgomery discovered the principle still earlier.
37. *Ibid.*, p. 199.
38. "Convair History," I-7.
39. *Ibid.*, I-8.
40. *Aircraft Year Book*, 1922, p. 189.
41. "Convair History," I-11.
42. *Ibid.*, I-12.
43. For the best account of the Bolling Commission and its work, see Holley, *Ideas and Weapons*, pp. 62–64.
44. "Convair History," II, 1–3. Fleet had to persuade I. M. Laddon, then chief of the Design Branch at McCook Field, to approve these changes, which contributed to reducing the price of the PT-1 from an initial $12,500 to $6,000 in 1927. Laddon subsequently became chief engineer for Consolidated.
45. W. G. Cunningham, *Location of the Aircraft Industry*, p. 39.
46. Stout's career is narrated in his autobiography, *So Away I Went* (Indianapolis, 1951) and in H. L. Smith, *Airways* (New York, 1942), pp. 332–337.
47. Stout, *So Away I Went*, p. 140.
48. *Ibid.*, pp. 323–326.

49. Interview given to the author by Frederick L. Salathé, July 24, 1965. Mr. Salathé participated in these experiments.

50. P. W. Brooks, *The Modern Airliner* (London, 1961), pp. 18–19.

51. This part of the Ford story is fully told in A. Nevins and F. E. Hill, *Ford: Expansion and Challenge* (New York, 1957), pp. 240–247.

52. A. Fokker and B. Gould, *Flying Dutchman* (New York, 1931), p. 248.

53. J. T. Neville, "The Story of Wichita," *Aviation*, 29, Nos. 3, 5, and 6, (Sept.–Dec. 1930), pp. 166–170, 291, 295, and 353–357, is still the most complete study of the Wichita phenomenon.

54. *Ibid.*, pp. 291–92.

55. *Ibid.*, p. 294.

56. *Ibid.*, p. 353.

57. *Ibid.*, p. 170.

58. R. Rankine, "Sikorsky and his Giant Airplanes," *Popular Aviation*, 15 (Sept. 1954), p. 145.

59. I. I. Sikorsky, *The Story of the Winged-S* (London, 1939), p. 173; transcript of interview, "Engineering the Humanities," by E. E. Wilson, June 14, 1962.

60. News Release S-7513, June 6, 1963, News Bureau, The Boeing Company. No criticism of Boeing is intended here. The culprit, if there was one, was the system of awarding contracts.

61. Glenn Martin to L. D. Gardner, July 1, 1921, Martin Papers, Library of Congress, Box 1.

62. Loening, *Our Wings Grow Faster*, pp. 114–15.

63. Loening to Chief, Bureau of Aeronautics, Navy Dept., Sept. 14, 1923, Loening Papers, Library of Congress, Box 5.

64. Loening, *Our Wings Grow Faster*, p. 124.

65. The fifth plane was classified by Douglas as DWD, since it differed slightly from the other four. One of the occupants of the plane that fell into the ocean was Henry H. Ogden, then a Technical Sergeant, and later an executive of Lockheed. Mr. Ogden gave his story to the author in an interview on April 26, 1963.

66. The purpose of the bombing tests was misunderstood and misrepresented at the time and has remained so ever since. They were not undertaken to "prove" whether warships could be sunk by aerial bombardment. The object was first to test the ability of aircraft to locate and attack targets at sea, and second to determine the effect of bombing on ships' structures, particularly the mining effect on hulls of near-misses. Unfortunately what should have been a scientific experiment yielding useful knowledge was turned into an emotion-charged demonstration that simply misled public opinion with regard to what the real problems were.

67. There is one biography of Moffett: E. Arpee, *From Frigates to Flat-Tops* (Lake Forest, Ill., 1953). His work is also sympathetically treated in E. E. Wilson, *Slipstream: The Autobiography of an Aircraftsman* (New York, 1965). Nothing equivalent is available for the heads of the Army Air Service, presumably because they have been so overshadowed by Mitchell.

Chapter 2

1. President's Aircraft Board, *Aircraft in National Defense*, Senate Document No. 18, 69ᵗʰ Congress, 1ˢᵗ Session (Washington, D. C., 1925).

2. E. W. Axe and Co., "The Aviation Industry in the United States," Ms., Axe-Houghton Economic Studies, Series B, No. 6 (New York, 1938), p. 18.

3. *Ibid.*, p. 12.

4. President's Aircraft Board, *Aircraft in National Defense*, Vol. 1, p. 58.

5. *Aircraft Year Book, 1926*, pp. 314–317.

6. President's Aircraft Board, *Aircraft in National Defense*, Vol. 4, pp. 1447–1448.

7. *Ibid.*, pp. 1418–1419.

8. *Ibid.*, pp. 1438–1439.

9. I. B. Holley, *Buying Aircraft: Material Procurement for the Army Air Forces. The United States Army in World War II*, Special Studies, No. 7 (Washington, D. C., 1964), p. 13; for the legislation of 1925–1926, see G. R. Simonson, "The Demand for Aircraft and the Aircraft Industry, 1907–1958," *Journal of Economic History*, 20, No. 3 (Sept. 1960), pp. 365–366.

10. E. E. Freudenthal, *The Aviation Business: From Kitty Hawk to Wall Street* (New York, 1940), p. 83; E. E. Wilson, *Air Power for Peace* (New York, 1945), p. 33.

11. Simonson, "Demand for Aircraft," p. 360; Axe and Co., "The Aviation Industry," p. 15.

12. The history of the NACA is told in G. W. Gray, *Frontiers of Flight: The Story of NACA Research* (New York, 1948). A shorter but equally good appraisal is J. C. Hunsaker, "Forty Years of Aeronautical Research," *Smithsonian Report, 1955*, No. 4237 (Washington, D. C., 1956), pp. 241–271.

13. Gray, *Frontiers of Flight*, p. 11, quotes Dr. Karl T. Compton, then president of M.I.T., as testifying in 1941 that the NACA had been composed of men of such high character and distinction as to render it completely free from any suspicion of political influence.

14. For a discussion of this point see Hunsaker, "Forty Years of Aeronautical Research," pp. 262–263. The NACA's first appropriation was $5,000. It rose rapidly but in the interwar years never exceeded an annual total of $2 million. See Holley, *Buying Aircraft*, p. 23.

15. Hunsaker, "Forty Years of Aeronautical Research," p. 257.

16. *Ibid.*, p. 258.

17. Ibid., p. 274.

18. R. Schlaifer and S. D. Heron, *The Development of Aircraft Engines and Fuels* (Cambridge, Mass., 1950), p. 11.

19. *Ibid.*, pp. 18–20.

20. C. F. Taylor, "Aircraft Propulsion: A Review of the Evolution of Aircraft Powerplants," *Smithsonian Report, 1962*, No. 4546 (Washington, D. C., 1963), pp. 274–275. This technique was devised by S. D. Heron. It seems to have been used first in the tungsten valve designed by

Thompson Products of Cleveland, Ohio, for the Pratt and Whitney Wasp in 1926.

21. Schlaifer and Heron, *Development of Aircraft Engines*, p. 31.
22. Taylor, "Aircraft Propulsion," p. 273. Ease of maintenance was also a major reason for the adoption of the air-cooled engine for virtually all commercial aircraft. The radial air-cooled engine was a development from the rotary engines used in Europe during the First World War. They were good engines, but they had to be abandoned because of engineering and maintenance problems created by the rotation of the entire engine.
23. W. A. Shrader, *Fifty Years of Flight* (Cleveland, Ohio, 1953), p. 23. The willingness of the Navy to encourage Lawrance at this early date should be evidence that the service was not run by "battleship admirals" who discouraged the growth of aviation.
24. C. F. Taylor, "Twenty-Five Years of Engine Development," *Aviation*, 40 (Aug. 1941), p. 228. Dr. Taylor was an engineer at McCook Field in the 1920's, closely associated with S. D. Heron. Later he became Professor of Automotive Engineering and head of the Sloan Automotive Laboratory at M.I.T.
25. Schlaifer and Heron, *Development of Aircraft Engines*, pp. 62–63. See also E. E. Wilson, *Slipstream: The Autobiography of an Aircraftsman* (New York, 1965), p. 34. Mr. Wilson was then Leighton's subordinate at the Bureau of Aeronautics.
26. Taylor, "Aircraft Propulsion," p. 270.
27. Schlaifer and Heron, *Development of Aircraft Engines*, pp. 18–19.
28. Wilson, *Slipstream*, p. 51; H. L. Smith, *Airways* (New York, 1942), p. 133.
29. The Niles Tool Company took $750,000 of Pratt and Whitney preferred stock in payment of its loans. These facts were clear on the record. Yet nine years later Alger Hiss, as counsel for the Nye Committee on the Munitions Industry, could state, and have the statement widely accepted, that Pratt and Whitney had made $11.5 million from the government on an investment of $1,000. See New York *Herald Tribune*, Sept. 17, 1934.
30. E. E. Wilson, *Kittyhawk to Sputnik* (Ann Arbor, Mich., 1958), Book I, pp. 56–57.
31. The best account of the development of the Wasp is H. Lippincott, "The Navy Gets an Engine," *Journal of the American Aviation Historical Society*, Vol. 6, pp. 247–258. See also Wilson, *Slipstream*, pp. 55, 72–75.
32. Wilson, *Slipstream*, p. 76; The Boeing Co., *Pedigree of Champions* (Seattle, Wash., 1963), pp. 20–22.
33. Thomas Wolfe, *Air Transportation: Traffic and Management* (New York, 1950), p. 23.
34. P. W. Brooks, *The Modern Airliner* (London, 1961), p. 43.
35. The early history of Lockheed is well summarized in Lockheed Aircraft Corp., *Of Men and Stars* (Burbank, Calif., April 1957), Ch. 2.
36. *Ibid.*, p. 16. Monocoque: "single shell." In monocoque construction the outer covering provides its own support, as compared with the framework of struts and braces required in the fabric fuselage.

37. Brooks, *The Modern Airliner*, pp. 5–7. Lockheed also claims for the Vega an engine cowling that became the basis for the NACA cowling.
38. *Ibid.*, p. 74.
39. "Fairchild Aviation Corporation," *Aero Digest*, 24, No. 1, p. 25.
40. Fairchild Engine and Airplane Corp., *Pegasus*, *19*, No. 6, p. 5.
41. The information on Ryan and the founding of the company was provided by the News Bureau, Ryan Aeronautical Company. Ryan was an Army pilot in the First World War and later flew on forest fire patrol.
42. W. G. Cunningham, *The Aircraft Industry: A Study in Industrial Location* (Los Angeles, 1951), p. 40. Ohio was second, with five firms; California was third.
43. C. L. Lawrance, *Our National Aviation Program* (New York, 1932), p. 4.
44. Convair Division, General Dynamics Corp., "Convair History," II-6, 7.
45. C. Maynard (ed.), *Flight Plan for Tomorrow: The Douglas Story. A Condensed History*, rev. ed. (Santa Monica, Calif., 1966), p. 12.
46. P. A. Dodd, *Financial Policies of the Aircraft Industry* (Philadelphia, Pa., 1933), p. 3.
47. The name "blimp" is derived from the British World War I classification for nonrigid airships: B-limp.
48. P. W. Litchfield, *Industrial Voyage* (Garden City, N.Y., 1954), p. 237.
49. Transcript of a recording by Jerome C. Hunsaker, April 1960, Aviation History Project, Oral History Research Office, Columbia University, Vol. 1, p. 76; J. C. Hunsaker, Second Annual Sight Lecture, Wings Club, May 26, 1965, transcript by courtesy of Eugene Emme, NASA Historian. The Naval Aircraft Factory was founded in 1916 to provide facilities for building larger flying boats than could be made by any existing aircraft firm. It continued through the Second World War, doing experimental work and manufacturing some naval planes.
50. R. K. Smith, *The Airships Akron and Macon* (Annapolis, Md., 1965), p. 3.
51. Litchfield, *Industrial Voyage*, p. 239.
52. J. S. Ames, Chairman, NACA, to E. Y. Mitchell, Assistant Secretary of Commerce, April 10, 1924, Bureau of Air Commerce File 711, National Archives.
53. Litchfield, *Industrial Voyage*, p. 239.
54. Smith, *Akron and Macon*, p. 18.
55. *Ibid.*, pp. 181–183. The largest dirigibles were as follows:

"Hindenburg"	7,070,000 cu. ft.
"Akron, Macon"	6,500,000 cu. ft.
"R-100, 101"	5,000,000 cu. ft.
"Graf Zeppelin"	3,700,000 cu. ft.
"Los Angeles"	2,500,000 cu. ft.

See H. Allen, *The Story of the Airship* (Akron, Ohio, 1942), p. 25.
56. Smith, *Akron and Macon*, pp. 84–89, 157.
57. This story is told in Nevil Shute Norway, *Slide Rule* (New York, 1954). Norway, better known as the novelist Nevil Shute, was an aeronautical engineer who worked for Vickers on the R-100. The R-101 was to initiate airship service between Britain and India. She crashed

in a storm near Beauvais, France. Among the dead was Lord Thompson, the British Secretary of State for Air, who had insisted on the flight being made in spite of warnings about the weather and the airworthiness of the ship.

58. Litchfield, *Industrial Voyage*, p. 249. The War and Navy Departments disagreed with Ickes but were unable to overrule him.
59. J. C. Hunsaker, Sight Lecture.
60. Hunsaker transcript, p. 81.
61. Smith, *Akron and Macon*, p. 170.

Chapter 3

1. North American Aviation, Inc., "Biography of J. H. Kindleberger" (Ms.), p. 8.
2. Data on the M-40 from Boeing News Bureau, S-2223, Oct. 6, 1952.
3. *Corporate and Legal History of United Airlines and Its Predecessors and Subsidiaries* (Chicago, 1953), p. 153.
4. For a summary of the financial arrangements of these mergers see J. B. Rae, "Financial Problems of the American Aircraft Industry, 1906–1940," *Business History Review*, 39, No. 1 (Spring 1965), pp. 107–109.
5. H. L. Smith, *Airways* (New York, 1942), pp. 136–137; F. J. Taylor, *High Horizons* (New York, 1962), p. 49.
6. Press release, Hamilton Standard Propeller Corp., January 8, 1943, Klemin Collection, Library of the University of California, Los Angeles, Box 140; *The Aircraft Industry*, Hearings before Subcommittee No. 4, Select Committee on Small Business, House of Representatives, 84ᵗʰ Congress, 2ⁿᵈ Session (Washington, D. C., 1956), Appendix 1, pp. 258–259.
7. E. E. Wilson, *Slipstream: The Autobiography of an Aircraftsman* (New York, 1965) p. 156.
8. J. T. Neville, "The Story of Wichita," p. 36. (This is a manuscript edition provided by the courtesy of the Beech Aircraft Corp.); Lockheed Aircraft Corp., *Of Men and Stars* (Burbank, Calif., June 1957), Ch. 4, p. 11.
9. L. Morris and K. Smith, *Ceiling Unlimited: The Story of American Aviation from Kitty Hawk to Supersonics* (New York, 1953), p. 278.
10. North American Aviation, Inc., "Brief History of North American Aviation, Inc., from the Date of Incorporation through December 31, 1934" (Ms.), p. 1.
11. "Curtiss-Wright Corporation," *Aero Digest*, 24, No. 4 (1941), pp. 28–29; W. A. Shrader, *Fifty Years of Flight: A Chronicle of the Aviation Industry in America 1903–1923* (Cleveland, Ohio, 1963), p. 45; G. Loening, *Our Wings Grow Faster* (Garden City, N.Y., 1935), p. 172.
12. "Brief History of North American Aviation," p. 4.
13. *Ibid.*, p. 5. North American had 19 per cent of the stock of Douglas Aircraft. Its sale in 1934 brought a profit of $1,200,000.
14. Morris and Smith, *Ceiling Unlimited*, p. 282; W. Price, "Merchant

of Speed," *Saturday Evening Post*, 221, No. 34 (Feb. 19, 1949), p. 50.

15. A. P. Sloan, *My Years with General Motors* (Garden City, N.Y., 1964), p. 362; "North American Aviation," *Aero Digest*, 24, No. 2 (Feb. 1934) p. 29.

16. D. J. Ingells, *The Plane that Changed the World* (Fallbrook, Calif., 1966), p. 11.

17. Sloan, *My Years with General Motors*, p. 364. Fokker for a while was in charge of European sales for Douglas Aircraft.

18. *Ibid.*, p. 364; "Brief History of North American Aviation," p. 13.

19. Smith, *Airways*, p. 148.

20. Morris and Smith, *Ceiling Unlimited*, p. 277.

21. Smith, *Airways*, pp. 147–148.

22. Fairchild Engine and Airplane Corp., *Pegasus*, 19, No. 6, p. 9.

23. J. B. Rae, *American Automobile Manufacturers* (Philadelphia, 1959), p. 183; there is a good review of the early history of Stinson in the Elizabeth Hiatt Gregory Collection, Library of the University of California, Los Angeles, Box 1, Folder 4.

24. "Fairchild Aviation Corporation," *Aero Digest*, 24, No. 1 (Jan. 1934), p. 25.

25. J. Niven, C. Canby, and V. Welsh (eds.), *Dynamic America: A History of General Dynamics Corporation* (New York, 1958), p. 245.

26. L. C. Dibble, "The Detroit Aircraft Corporation," *Automotive Industries*, 40 (June 15, 1929), p. 921.

27. Lockheed Aircraft Corp., *Of Men and Stars* (May, 1957), Ch. 3, p. 7.

28. Dibble, "Detroit Aircraft Corporation," p. 920.

29. P. A. Dodd, *Financial Policies of the Aircraft Industry* (Philadelphia, Pa., 1933), p. 4.

30. Neville, "Story of Wichita," p. 30.

31. A. F. Haiduck, "Bellanca Aircraft Corporation," *Aeronautical Engineering Review*, 1 (Nov. 1942), p. 43.

32. *Aviation and Aeronautical Engineering*, 13, p. 318.

33. G. R. Simonson, "The Demand for Aircraft and the Aircraft Industry," *Journal of Economic History*, 20, No. 3 (Sept. 1960), p. 336.

34. Of 286 aircraft manufacturers in 1929, only seven had any substantial government business and these were also the principal builders of transport planes. The others were all aiming for the small-plane market. See Simonson, "Demand for Aircraft" p. 367.

35. Lockheed Aircraft Corp., *Of Men and Stars*, Ch. 3, p. 14; Gross Papers, Manuscripts Division, Library of Congress, Box 4, Lockheed Aircraft Co. analysis, March 31, 1932.

36. Mr. Squier's part in the affairs of Lockheed was related by him to the author on July 29, 1962. A transcript of this interview may be found in the Honnold Library of The Claremont Colleges, in the collection made by the Oral History Program of the Claremont Graduate School.

37. Lockheed Aircraft Corp., *Of Men and Stars*, Ch. 1, p. 4.

38. "Chronology of World, U.S. Aircraft Industry, and North American Aviation, Inc., Events Prior to World War II," North American Aviation Staff Office, Dept. 191, May 19, 1959.

39. "Brief History of North American Aviation," p. 17.

40. *Ibid.*, p. 7.

41. This information comes from an interview given by Mr. Wilson to the author, Aug. 14, 1962.

42. E. E. Wilson, *From Kitty Hawk to Sputnik* (Ann Arbor, Mich., 1958) Book II, p. 219.

43. The best analysis is Smith, *Airways*, Chs. 17–21; a more recent study is C. J. Kelly, Jr., *The Sky's the Limit* (New York, 1963), pp. 69–96.

44. Privately operated mail routes were fully restored by May 8, 1934.

45. Simonson, "Demand for Aircraft," p. 369.

46. Taylor, *High Horizons*, p. 97.

47. "Brief History of North American Aviation," p. 17. Information on North American was given in a recorded interview by John L. Atwood, April 2, 1964. Transcript may be found in the Honnold Library of The Claremont Colleges.

48. North American Aviation, Inc., "Kindelberger Biography."

49. *Stinson Plane News*, 6, No. 6, in Gregory Collection, Box 1, Folder 4.

50. A. M. Schlesinger, Jr., *The Coming of the New Deal* (Boston, Mass., 1959), Ch. 28.

51. This is the purpose of E. E. Freudenthal's *The Aviation Business: From Kitty Hawk to Wall Street* (New York, 1940). The book is an excellent collection of data, but it is a definite plea for nationalization.

52. Wilson, *Kitty Hawk to Sputnik*, Book II, p. 254.

53. R. E. G. Davies, *A History of the World's Airlines* (London, 1964), p. 251.

54. H. Mansfield, *Vision* (New York, 1956), p. 106; Taylor, *High Horizons*, p. 83.

55. Smith, *Airways*, pp. 252–253. To celebrate the restoration of private services Frye broke his own record, flying a Northrop Gamma research plane with mail from Los Angeles to Newark in eleven and one-half hours on May 8, 1934.

Chapter 4

1. J. K. Northrop, "Aviation History 1903–1960," address before the National Air Council, Washington, D. C., Nov. 3, 1948, p. 8.

2. P. W. Brooks, *The Modern Airliner* (London, 1961), p. 73.

3. Northrop, "Aviation History," p. 8. Northrop states that as of 1948 lift had been doubled and drag reduced by three-fourths since the days of the Wrights. Since no radical change in airframe design had occurred since 1933, his figures may be taken as reasonably accurate for that date.

4. N. W. Hoff, "Thin Shells in Aerospace Structures," *Aeronautics and Astronautics*, 5, No. 2 (Feb. 1967), p. 27.

5. Brooks, *The Modern Airliner*, p. 72.

6. I. B. Holley, *Buying Aircraft: Material Procurement for the Army Air Forces. The United States Army in World War II*, Special Studies, No. 7 (Washington, D. C., 1964), p. 13.

7. W. F. Craven and J. L. Cate, *The Army Air Forces in World War II*, Vol. 6, *Men and Planes* (Chicago, 1955), p. 177.

8. J. C. Hunsaker, "Forty Years of Aeronautical Research," *Smithsonian Report, 1955,* No. 4237 (Washington, D. C., 1956), p. 262.

9. Brooks, *The Modern Airliner*, p. 72.

10. Holley, *Buying Aircraft*, p. 21 n.

11. J. Niven, C. Canby, and V. Welsh (eds.), *Dynamic America: A History of General Dynamics Corporation* (New York, 1958), p. 146.

12. The Boeing Co., *Pedigree of Champions* (Seattle, Wash., 1963), p. 31. The fuselages of these all-metal planes were actually semi-monocoque, with the outer skin stiffened by reinforcing frames. See Hoff, "Thin Shells in Aerospace Structures," p. 28.

13. E. E. Wilson, *From Kitty Hawk to Sputnik* (Ann Arbor, Mich., 1958), Book II, pp. 209–210.

14. David L. Bruce, report on "Universal Propeller" built by Paragon Engines, Inc.; may be found in Air Force Museum, Wright-Patterson Air Force Base. This propeller was tested on Nov. 29, 1926, at McCook Field.

15. "Boeing Aircraft Co., 25th Anniversary," *Aero Digest, 39,* No. 1 (July 1941), p. 144; Brooks, *The Modern Airliner*, p. 78.

16. Wilson, *Kitty Hawk to Sputnik*, Book II, pp. 295–298.

17. For specifications of these planes see The Boeing Co., *Pedigree of Champions*, pp. 32–36.

18. *Ibid.*, p. 35.

19. F. J. Taylor, *High Horizons* (New York, 1962), p. 75.

20. See The Boeing Co., *Pedigree of Champions*, p. 32, and "Historical Planes of the Martin Company," Release 910-L, in Air Force Museum, Wright-Patterson Air Force Base.

21. *The Martin Company*, pamphlet (Baltimore, Md., 1960).

22. W. G. Cunningham, *The Aircraft Industry: A Study in Industrial Location* (Los Angeles, 1951), p. 22.

23. Holley, *Buying Aircraft*, p. 37.

24. See Douglas Aircraft Co., Inc., Service Information Summary, *Fiftieth Anniversary of Naval Aviation* (El Segundo, Calif., 1962), pp. 9, 135.

25. Lockheed Aircraft Corp., *Of Men and Stars* (Burbank, Calif.), Ch. 1, p. 4; Ch. 4, p. 12.

26. *Ibid.*, Ch. 1, p. 8.

27. *Ibid.*, Ch. 1, p. 5; Ch. 4, p. 7. From 1933 to 1937 Brashears sold $1.5 million of Lockheed stock.

28. Gregory Collection, University of California, Los Angeles, Box 1, Folder 3, description of Lockheed Electra, March 2, 1936.

29. Lockheed Aircraft Corp., *Of Men and Stars*, Ch. 1, p. 11.

30. *Ibid.*, Chapter 4, p. 7.

31. Holley, *Buying Aircraft*, p. 21 n.

32. C. Maynard (ed.), *Flight Plan for Tomorrow: The Douglas Story. A Condensed History*, rev. ed. (Santa Monica, Calif., 1966), pp. 12–13.

33. *Ibid.*, p. 21.

34. The information on this credit was given in a recorded interview on

Oct. 10, 1963, by Richard Millar, an investment banker who had helped with the Douglas stock issue and then served for five years as chairman of the Finance Committee of Douglas Aircraft.

35. Taylor, *High Horizons*, p. 76.
36. R. Hubler, *Big Eight: The Biography of an Airplane* (New York, 1960), pp. 34–35; Maynard, *Flight Plan for Tomorrow*, p. 19; recorded interview by Arthur E. Raymond, Feb. 17, 1964.
37. The information on the Douglas engineering staff is from the Arthur E. Raymond transcript, Honnold Library, The Claremont Colleges, pp. 5 and 6.
38. Richard Millar transcript, Honnold Library, The Claremont Colleges, p. 5.
39. "Flutter": an oscillation of definite period but unstable character, "Nomenclature for Aeronautics," *Report No. 474*, NACA (Washington, D. C., 1936), p. 15. Wing flutter was a major problem in the early days of designing internally braced metal wings.
40. Brooks, *The Modern Airliner*, p. 81. The wing flaps provide greater lift at the cost of higher drag. They permit low-speed take-off and landing.
41. Raymond transcript, p. 11; Hubler, *Big Eight*, p. 37.
42. Maynard, *Flight Plan for Tomorrow*, p. 22.
43. *Ibid.*, p. 20.
44. Hubler, *Big Eight*, p. 45.
45. Maynard, *Flight Plan for Tomorrow*, p. 236.
46. C. J. McCarthy, "Naval Aircraft Design in the Mid-1930's," in Doyce B. Nunis, Jr. (ed.), "Recollections of the Early History of Naval Aviation: A Session in Oral History," *Technology and Culture*, 4, No. 2, (Spring 1963), p. 172.
47. Douglas Aircraft Co., Inc., *Fifty Years of Naval Aviation*, p. 135.
48. *Ibid.*, p. 76; R. Hill, "The Brewster Aeronautical Corporation," *Aeronautical Engineering Review*, 1 (Nov. 1942), p. 47.
49. Taylor, *High Horizons*, pp. 76–77.
50. H. Hagedorn, "Managerial Implications of a Technological Revolution. How the British Aircraft Industry Accommodated to the Metal Monoplane," Ms. in Royal Aeronautical Society (London, 1956).
51. M. M. Postan, D. Hay, and J. D. Scott, *Design and Development of Weapons*, History of the Second World War, United Kingdom Civil Series (London, 1964), p. 33.
52. There was another NACA study of jet propulsion at this time, made at the request of the aircraft industry, but the result was essentially a repetition of the Buckingham Report of 1923. Higher speeds could be contemplated, but they were still not high enough to make the jet engine acceptable. See Hunsaker, *Forty Years of Aeronautical Research*, p. 265.
53. Transcript of interview with Frank Collbohm, April 1960, Aviation Project, Vol. 2, Oral History Research Office, Columbia University.
54. Postan, Hay, and Scott, *Design and Development of Weapons*, p. 104.
55. Taylor, *High Horizons*, pp. 60–61.

Chapter 5

1. I. B. Holley, *Buying Aircraft: Material Procurement for the Army Air Forces. The United States Army in World War II*, Special Studies, No. 7 (Washington, D. C., 1964), pp. 33–34.

2. Between 1934 and 1939 the aircraft industry spent $44,000,000; W. F. Craven and J. L. Cate, *The Army Air Forces in World War II*, Vol. 6, *Men and Planes* (Chicago, 1955), p. 181.

3. This aspect of the aircraft business was pointed out by Frank R. Collbohm, president of the RAND Corporation, in an interview on June 6, 1961. He expressed the opinion that the fixed-price contract made for better engineering; it cost too much to make mistakes.

4. E. W. Axe and Co., "The Aviation Industry in the United States" (Ms.), Axe-Houghton Economic Studies, Series B, No. 6 (New York, 1938), p. 101.

5. Holley, *Buying Aircraft*, p. 17.

6. G. R. Simonson, "The Demand for Aircraft, and the Aircraft Industry," *Journal of Economic History*, 20, No. 3, (Sept. 1960), p. 370; *Aviation Facts and Figures, 1958*, p. 113. Total exports climbed sharply after 1937, but this may be taken as the last year before the pressure of European military orders affected the figures.

7. "Brief History of North American Aviation," p. 19.

8. C. J. McCarthy, "Naval Aircraft Design in the Mid-1930's," *Technology and Culture*, 4, No. 2, p. 169.

9. C. L. Lawrance, *Our National Aviation Program*, (New York, 1932), p. 2. The actual total was 2,800: 812 military and 1,988 civilian.

10. *Ibid.*, p. 3.

11. *Ibid.*, p. 13.

12. Holley, *Buying Aircraft*, p. 10.

13. *Ibid.*, p. 11. This figure is actually for 1938 but it does not change the main point.

14. *Ibid.*, p. 17; Axe and Co., "The Aviation Industry," p. 88.

15. *Aviation Facts and Figures, 1956*, p. 7; J. B. Rae, *The American Automobile* (Chicago, 1965), p. 238.

16. Axe and Co., "The Aviation Industry," p. 2.

17. *Aviation Facts and Figures, 1956*, p. 12.

18. G. L. Martin, "The Development of Aircraft Manufacture," *Aviation Engineering*, 5, Dec. 1931, p. 30.

19. *Ibid.*, pp. 24 and 29. Even the form in which the metal was used had to be considered in plant design. Duralumin was used in sheet form because inventory studies showed this to be most economical.

20. E. E. Wilson, *Air Power for Peace* (New York, 1945), pp. 75–76.

21. Holley, *Buying Aircraft*, p. 31.

22. McCarthy, "Naval Aircraft Design in the Mid-1930's," p. 171.

23. President's Air Policy Commission, *Survival in the Air Age: A Report* (Washington, D. C., 1948), p. 50. This document is ordinarily referred to as the Finletter Report.

24. J. S. Day, *Subcontracting in the Airframe Industry* (Cambridge, Mass., 1956), p. 18.

25. *Ibid.*, p. 5.
26. W. G. Cunningham, *The Aircraft Industry: A Study in Industrial Location* (Los Angeles, 1951), p. 21.
27. *Aviation Facts and Figures, 1958*, p. 53.
28. *Ibid.*, p. 56.
29. M. Derber and E. Young, *Labor and the New Deal* (Madison, Wis., 1957), p. 23.
30. Donald W. Douglas transcript, Oral History Research Office, Columbia University.
31. Lockheed Aircraft Corp., *Of Men and Stars* (Burbank, Calif.), Ch. 5, p. 7.
32. Holley, *Buying Aircraft*, p. 21. Most of the rest of the military contracts went to Consolidated, Chance Vought, Grumman, and Martin. The listing of the leaders is based on numbers of aircraft delivered, but most of North American's production at this time consisted of trainers.
33. There was not even an assurance of retaining leadership. Curtiss-Wright appears among the first four manufacturers of military aircraft in the 1930's. A decade later it was out of the airframe business altogether and had lost its position as Pratt and Whitney's principal rival in the engine field.
34. M. I. Peale, "The Story of Republic Aviation," courtesy of Republic Aviation Corporation. This is a reprint of a series of articles published in the *Christian Science Monitor* (Feb. 1959).
35. This account of Bell's career comes from the following sources: a recorded interview with Bell, Sept. 23, 1951, Aviation Project, No. 388, Vol. 7, Oral History Research Office, Columbia University; Bell Aerosystems Company, *Rendezvous, 4*, No. 4; *Bell Aircraft News—20th Anniversary Edition*, July 10, 1955.
36. *Bell Aircraft News*, July 10, 1955, p. 2.
37. Production of civil aircraft, including commercial transports, rose steadily from 803 in 1932 to 3,661 in 1939 (*Aviation Facts and Figures, 1956*, pp. 6–7). Since the number of transports in service actually declined somewhat during this period, because of the introduction of bigger and faster models, the increase in units produced was in the field of small private planes.
38. Simonson, "Demand for Aircraft," p. 371.
39. CAA File 821.1 (Bureau of Air Commerce), Aug. 7, 1935, National Archives. The functions of the Bureau were transferred to the Civil Aeronautics Authority by the Civil Aeronautics Act of 1938.
40. *Ibid.*, R. E. Gross to Eugene L. Vidal, Chief, Bureau of Air Commerce, May 31, 1935.
41. Holley, *Buying Aircraft*, p. 575.
42. "Twenty-Five Years of Progress," *The Beechcrafter, 10*, No. 5 (June 1957), p. 4.
43. Information on Piper supplied by Public Relations Department, Piper Aircraft Corp.
44. A. P. Sloan, Jr., *My Years with General Motors* (Garden City, N.Y., 1964), p. 369.
45. R. Schlaifer and S. D. Heron, *The Development of Aircraft Engines*

and Fuels (Cambridge, Mass., 1950), p. 259. Packard at its own expense developed an air-cooled diesel, but it was not successful.

46. *Ibid.*, p. 271.

47. For a good summary, see C. J. Kelly, Jr., *The Sky's the Limit* (New York, 1963), Ch. XII.

48. I. I. Sikorsky, *The Story of the Winged-S* (London, 1939), pp. 202–203.

49. *Ibid.*, p. 210.

50. *Ibid.*, p. 207.

51. *Ibid.* Improved versions, S-42A and S-43, had four Pratt and Whitney 750 h.p. Hornet engines and a top speed of 194 m.p.h. They carried 32 passengers.

52. E. E. Wilson interview, June 14, 1962.

53. Convair Division, General Dynamics Corp., "Convair History," III-7.

54. *Ibid.*, IV-10.

55. *Ibid.*, III-2,3.

56. *Ibid.*, III-3.

57. *Ibid.*, III-4. Consolidated engineers claimed that Martin underbid them by half a million on the order and lost a million. They were probably consoling themselves. The order was for nine planes, and a loss of $1 million on an order this size seems unlikely.

58. *Ibid.*, V-1.

59. *Ibid.*, the loss was $177,449 in 1931 and $318,947 in 1932.

60. *Ibid.*, III-3.

61. J. Niven, C. Canby, and V. Welsh (eds.), *Dynamic America: A History of General Dynamics Corporation* (New York, 1958), p. 254.

62. Cunningham, *Location of the Aircraft Industry*, p. 43.

63. "Convair History," VI-2.

64. R. E. G. Davies, *A History of the World's Airlines* (London, 1964), p. 148. The first flight carried mail only. Passenger service began in 1936.

65. Glenn Martin to G. H. Humpstone, New York City, Dec. 28, 1937, Martin Papers, Library of Congress, Box 3. The PBM was an improvement on but generally similar to the PBY. Its most conspicuous difference was that it had no wing struts.

66. Martin to Charles P. Crane, Indio, Calif., Dec. 28, 1938, Martin Papers, Library of Congress, Box 3.

67. Description in Elizabeth Hiatt Gregory Collection, University of California, Los Angeles, Box 4, Folder 5.

68. The Boeing Co., *Pedigree of Champions* (Seattle, Wash., 1963), p. 43. The second series, 314A, had a cruising speed of 184 m.p.h.

69. H. Mansfield, *Vision* (New York, 1956), pp. 146–149.

70. Tests made in 1937 showed an increase in speed of over 25 per cent in flights above 25,000 feet. See Ms. by S. L. Chapin and T. Smith, "A History of Pressurized Flight" (1962), 12-5.

71. *Ibid.*, 14-2,3.

72. *Ibid.*, 18-4.

73. *Ibid.*, 12-15.

74. Douglas Aircraft Co., Inc., *Annual Report*, 1952, p. 11. The DC-4 came on the scene a little late because Douglas' first four-motored transport

design, confusingly numbered DC-4E, proved unsatisfactory. Five airlines (American, Eastern, Pan American, TWA, and United) put up $500,000 to finance this design, and its failure sent TWA and Pan American to Boeing. To add to the confusion, there was also a twin-engined DC-5 before the DC-4. It was a high-wing monoplane, and only twelve were built.

75. Chapin and Smith, "History of Pressurized Flight," 17-12.
76. For the story of Garrett and AiResearch see S. L. Chapin, "Garrett and Pressurized Flight: A Business Built on Thin Air," *Pacific Historical Review*, 35, No. 3 (Aug. 1966), pp. 329–343.
77. Mansfield, *Vision*, pp. 81–83. The term "battleship of the air" was of course a misnomer since the strategic and tactical functions of the battleship and the big bomber were entirely different.
78. Craven and Cate, *Men and Planes*, p. 202.
79. Mansfield, *Vision*, pp. 116–119.
80. Craven and Cate, *Men and Planes*, p. 203. The B-17 was not the first four-engined bomber. This distinction clearly belongs to the planes built by Sikorsky for Russia in the First World War.
81. *Ibid.*, p. 202.
82. R. G. Hubler, *Big Eight: The Biography of an Airplane* (New York, 1960), p. 147.
83. Craven and Cate, *Men and Planes*, p. 203.
84. Mansfield, *Vision*, p. 158.
85. Press release from Harold Mansfield, Boeing Aircraft Co., May 1940, Klemin Collection, University of California, Los Angeles, Box 81. The claim to priority is corroborated by Chapin and Smith, "History of Pressurized Flight," 17-1.
86. Chapin and Smith, "History of Pressurized Flight," 15-2.
87. Lockheed Aircraft Corp., *Of Men and Stars*, Ch. 5, p. 2; P. W. Brooks, *The Modern Airliner* (London, 1961), p. 84.
88. Bernice K. Platt, "The Saga of Vega," *Aircraftsman*, 8, pp. 5–7.
89. Brooks, *The Modern Airliner*, p. 101.
90. Chapin and Smith, "History of Pressurized Flight," 18–6.
91. Mansfield, *Vision*, p. 150.
92. Lockheed Aircraft Corp., *Of Men and Stars*, Ch. 5, p. 3.
93. "Convair History," VI-6.
94. Pratt and Whitney Aircraft Division, United Aircraft Corp., *The Pratt and Whitney Aircraft Story*, 2nd ed. (Hartford, Conn., 1952), p. 127.
95. Craven and Cate, *Men and Planes*, p. 187.
96. E. E. Wilson, *From Kitty Hawk to Sputnik* (Ann Arbor, Mich., 1958), Book II, pp. 287–288.

Chapter 6

1. W. F. Craven and J. L. Cate, *The Army Air Forces in World War II*, Vol. 6., *Men and Planes* (Chicago, 1955), p. 183.
2. *Ibid.*, p. 184.
3. *Ibid.*, p. 177; I. B. Holley, *Buying Aircraft: Material Procurement for*

the Army Air Forces. The United States Army in World War II, Special Studies, No. 7 (Washington, D. C., 1964), p. 156. Chapter VII of *Buying Aircraft* provides a valuable factual account and appraisal of industrial mobilization planning.

4. Craven and Cate, *Men and Planes,* p. 177.
5. H. Mansfield, *Vision* (New York, 1956), p. 153; The Boeing Co., *Pedigree of Champions* (Seattle, Wash., 1963), p. 49; S. L. Chapin and T. Smith, "A History of Pressurized Flight," Ms. (1962), 18-7.
6. Holley, *Buying Aircraft,* p. 77.
7. Craven and Cate, *Men and Planes,* p. 186.
8. Northrop Corp., *Northrop Highlights* (Beverly Hills, Calif., n.d.).
9. McDonnell Aircraft Corp., *McDonnell Airscoop* (July 1959).
10. Craven and Cate, *Men and Planes,* p. 191.
11. *Ibid.* p. 301.
12. Lockheed Aircraft Corp., *Of Men and Stars* (Burbank, Calif.) Ch. 5, p. 3.
13. *Ibid.,* p. 6.
14. North American Aviation, Inc., "Brief History of Operations Immediately Prior to and During World War II" (Ms.); "Biography of J. H. Kindelberger" (Ms.), n.d., pp. 18–19.
15. F. G. Swanborough, *United States Military Aircraft since 1909* (London and New York, 1963), pp. 344, 348–349; John L. Atwood transcript, Honnold Library, The Claremont Colleges, p. 6.
16. North American Aviation, Inc., Staff Office, "History of the Aviation Industry," Ms. (1958, rev. 1959).
17. North American Aviation, "Brief History, 1935–45," pp. 14–15.
18. This sketch of Vultee is taken from Convair Division, General Dynamics Corp., "Convair History," VII-5.
19. *Ibid.,* VII-6.
20. *Ibid.,* VII-7.
21. *Ibid.,* VII-8. Y designated a model bought for service testing.
22. Pratt and Whitney Aircraft Division, United Aircraft Corp., *Pratt and Whitney Aircraft Story,* 2nd ed. (Hartford, Conn., 1952), p. 127.
23. Craven and Cate, *Men and Planes,* p. 178.
24. *Ibid.,* p. 300.
25. E. E. Wilson, *From Kitty Hawk to Sputnik* (Ann Arbor, Mich., 1958), Book II, p. 313; *Pratt and Whitney Aircraft Story,* p. 199.
26. *Aviation Facts and Figures, 1958,* p. 7.
27. *Ibid.,* p. 10. The figure for civil aircraft is estimated.
28. *Ibid.,* p. 53; Craven and Cate, *Men and Planes,* p. 187.
29. Craven and Cate, *Men and Planes,* p. 189. This was an overestimate. It assumed two and one-half shifts and freezing of designs to a degree that experience showed to be impractical.
30. *Ibid.,* p. 188; W. G. Cunningham, *The Aircraft Industry: A Study in Industrial Location* (Los Angeles, 1951), p. 1251, has 8.8 per cent of the airframe and 10.8 per cent of the engine capacity within the defense zone (200 miles inland) in 1940. The discrepancy indicates that increased capacity was secured at first by additions to existing plant, without change of location.

31. Craven and Cate, *Men and Planes*, p. 174.
32. Swanborough, *U.S. Military Aircraft*, p. 186.
33. Douglas Aircraft Co., Inc., *Fiftieth Anniversary of Naval Aviation* (El Segundo, Calif., 1962), p. 76.
34. Craven and Cate, *Men and Planes*, p. 263.
35. Mansfield, *Vision*, pp. 152–154.
36. "Convair History," VI-6,7. Experimental contracts of this kind could be negotiated without competitive bidding, and this normally gave the selected firm a decisive advantage in getting the production contract. For the complexities of military procurement see Holley, *Buying Aircraft*, Ch. VI.
37. "Convair History," VI-8.
38. C. Maynard (ed.), *Flight Plan for Tomorrow: The Douglas Story. A Condensed History*, rev. ed. (Santa Monica, Calif., 1966), p. 42.
39. Swanborough, *U.S. Military Aircraft*, pp. 352–353.
40. *Ibid.*, p. 334.
41. *Bell Aircraft News*, July 10, 1955, p. 4.
42. Lockheed Aircraft Corp., *Of Men and Stars*, Ch. 5, p. 8.
43. The twin fuselage was adopted because tests showed that effective control required the rudders to be directly behind the engines.
44. Lockheed Aircraft Corp., *Of Men and Stars*, Ch. 4, p. 7.
45. *Ibid.*, Ch. 5, p. 12; Transcript of interview with H. H. Ogden, April 26, 1963, Honnold Library, The Claremont Colleges.
46. Swanborough, *U.S. Military Aircraft*, p. 406; Republic Aviation Corp., "Company History" (Farmingdale, N.Y., n.d.), pp. 13–14.
47. This account of the origin of the P-51 is in the interview with J. L. Atwood, April 2, 1964, Honnold Library, The Claremont Colleges.
48. There is a very lucid analysis of the origins of the 50,000-plane program in Holley, *Buying Aircraft*, pp. 209–228.
49. *Ibid.*, p. 228.
50. Craven and Cate, *Men and Planes*, p. 265.
51. T. P. Wright, "50,000 Planes a Year," *Aviation*, 39, No. 7, p. 34. The author was vice-president of engineering, Curtiss-Wright Corporation.
52. *Ibid.*, p. 98. See also Cunningham, *Location of the Aircraft Industry*, p. 76.
53. Craven and Cate, *Men and Planes*, p. 303.
54. North American Aviation, "Brief History, 1935–45," pp. 14–15.
55. *Ibid.*, p. 43.
56. Cunningham, *Location of the Aircraft Industry*, p. 82.
57. Lockheed Aircraft Corp., *Of Men and Stars*, Ch. 5, p. 17.
58. Mansfield, *Vision*, p. 163.
59. *Ibid.*, pp. 167–168.
60. W. F. Craven and J. L. Cate, *The Army Air Forces in World War II*, Vol. 5, *The Pacific-Matterhorn to Nagasaki* (Chicago, 1953), p. 6.
61. Mansfield, *Vision*, p. 172.
62. Craven and Cate, *Matterhorn to Nagasaki*, p. 7.
63. Craven and Cate, *Men and Planes*, pp. 210–211.
64. *Aviation Facts and Figures, 1958*, p. 7.
65. The 50,000 figure would have been attained in 1942, except that the

increasing emphasis on big bombers resulted in fewer units than had originally been planned but greater total airframe weight.

66. Craven and Cate, *Men and Planes,* p. 310.

Chapter 7

1. I. B. Holley, *Buying Aircraft: Material Procurement for the Army Air Forces. The United States Army in World War II,* Special Studies, No. 7 (Washington, D. C., 1964), p. 293 n.
2. W. F. Craven and J. L. Cate, *The Army Air Forces in World War II,* Vol. 6, *Men and Planes* (Chicago, 1955), p. 306. For a detailed discussion of military procurement policies at this time and especially the question of fixed-price vs. negotiated contracts, see R. E. Smith, *The Army and Economic Mobilization. The U.S. Army in World War II. The War Department,* Vol. 4, Pt. 5 (Washington, D. C., 1959), Chs. XI, XII.
3. Smith, *The Army and Economic Mobilization,* p. 292.
4. North American Aviation, Inc., "Brief History of Operations Immediately Prior to and During World War II," p. 29.
5. For an analysis of these methods see W. G. Cunningham, *The Aircraft Industry: A Study in Industrial Location* (Los Angeles, 1951), pp. 78–97, and G. R. Simonson, "Demand for Aircraft and the Aircraft Industry," *Journal of Economic History,* 20, No. 3 (Sept. 1960), pp. 372–374.
6. J. S. Day, *Subcontracting in the Airframe Industry* (Cambridge, Mass., 1956), p. 18.
7. *Ibid.,* p. 16; Simonson, "Demand for Aircraft," p. 373.
8. W. G. Cunningham, *Location of the Aircraft Industry,* p. 77.
9. Holley, *Buying Aircraft,* p. 297. Dr. Holley points out that the 20 per cent depreciation provision was not an unlimited boon to the manufacturers. A prolonged emergency would leave them to meet a full tax burden with no write-off.
10. *Ibid.,* p. 298; Craven and Cate, *Men and Planes,* p. 308; W. G. Cunningham, *Location of the Aircraft Industry,* p. 77.
11. Holley, *Buying Aircraft,* p. 299.
12. Craven and Cate, *Men and Planes,* p. 308.
13. Smith, *The Army and Economic Mobilization,* p. 263.
14. Simonson, "Demand for Aircraft," p. 373.
15. Lockheed Aircraft Corp., *Of Men and Stars* (Burbank, Calif., July 1957), Ch. 5, p. 16.
16. This information of the expansion of North American is taken from North American Aviation, "Brief History, 1933–1945." pp. 34 ff.
17. John L. Atwood transcript, Honnold Library, The Claremont Colleges, p. 11.
18. *Aviation Facts and Figures, 1958,* p. 54.
19. Convair Division, General Dynamics Corp., "Convair History," VII-4.
20. Richard Millar transcript, Honnold Library, The Claremont Colleges, p. 3.
21. *Ibid.,* p. 7; "Convair History," VII-9.

22. "Convair History," VII-7.
23. Millar transcript, p. 7.
24. "Convair History," VII-10. This Downey factory later became the Space Division of North American.
25. *Ibid.*, VI-8.
26. *Ibid.*, VI-11.
27. *Ibid.*, VI-12. Fleet claimed that in 1941 his income was $1,700,000, of which the Federal government took 93 per cent and the State of California 6 per cent, leaving him $17,000 to live on. If this was literally true, he should have fired his tax accountant. The author tried several times to get Mr. Fleet's version of his career with Consolidated but never received any response.
28. *Ibid.*, VI-13, VII-11.
29. Millar transcript, p. 10.
30. "Convair History," VIII-6.
31. Motor vehicle production for 1940 was 4,472,286, the highest since 1929.
32. E. E. Wilson, *From Kitty Hawk to Sputnik* (Ann Arbor, Mich., 1958), Book II, pp. 328–329.
33. A. Nevins and F. E. Hill, *Ford: Decline and Rebirth, 1933–1962* (New York, 1962), pp. 175–176.
34. Pratt and Whitney Aircraft Division, United Aircraft Corp., *Pratt and Whitney Aircraft Story*, 2nd ed. (Hartford, Conn., 1952), pp. 132–133.
35. Nevins and Hill, *Ford: Decline and Rebirth*, p. 179.
36. *Ibid.*, p. 178.
37. *Pratt and Whitney Aircraft Story*, p. 132.
38. Transcript of interview with H. Mansfield Horner, president of United Aircraft, May 1960, Aviation Project, Oral History Research Office, Columbia University.
39. Nevins and Hill, *Ford: Decline and Rebirth*, p. 174.
40. Craven and Cate, *Men and Planes*, p. 320.
41. For appraisals of the Reuther plan see Craven and Cate, *Men and Planes*, pp. 322–324, and Holley, *Buying Aircraft*, pp. 310–313.
42. The drama of the Battle of Britain created a strong impression of an acute shortage of fighter planes. Actually the supply of trained pilots gave the British more concern than the supply of planes.
43. *Freedom's Arsenal: The Story of the Automotive Council for War Production* (Detroit, Mich., 1950), p. 2.
44. *Ibid.*, pp. 8, 9.
45. *Ibid.*, p. 11.
46. *Ibid.*, p. 39.
47. Holley, *Buying Aircraft*, p. 308. The original plan was to have only two central assembly plants, but it became evident that they would have to be so big as to strain the resources of any community they were placed in.
48. Nevins and Hill, *Ford: Decline and Rebirth*, p. 177.
49. C. E. Sorensen, *My Forty Years with Ford* (New York, 1956), p. 279.
50. *Ibid.*
51. *Ibid.*, p. 280.

52. Nevins and Hill, *Ford: Decline and Rebirth,* pp. 185–186.
53. Craven and Cate, *Men and Planes,* p. 313. Nevins and Hill, *Ford: Decline and Rebirth,* p. 188, give the schedule established in Sept. 1941, as 75 "fly-aways" and 150 "knock-downs." The discrepancy is unimportant because production schedules were in constant flux.
54. Nevins and Hill, *Ford: Decline and Rebirth,* pp. 190, 192. The authors defend the Ford position by arguing that Consolidated had a highly trained and skilled work force while Ford had to recruit unskilled labor for Willow Run. Since Consolidated's payroll rose from 3,000 early in 1940 to 24,000 in the fall of 1941 ("Convair History," VI-10), this argument seems dubious.
55. Sorensen, *My Forty Years with Ford,* p. 285.
56. *Ibid.,* p. 289.
57. Craven and Cate, *Men and Planes,* p. 325.
58. Holley, *Buying Aircraft,* p. 316.
59. *Freedom's Arsenal,* p. 61.
60. Craven and Cate, *Men and Planes,* p. 352. The production of civilian planes was 6,785 in 1940 and 6,844 in 1941.
61. *Freedom's Arsenal,* p. 41.
62. Holley, *Buying Aircraft,* p. 325.
63. *Ibid.,* p. 326.
64. The first educational orders given to the automobile industry to familiarize it with aircraft manufacture were placed with Ford, Chrysler, and Hudson in 1941. Craven and Cate, *Men and Planes,* p. 301.

Chapter 8

1. Actual production was 47,675 in 1942 and 85,433 in 1943: *Aviation Facts and Figures, 1958,* p. 6.
2. The totals were 275.8 million pounds in 1942 and 654.2 million pounds in 1943 (*Ibid.,* p. 10). The weight of the average airframe rose from 4,520 pounds in 1942 to 8,900 pounds in 1943 (I. B. Holley, *Buying Aircraft: Material Procurement for the Army Air Forces. The United States Army in World War II,* Special Studies, No. 7, (Washington, D. C., 1964), p. 243). From these figures it is evident that measuring production by the number of units alone was not only meaningless but misleading.
3. W. F. Craven and J. L. Cate, *The Army Air Forces in World War II,* Vol. 6, *Men and Planes* (Chicago, 1955), pp. 289–290.
4. *Bell Aircraft News,* July 10, 1955, p. 4.
5. Craven and Cate, *Men and Planes,* p. 315.
6. Holley, *Buying Aircraft,* p. 321.
7. Convair Division, General Dynamics Corp., "Convair History" (Ms.), VIII-8.
8. Craven and Cate, *Men and Planes,* pp. 221–222.
9. Lockheed Aircraft Corp., *Of Men and Stars* (Burbank, Calif., July 1957), Ch. 5, p. 18.
10. Lockheed Aircraft Corp., *Of Men and Stars* (Aug.–Sept. 1957), Ch. 6, p. 6.

11. *History of the Aircraft War Production Council, East Coast, Inc.* (New York, 1947), pp. 1–3; see also *A History of Eastern Aircraft Division, General Motors* (New York, 1944).

12. "Convair History," VIII-2.

13. *Ibid.*, VIII-10, 11.

14. Lockheed Aircraft Corp., *Of Men and Stars*, Ch. 6, p. 18.

15. North American Aviation, Inc., "Brief History of Operations Immediately Prior to and During World War II," pp. 96–97.

16. Lockheed Aircraft Corp., *Of Men and Stars*, Ch. 6, p. 6; J. S. Day, *Subcontracting in the Airframe Industry* (Cambridge, Mass., 1956), p. 16.

17. Craven and Cate, *Men and Planes*, pp. 229–230; there is a particularly lucid exposition of this problem entitled "More Airplanes or Better," in Holley, *Buying Aircraft*, pp. 512–518.

18. M. M. Postan, *British War Production*, History of the Second World War, United Kingdom Civil Series (London, 1952), p. 123.

19. Craven and Cate, *Men and Planes*, p. 355; Holley, *Buying Aircraft*, p. 529.

20. W. G. Cunningham, *The Aircraft Industry: A Study in Industrial Location* (Los Angeles, 1951), p. 95.

21. *Ibid.*, p. 94.

22. Holley, *Buying Aircraft*, p. 538.

23. *Aviation Facts and Figures, 1956*, p. 17; the highest figure reached was 2,100,000 in November 1943: G. R. Simonson, "Demand for Aircraft and the Aircraft Industry," *Journal of Economic History*, 20, No. 3 (Sept. 1960), p. 377.

24. Lockheed Aircraft Corp., *Of Men and Stars*, Ch. 6, pp. 15–16.

25. The North American labor picture is in North American Aviation, Inc., "Brief History, 1935–1945," pp. 102–108.

26. *Ibid.*, p. 81.

27. *Aviation Facts and Figures, 1956*, p. 7.

28. Holley, *Buying Aircraft*, p. 448.

29. North American Aviation, "Brief History, 1935–1945," p. 117.

30. Holley, *Buying Aircraft*, pp. 451–452.

31. This account is based on E. E. Wilson, *Slipstream: The Biography of an Aircraftsman* (New York, 1965), pp. 243–244.

32. Pratt and Whitney Aircraft Division, United Aircraft Corp., *Pratt and Whitney Aircraft Story*, 2nd ed. (Hartford, Conn., 1952), pp. 134–135. This account makes F. B. Rentschler the chief architect of this price adjustment plan.

33. North American Aviation, "Brief History, 1935–1945," p. 123.

34. Holley, *Buying Aircraft*, p. 434.

35. Simonson, "Demand for Aircraft," p. 376. These companies, in the order of airframe weight produced during the war, were as follows: Douglas, Convair, Boeing, North American, Lockheed, Curtiss, Martin, Republic, Grumman, Bell, Chance Vought, and Fairchild. Ford and the Eastern Aircraft Division of General Motors have been omitted as being strictly temporary producers.

36. Craven and Cate, *Men and Planes*, p. 331.

37. Simonson, "Demand for Aircraft," p. 376.

38. *Ibid.*
39. *Freedom's Arsenal: The Story of the Automotive Council for War Production* (Detroit, Mich., 1950), p. 193.
40. *Ibid.,* pp. 199–200; Holley, *Buying Aircraft,* p. 549.
41. For a defense of the company, see A. Nevins and F. E. Hill, *Ford: Decline and Rebirth, 1933–1962* (New York, 1962), pp. 186 ff. There is an excellent and dispassionate analysis in Holley, *Buying Aircraft,* pp. 518–529.
42. Holley, *Buying Aircraft,* p. 523.
43. C. E. Sorensen, *My Forty Years with Ford* (New York, 1956), p. 298.
44. Nevins and Hill, *Ford: Decline and Rebirth,* p. 215.
45. *Ibid.,* p. 218.
46. Holley, *Buying Aircraft,* p. 522.
47. Craven and Cate, *Men and Planes,* p. 355.
48. *Ibid.,* p. 329.
49. Nevins and Hill, *Ford: Decline and Rebirth,* p. 223. This total includes "fly-aways" and "knock-downs."
50. This was a standard procedure and was normally followed by a firm contract. However, in judging the performance of industry in wartime production, it is important to remember that while much of the plant and equipment was provided by government funds, many firms made heavy commitments of their own resources on the strength of letters of intent, with no absolute assurance that they would be reimbursed.
51. Nevins and Hill, *Ford: Decline and Rebirth,* p. 200.
52. *Ibid.,* p. 208.
53. *History of Eastern Aircraft Division,* pp. 17–20.
54. Craven and Cate, *Men and Planes,* p. 355.
55. See Lynn T. White, "Eilmer of Malmesbury, an Eleventh Century Aviator," *Technology and Culture,* 2, No. 2 (Spring 1961), pp. 97–111. The evidence that Eilmer actually flew is convincing, even though he crash-landed and broke both his legs.
56. Holley, *Buying Aircraft,* p. 552; *Cunningham, Location of the Aircraft Industry,* p. 96. Cunningham lists as the major glider manufacturers:
    1. Aircraft companies: Cessna, Commonwealth, Aeronca, Taylorcraft, Piper, Waco.
    2. Glider companies: Schweizer Aircraft, Astoria, Long Island; Laister-Kauffman Aircraft, St. Louis, Mo.; G and A Aircraft (subsidiary of Firestone Tire and Rubber), Willow Grove, Pa.
    3. Non-aircraft companies: Ford Motor Company, Iron Mountain, Mich.; Gibson Refrigerator, Greenville, Mich.; Pratt, Read and Co. (piano manufacturers), Deep River, Conn.
57. For the story of the autogiro, see Juan de la Cierva and Don Rose, *Wings of Tomorrow: The Story of the Autogiro* (New York, 1931).
58. R. G. Hubler, *Straight Up: The Story of Vertical Flight* (New York, 1961), p. 59. This book has a thorough survey of the early helicopter experiments. The author quotes the Civil Aeronautics Authority as listing 47 abortive experiments up to the end of 1938.
59. Holley, *Buying Aircraft,* p. 578.

60. E. E. Wilson transcript, Naval History Project, No. 480, Oral History Research Office, Columbia University (1962), Vol. 1, p. 850. Wilson, it will be recalled, had been in charge of Sikorsky Aircraft when its flying-boat business was terminated. It was on his recommendation that United Aircraft financed Sikorsky's experiments with helicopters.

61. Hubler, *Straight Up*, p. 56.

62. R. Schlaifer and S. D. Heron, *The Development of Aircraft Engines and Fuels*, (Cambridge, Mass., 1956), p. 444.

63. *Ibid.* p. 329.

64. *Ibid.*, pp. 446–447.

65. *Ibid.*, pp. 448–449; R. L. Perry, "Innovation and Military Requirements: A Comparative Study," USAF Project RAND, Memorandum RM-5182-PR, (Aug. 1967) p. 29.

66. Lockheed Aircraft Corp., *Of Men and Stars*, Chap. 7, p. 6.

67. *Pratt and Whitney Aircraft Story*, pp. 154–155.

68. Schlaifer and Heron, *Development of Aircraft Engines*, p. 453.

69. J. C. Hunsaker, "Forty Years of Aeronautical Research," *Smithsonian Report, 1955*, No. 4237 (Washington, D. C., 1956), p. 264. In 1939 the growth of interest in the military possibilities of rocket propulsion resulted in the National Academy of Sciences, at the request of the War Department, initiating what is now the Jet Propulsion Laboratory at the California Institute of Technology.

70. Schlaifer and Heron, *Development of Aircraft Engines*, p. 462. The flight took place on May 15, 1941.

71. *Bell Aircraft News—20th Anniversary Edition*, p. 4.

72. Hunsaker, "Forty Years of Research," p. 265; transcript of interview with H. Mansfield Horner, president, United Aircraft, May 1960, Aviation Project, Oral History Research Office, Columbia University, Vol. II, p. 13.

73. Perry, "Innovation and Military Requirements," p. 30. The author points out, however, that the General Electric improvements were paralleled by Rolls-Royce, which also had supercharger experience.

74. Letter from General Laurence C. Craigie to author, Oct. 24, 1967. There was another experimental plane designated XP-59. The A was added for the jet to conceal the fact that this plane was a quite different experiment. When the XP-59A was shipped from the factory in Buffalo, a dummy propeller was put on the nose to help maintain secrecy.

75. Lockheed Aircraft Corp., *Of Men and Stars*, Ch. 7, p. 8.

76. Holley, *Buying Aircraft*, p. 562.

77. Schlaifer and Heron, *Development of Aircraft Engines*, p. 472.

78. Simonson, "Demand for Aircraft," p. 377.

79. *Ibid.*, p. 372.

80. Goodyear Aircraft News Service, "Goodyear in Aeronautics," undated release.

81. The Boeing Co., *Pedigree of Champions* (Seattle, Wash., 1963), p. 40. The G model was also slower, understandably so in view of the additional weight it had to carry.

82. Holley, *Buying Aircraft*, p. 550.

83. Northrop Corp., *Northrop Highlights* (Beverly Hills, Calif., n.d.), p. 2.

84. Craven and Cate, *Men and Planes*, p. 224.
85. Fairchild Engine and Airplane Corp., *Pegasus, 19*, No. 6 (Dec. 1952), pp. 9–10.
86. Craven and Cate, *Men and Planes*, p. 316.
87. *Ibid.*, pp. 221–222; *Aviation Week, 48*, No. 6 (April 26, 1948), p. 14.
88. Holley, *Buying Aircraft*, p. 555.
89. Craven and Cate, *Men and Planes*, p. xix.

Chapter 9

1. G. R. Simonson, "The Demand for Aircraft and the Aircraft Industry," *Journal of Economic History, 20*, No. 3, 1960, pp. 377–378.
2. I. B. Holley, *Buying Aircraft: Material Procurement for the Army Air Forces. The United States Army in World War II*, Special Studies, No. 7 (Washington, D. C., 1964), p. 452.
3. Convair Division, General Dynamics Corp., "Convair History" (Ms.), X-1.
4. The postwar readjustment at Boeing is described in H. Mansfield, *Vision* (New York, 1956), pp. 261 ff.
5. *Aviation Week, 47*, No. 1 (July 17, 1947), p. 22.
6. The Boeing Co., *Pedigree of Champions* (Seattle, Wash., 1963), p. 56.
7. *Ibid.*, p. 79.
8. Mansfield, *Vision*, p. 264; *Aviation Week, 52*, No. 12 (March 20, 1950), p. 41.
9. Mansfield, *Vision*, p. 274. The B-47 had six jet engines with a total thrust of 7,700 pounds, arranged with two in pairs near the center of each wing, and the other two mounted singly close to the wing tips.
10. *Ibid.*, pp. 279 and 311.
11. R. G. Hubler, *Big Eight: The Biography of an Airplane* (New York, 1960), p. 56.
12. C. Maynard (ed.), *Flight Plan for Tomorrow: The Douglas Story. A Condensed History*, rev. ed. (Santa Monica, Calif., 1966), pp. 30–32; P. W. Brooks, *The Modern Airliner* (London, 1961), pp. 98–100.
13. Maynard, *Flight Plan for Tomorrow*, p. 50.
14. Hubler, *Big Eight*, p. 19.
15. R. E. Gross to Lynn Bollinger, Harvard Business School, Dec. 6 and Dec. 15, 1944, Gross Papers, Library of Congress, Box 13.
16. Lockheed Aircraft Corp., *Of Men and Stars* (Burbank, Calif.), Ch. 7, p. 12.
17. *Ibid.*, p. 4.
18. *Ibid.*, Ch. 8, p. 2. It should be explained at this point that the Bureau of Air Commerce disappeared in 1938 in one of F. D. Roosevelt's sleight-of-hand operations on the administrative branch of the government. It was replaced by two agencies, the Civil Aeronautics Board, which assigned routes and regulated rate structures, and the Civil Aeronautics Administration, later the Federal Aviation Agency, which had charge of safety, promotional activities, etc. It is not clear what, if anything, was gained by the change.

19. A. E. Raymond transcript, Honnold Library, The Claremont Colleges, p. 19.
20. Brooks, *Modern Airliner*, p. 104; R. E. Gross to J. C. Franklin, New York City, Nov. 7, 1950, Gross Papers, Box 9.
21. Lockheed Aircraft Corp., *Of Men and Stars*, Ch. 8, pp. 4–5.
22. This story is told in a Lockheed publication, "The Lockheed Story" (June 1956).
23. North American Aviation, Inc., "Biography of J. H. Kindelberger" (Ms.), pp. 40–41.
24. North American Aviation, Inc., *Annual Report, 1949*, pp. 8 and 9; J. L. Atwood, address to New York Society of Security Analysts, *Los Angeles Times*, July 8, 1963.
25. Atwood to N.Y. Society of Security Analysts, April 25, 1955; North American Aviation, "Kindelberger Biography," pp. 44 and 45.
26. North American Aviation, *Annual Report, 1947*, p. 7; North American Aviation, "Kindelberger Biography," pp. 44–47.
27. North American Aviation, *Annual Report, 1948*, p. 10. General Motors sold its holdings in Bendix Aviation at the same time, some 400,000 shares representing a 19 per cent interest, for $12 million. For the reasons behind this step, see A. P. Sloan, *My Years with General Motors* (Garden City, N.Y., 1964), pp. 372–374.
28. *Ibid.*, p. 374.
29. J. L. Atwood says that General Motors never tried to manage North American except for some requirements on legal matters and financial reporting; J. L. Atwood transcript, Honnold Library, The Claremont Colleges, p. 13.
30. This sketch is taken from North American Aviation, "Kindelberger Biography," and the *Los Angeles Times*, July 28, 1962.
31. Breech was board chairman of North American until 1942; he then became president of Bendix Aviation.
32. This is based on the Atwood transcript.
33. "North American Aviation, Inc.," *Management Audit*, 7, No. 11, pp. 10, 11.
34. "Convair History," X-1.
35. *Ibid.*, p. 2.
36. *Ibid.*, p. 3.
37. *Aviation Week, 48*, No. 1 (Jan. 5, 1948), p. 17.
38. "Convair History," X-6.
39. This is the official figure. *Aviation Week, 48*, No. 19 (May 10, 1948), p. 34, gives the Convair deficit as $42 million.
40. *Aviation Week, 47*, No. 11 (Sept. 15, 1947), p. 18; "Convair History," X-5.
41. "Convair History," X-6.
42. *Ibid.*, p. 4.
43. This account is based on W. F. Craven and J. L. Cate, *The Army Air Forces in World War II*, Vol. 6, *Men and Planes* (Chicago, 1955), pp. 244–246.
44. "Convair History," X-9.
45. *Ibid.*, p. 11. See also transcript of interview with R. C. Sebold, former

vice-president of engineering, Convair-Fort Worth, Nov. 13, 1962, pp. 9–12, Honnold Library, The Claremont Colleges.

46. R. E. Gross to Guy W. Vaughan, March 29, 1949; Vaughan to Gross, April 19, 1949, Gross Papers, Box 13.

47. General Dynamics Corp., *Annual Report, 1953*, p. 11.

48. Martin Papers, Library of Congress, Box 79, Engineering Report 2009, Sept. 26, 1944; Box 73, Statement before the Senate Banking and Currency Committee, Jan. 15, 1948.

49. Martin Papers, Box 76, T. L. North, "Report on the Commercial Aircraft Picture," Feb. 11, 1946.

50. *Aviation Week*, 52, No. 12 (March 20, 1950), p. 41; Martin Papers, Box 76, U.S. Circuit Court of Appeals, 6th Circuit, No. 12130, May 31, 1955.

51. Martin Papers, Statement before the Senate Banking and Currency Committee.

52. Martin Papers, Box 73, Glenn L. Martin to Louis A. Johnson, Secretary of Defense, May 4, 1949.

53. *Ibid.*, Box 71, Martin to Senator Millard, Tydings, March 15 and 16, 1949; to W. S. Symington, Secretary of Air, Feb. 7, 1949.

54. *Aviation Week*, 51, No. 4 (July 25, 1949), p. 12; Martin Papers, Box 71, Report of management study by Robert Heller and Associates, Cleveland, Ohio, April 12, 1948.

55. *Aviation Week*, 52, No. 21 (May 22, 1950), p. 9; Martin Papers, Box 74, Minutes of Director's meeting, Sept. 28, 1953.

56. *The Martin Company*, pamphlet (Baltimore, Md., 1960), pp. 44–45; Martin Papers, Box 71, Minutes of Director's meeting, Feb. 16, March 16, Oct. 18, 1951.

57. Martin Papers, Box 77, Minutes of Director's meeting, Dec. 15, 1950; Box 72, Minutes of special stockholders' meeting, April 2, 1952; Box 74, President's letter to stockholders, Feb. 16, 1953.

58. *The Martin Company*, p. 40.

59. W. G. Cunningham, *The Aircraft Industry: A Study in Industrial Location* (Los Angeles, 1951), p. 150.

60. For details see *Bell Aircraft News—20th Anniversary Edition*, July 10, 1955; Bell transcript, Aviation Project, Oral History Research Office, Columbia University, Vol. VII, No. 388, pp. 190–192.

61. *Aviation Week*, 47, No. 19 (Nov. 10, 1946), p. 57.

62. Republic Aviation Corp., "Company History," n.d.

63. Northrop Corp., *Northrop Highlights*, n.d.; *Aviation Week*, 52, No. 20 (May 15, 1950), p. 5.

64. *Aviation Week*, 53, No. 18 (Oct. 30, 1950), p. 7.

65. Ryan Aeronautical Co. News Bureau, "The Ryan Aeronautical Company Story," n.d.

66. McDonnell Aircraft Corp., *Annual Report, 1960*, p. 8.

67. Ling-Temco-Vought, Inc., "The Texas Aircraft Industry, 1940–1959" (Ms.), p. 42.

68. Fairchild Engine and Airplane Corp., *Pegasus, 19*, No. 6 (Dec. 1952), pp. 13–16.

69. *Ibid.*, p. 16. The C-82 had a gross weight of 27 tons and carried a payload of 20,000 pounds. The C-119 series began at 32 tons with the

same payload and grew to the C-119H, 43 tons and 28,000 pounds load.

70. *Aviation Week*, 51, No. 3 (July 18, 1949), p. 13.
71. *Chance Vought News*, Historical Supplement.
72. H. Mansfield Horner transcript, Aviation Project, Oral History Research Office, Columbia University, p. 19.
73. *Aerospace Facts and Figures, 1964*, p. 25.
74. Pratt and Whitney Aircraft Division, United Aircraft Corp., *The Pratt and Whitney Aircraft Story*, 2nd ed. (Hartford, Conn., 1952), pp. 168–169.
75. *Aviation Week*, 52, No. 6 (Feb. 6, 1950), p. 32; Vaughan to R. E. Gross, April 21, 1949, Gross Papers, Box 23.
76. *Aviation Week*, 47, No. 19 (Nov. 10, 1947), p. 11; 55, No. 1 (July 2, 1951), p. 17. The Hughes Aircraft Company is engaged entirely in electronics and missiles.
77. President's Air Policy Commission, *Survival in the Air Age* (Washington, D. C., 1948), pp. 24–25.
78. *Ibid.*, pp. 48–49.
79. *Ibid.*, p. 48.
80. *Fortune*, 37 (March 1948), p. 148.
81. "Convair History," X-11.
82. *Aviation Week*, 50, No. 23 (June 6, 1949), p. 10; 51, No. 8 (Aug. 22, 1949), pp. 13–15.
83. *Ibid.*, 51, No. 16 (Oct. 17, 1949), pp. 12–13. A good summation of the controversy over strategy appears in an article by Bernard Brodie in the *Los Angeles Times*, Dec. 3, 1967.
84. President's Air Policy Commission, *Survival in the Air Age*, p. 67.
85. W. G. Cunningham, *Location of the Aircraft Industry*, p. 182.
86. *Aviation Week*, 50, No. 16 (April 18, 1949), p. 38.
87. *Ibid.*, 52, No. 4 (Jan. 23, 1950), pp. 13–14.
88. *Ibid.*, 52, No. 8 (Feb. 20, 1950), p. 26.
89. *Ibid.*, 53, No. 2 (July 10, 1950), p. 2; R. E. Gross to Guy W. Vaughan, Sept. 6, 1950, Gross Papers, Box 9.
90. *Aerospace Facts and Figures, 1964*, p. 25.
91. *Aviation Week*, 53, No. 4 (July 24, 1950), p. 13.
92. Simonson, "Demand for Aircraft," p. 380.
93. *Aviation Week*, 55, No. 1 (July 2, 1951), p. 37.
94. Simonson, "Demand for Aircraft," p. 379.
95. This description of Lockheed in 1949–1950 comes from Lockheed Aircraft Corp., *Of Men and Stars*, Ch. 8, pp. 10–12.
96. Gross Papers, Box 13, Gross to Fred E. Robinson, president, National Aviation Corp., April 27, 1950.
97. Lockheed Aircraft Corp., *Of Men and Stars*, Ch. 9, p. 3.
98. *Aviation Week*, 54, No. 8 (Feb. 19, 1951), p. 12.

Chapter 10

1. Most of the history of military missiles is necessarily secret. For space exploration there is an excellent history of Project Mercury: Loyd S.

Swenson, Jr., James M. Grimwood, and Charles C. Alexander, *This New Ocean* (NASA, Washington, D. C., 1966).

2. *Bell Aircraft News—20ᵗʰ Anniversary Edition,* p. 10; Lawrence Bell transcript, Aviation Project, VII-4, Oral History Research Office, Columbia University, p. 190. R. G. Hubler, *Straight Up: The Story of Vertical Flight* (New York, 1961) gives an excellent, concise history of the helicopter in both America and Europe.

3. Hubler, *Straight Up,* p. 132.

4. The Boeing Co., Vertol Division, *Missions and Milestones* (Morton, Pa., 1963), pp. 3–4.

5. Hubler, *Straight Up,* p. 69.

6. *McDonnell Airscoop,* March 1, 1959.

7. Hubler, *Straight Up,* pp. 84 and 231.

8. *Los Angeles Times,* May 5, 1964.

9. Hubler, *Straight Up,* p. 232. C. H. Kaman, "The Kaman Aircraft Corporation," reprint of articles written for the *Christian Science Monitor* (July 1–3, 1958), pp. 1–2.

10. Kaman, "Kaman Aircraft Corporation," p. 5.

11. Hubler, *Straight Up,* p. 233.

12. VTOL: Vertical Take-Off and Landing; STOL: Short Take-Off and Landing.

13. *Aerospace Facts and Figures, 1964,* p. 38.

14. Hubler, *Straight Up,* pp. 143–146.

15. The Comet was tested in 1949 and went into service in 1952. The sealing of the cabin windows failed at high altitudes, causing the fuselage to explode.

16. The Boeing Co., *Pedigree of Champions* (Seattle, Wash., 1963), p. 64.

17. P. W. Brooks, *The Modern Airliner* (London, 1961), pp. 130–131.

18. C. Maynard (ed.), *Flight Plan for Tomorrow: The Douglas Story. A Condensed History,* rev. ed. (Santa Monica, Calif., 1966), p. 33. R. G. Hubler, *Big Eight: The Biography of an Airplane* (New York, 1960), p. 87. This book provides a detailed narrative of the development of the DC-8, with a clear analysis of the problems that were encountered.

19. Douglas Aircraft Co., Inc., *Annual Report,* 1952, p. 6.

20. C. R. Smith transcript, Aviation Project, Oral History Research Office, Columbia University, Vol. VI, pp. 36–37.

21. *Ibid.,* p. 38.

22. *Aviation Week,* 59, No. 16 (Oct. 19, 1952), p. 13.

23. *Ibid.,* pp. 73–74; Maynard, *Flight Plan for Tomorrow,* pp. 81–83.

24. Hubler, *Big Eight,* pp. 75–76; Maynard, *Flight Plan for Tomorrow,* p. 88.

25. Hubler, *Big Eight,* p. 99.

26. *Ibid.,* p. 148.

27. Maynard, *Flight Plan for Tomorrow,* p. 33.

28. A. E. Raymond transcript, Honnold Library, The Claremont Colleges, p. 18. Hubler, *Big Eight,* p. 149, says that in the spring of 1958 development costs on the DC-8 exceeded $200 million.

29. Convair Division, General Dynamics Corp., "Convair History," XI-6.

30. *Ibid.,* p. 7.

31. *Ibid.,* p. 11.

32. This description of the B-58 is in J. Niven, C. Canby, and V. Welsh, *Dynamic America: A History of General Dynamics Corporation* (New York, 1958), p. 365. See also R. C. Sebold transcript, Honnold Library, The Claremont Colleges, pp. 14–15.

33. Hubler, *Big Eight*, pp. 111–112.

34. Lockheed Aircraft Corp., *Of Men and Stars*, Ch. 8, (Burbank, Calif., Oct. 1957), p. 11; R. E. Gross to E. B. Lurie, New York City, Aug. 1, 1952, Gross Papers, Box 9.

35. Lockheed Aircraft Corp., *Of Men and Stars*, Ch. 9 (Jan. 1958), p. 5.

36. Gross Papers, Box 9, R. E. Gross to Clive Church, San Francisco, Aug. 31, 1955.

37. *Ibid.*, R. E. Gross to Sinclair Weeks, Secretary of Commerce, Jan. 22, 1953.

38. *Ibid.*, Gross to Frederick M. Warburg, June 29, 1950; to Blakeslee Barron, Feb. 8, 1955.

39. Lockheed Aircraft Corp., *Of Men and Stars*, Ch. 9, pp. 5, 6.

40. *Ibid.*, p. 11; R. E. Gross to Don Daseke, Midwest Investors Service, Nov. 18, 1955, Gross Papers, Box 9.

41. Lockheed Aircraft Corp., *Of Men and Stars*, Ch. 9, p. 12.

42. Brooks, *The Modern Airliner*, p. 119.

43. Transcript of interview with Kenneth R. Jackman, March 7, 1963, p. 16, Honnold Library, The Claremont Colleges. The problems of the British aircraft industry since the Second World War have been due to faulty public policy rather than to any lack of engineering skill. There is an excellent analysis of British aviation policy in R. Higham, "Some Lessons of British Air-Transport Experience," *Transportation: A Service* (New York, 1968), pp. 203–212.

44. This changeover is ably analyzed in G. R. Simonson, "Missiles and Creative Destruction in the American Aircraft Industry, 1956–1961," *Business History Review*, 38, No. 3 (Autumn 1964), pp. 302–314.

45. *Ibid.*, p. 307.

46. *Aerospace Facts and Figures, 1964*, pp. 77 and 81; Victor R. Fuchs, *Changes in the Location of Manufacturing Industry in the United States Since 1929* (New Haven, Conn., 1962), p. 92. Automobile manufacturing employed 695,475 people in 1954. Fuchs gives 822,470 for the aircraft industry in that year. The discrepancy with the figure given in the text is due to differences in classifying "aircraft and parts."

47. Rockwell-Standard was a consolidation of the Timken-Detroit Axle Co. and the Standard Spring Co. Its products included axles, brakes, springs, tools, and stainless steel household equipment.

48. Hubler, *Big Eight*, p. 149.

49. *Aviation Facts and Figures, 1958*, p. 112.

50. *Aerospace Facts and Figures, 1964*, p. 25.

51. *Ibid.*, p. 6.

52. J. L. Atwood, "Some Aspects and Problems of the Aircraft Industry," address at Eighth Stanford Business Conference, July 28, 1949, p. 7.

53. L. C. Philmus, "The Airplane: The Only Way to Fly," *Engineering Opportunities*, 4, No. 10 (Oct. 10, 1966), p. 46.

Sources

Manuscripts

The Manuscripts Division, Library of Congress, has the papers of Robert E. Gross, Grover Loening, and Glenn L. Martin.

The papers of Alexander Klemin, distinguished aeronautical engineer, are in the Special Collections Department of the Library of the University of California, Los Angeles, which also houses the Elizabeth Hiatt Gregory Collection, an extensive compilation of documents on the history of aviation.

The Millar-Northrop Library of Aviation in the Occidental College Library contains manuscripts and documents contributed by Richard Millar and John K. Northrop, both personal papers and other materials in the history of American aviation.

Documents

Unpublished:

Records of the Bureau of Air Commerce and Civil Aeronautics Board, National Archives.

Convair Division, General Dynamics Corporation, "Convair History," compiled by Howard O. Welty, and "Historical Background of Convair."

North American Aviation, Inc., "Biography of J. H. Kindelberger," "Brief History of North American Aviation, Inc., from the Date of Incorporation through December 31, 1934," "Brief History of Operations Immediately Prior to and During World War II," "History of the Aviation Industry."

Chapin, Seymour L., and Smith, Thomas M., "A History of Pressurized Flight" (1962).

Hunsaker, J. C., "Second Annual Sight Lecture," The Wings Club, May 26, 1965.

Published:
President's Aircraft Board, *Aircraft in National Defense,* Senate Document No. 18, 69th Congress, 1st Session (Washington, D. C., 1925).
President's Air Policy Commission, *Survival in the Air Age* (Washington, D. C., 1948).
U.S. Congress, *The Aircraft Industry,* Hearings before Subcommittee No. 4, Select Committee on Small Business, House of Representatives, 84th Congress, 2nd Session (Washington, D. C., 1956).
U.S. Congress, *National Aviation Policy,* Senate Report 949, 80th Congress, 2nd Session, (Washington, D. C., 1948).

Recorded Interviews

The Oral History Research Office of Columbia University has an extensive collection of transcripts of interviews with individuals connected with the history of aviation, listed under Aviation Project No. 388 and Naval History Project No. 480. Specific references are made in the notes.

The Oral History Program of the Claremont Graduate School has transcripts of interviews on the history of the aircraft industry with the following men:

John L. Atwood (North American)
Kenneth R. Jackman (Convair)
Joseph S. Marriott (FAA)
Richard Millar (Douglas, Northrop, Vultee)
Henry H. Ogden (Lockheed)
Arthur E. Raymond (Douglas)
Frederick Salathé, Jr. (Pacific Exploration Company)
Raymond C. Sebold (Convair)
Carl Squier (Lockheed)
Thomas Wolfe (United Airlines and Pan American Airways)

In addition, the author has notes on unrecorded interviews with Frank R. Collbohm (Douglas), John K. Northrop, Nathaniel Paschall (Boeing, Douglas), and Eugene E. Wilson (United Aircraft).

Books

Allen, Hugh, *Goodyear Aircraft* (Cleveland, Ohio, 1947).
Arpee, Edward, *From Frigates to Flat-Tops* (Lake Forest, Ill., 1953).
Axe, E. W., and Co., "The Aviation Industry in the United States" (Ms.), Axe-Houghton Economic Studies, Series B, No. 6 (New York, 1938).
Bartlett, Robert M., *Sky Pioneer: The Story of Igor I. Sikorsky* (New York, 1947).
The Boeing Co., *Pedigree of Champions* (Seattle, Wash., 1963).
Bollinger, Lynn, and Lilley, Tom, *The Financial Position of the Aircraft*

Industry, Business Research Studies, No. 28, Vol. 30, No. 3, Harvard Business School (Cambridge, Mass., 1943).

Brooks, Peter W., *The Modern Airliner* (London, 1961).

Cierva, Juan de la, and Rose, Don, *Wings of Tomorrow: The Story of the Autogiro* (New York, 1931).

Craven, Wesley F., and Cate, James L., *The Army Air Forces in World War II*, Vol. 6, *Men and Planes* (Chicago, 1955); Vol. 7, *Services Around the World* (Chicago, 1958).

Cunningham, Frank, *Skymaster: The Story of Donald Douglas and Douglas Aircraft Co.* (Philadelphia, 1943).

Cunningham, William G., *The Aircraft Industry: A Study in Industrial Location* (Los Angeles, 1951).

Davies, R. E. G., *A History of the World's Airlines* (London, 1964).

Day, John S., *Subcontracting in the Airframe Industry* (Cambridge, Mass., 1956).

Douglas Aircraft Co., Inc., Service Information Summary, *Fiftieth Anniversary of Naval Aviation* (El Segundo, Calif., 1962).

Fokker, Anthony H. G., and Gould, Bruce, *Flying Dutchman* (New York, 1931).

Freudenthal, Elsbeth E., *The Aviation Business: From Kitty Hawk to Wall Street* (New York, 1940).

General Motors Corp., *History of the Eastern Aircraft Division* (New York, 1944).

Gray, George W., *Frontiers of Flight: The Story of NACA Research* (New York, 1948).

Hatch, Alden, *Glenn Curtiss: Pioneer of Naval Aviation* (New York, 1942).

Heron, S. D., *History of the Aircraft Piston Engine* (Detroit, Mich., 1961).

History of the Aircraft War Production Council, East Coast, Inc. (New York, 1947).

Holley, Irving B., Jr., *Buying Aircraft: Material Procurement for the Army Air Forces. The United States Army in World War II*, Special Studies, No. 7 (Washington, D. C., 1964).

———, *Ideas and Weapons* (New Haven, Conn., 1953).

Hubler, Richard G., *Big Eight: The Biography of an Airplane* (New York, 1960).

———, *Straight Up: The Story of Vertical Flight* (New York, 1961).

Ingells, Douglas J., *The Plane that Changed the World* (Fallbrook, Calif., 1966).

Kelly, C. J., Jr., *The Sky's the Limit* (DC-3) (New York, 1963).

Lawrance, Charles L., *Our National Aviation Program* (New York, 1932).

Levine, Isaac Don., *Mitchell: Pioneer of Air Power* (New York, 1943).

Litchfield, P. W., *Industrial Voyage* (Goodyear), (Garden City, N.Y., 1954).

Lockheed Aircraft Corp., *Of Men and Stars* (Burbank, Calif., 1957–1958).

Loening, Grover, *Our Wings Grow Faster* (Garden City, N.Y., 1935).

Mansfield, Harold, *Vision* (Boeing) (New York, 1956).

Maynard, Crosby, *Flight Plan for Tomorrow: The Douglas Story. A Condensed History*, rev. ed. (Santa Monica, Calif., 1966).

Mingos, Howard, *The Birth of an Industry* (New York, 1930).

Morris, Lloyd, and Smith, Kendall, *Ceiling Unlimited: The Story of American Aviation from Kitty Hawk to Supersonics* (New York, 1953).

Nevins, Allan, and Hill, Frank E., *Ford: Decline and Rebirth, 1933–1962* (New York, 1963).

Nicolson, Harold, *Dwight Morrow* (New York, 1935).

Niven, John; Canby, Courtlandt; and Welsh, Vernon (eds.), *Dynamic America: A History of General Dynamics Corporation* (New York, 1958).

Postan, M. M., *British War Production*. History of the Second World War, United Kingdom Civil Series (London, 1952).

Postan, M. M.; Hay, D.; and Scott, J. D., *Design and Development of Weapons*. History of the Second World War, United Kingdom Civil Series (London, 1964).

Pratt and Whitney Aircraft Division, United Aircraft Corporation, *The Pratt and Whitney Aircraft Story*, 2nd ed. (Hartford, Conn., 1952).

Schlaifer, Robert, and Heron, S. D., *The Development of Aircraft Engines and Fuels* (Cambridge, Mass., 1950).

Shrader, Welman A., *Fifty Years of Flight: A Chronicle of the Aviation Industry in America, 1903–1953* (Cleveland, Ohio, 1963).

Sikorsky, Igor I., *The Story of the Winged-S* (London, 1939).

Sloan, A. P., *My Years with General Motors* (Garden City, N.Y., 1964).

Smith, Henry L., *Airways* (New York, 1942).

Smith, Richard K., *The Airships Akron and Macon* (Annapolis, Md., 1965).

Sorensen, C. E., with Williamson, S. T., *My Forty Years with Ford* (New York, 1956).

Stout, William B., *So Away I Went* (Indianapolis, 1951).

Swanborough, F. G., *United States Military Aircraft since 1909* (London and New York, 1963).

Taylor, Frank J., *High Horizons* (New York, 1962).

United Air Lines, *Corporate and Legal History of United Air Lines and Its Predecessors and Subsidiaries* (Chicago, 1953).

Wilson, Eugene E., *Air Power for Peace* (New York, 1945).

——, *From Kitty Hawk to Sputnik* (Ann Arbor, Mich., 1958).

——, *Slipstream: The Autobiography of an Aircraftsman* (New York, 1965).

Wolfe, Thomas, *Air Transportation: Traffic and Management* (New York, 1950).

Woods, G. B., *The Aircraft Manufacturing Industry* (New York, 1946).

Articles

Atwood, J. L., "Some Aspects and Problems of the Aircraft Industry," address at Eighth Stanford Business Conference, July 28, 1947.

Au Werter, Jay F., "Pratt and Whitney Expands," *Aviation*, 39, No. 7 (July 1940).

"Boeing Aircraft Co., 25th Anniversary," *Aero Digest*, 39, No. 1 (July 1941).

Bollinger, Lynn; Lilley, Tom; and Lombard, A. E., Jr., "Preserving American Air Power," *Harvard Business Review*, 23 (Spring 1945).

Burden, W. A., "Postwar Status of the Aircraft Industry," *Harvard Business Review*, 23 (Winter 1945).

Cerny, W. J., "Northrop Aircraft, Inc." *Aeronautical Engineering Review,* *1* (Nov. 1942).

Chapin, Seymour L., "Garrett and Pressurized Flight: A Business Built on Thin Air," *Pacific Historical Review, 35,* No. 3 (Aug. 1966).

"Curtiss-Wright Chronological History," *Aero Digest, 39,* No. 4 (Oct. 1941).

"Curtiss-Wright Corporation," *Aero Digest, 24,* No. 4 (April 1934).

Davis, Forrest, "See You Tomorrow in London" (Martin), *Saturday Evening Post, 210,* Pt. 1 (Aug. 31, 1937).

Dibble, Lewis C., "The Detroit Aircraft Corporation," *Automotive Industries, 40* (June 15, 1929).

"Fairchild Aviation Corporation," *Aero Digest, 24,* No. 1 (Jan. 1934).

Ganahl, Frank de., "Fleetwings, Inc.," *Aeronautical Engineering Review,* *1* (Nov. 1942).

Haiduck, Andrew F., "Bellanca Aircraft Corporation," *Aeronautical Engineering Review,* 1 (Nov. 1942).

Hill, Ray, "The Brewster Aeronautical Corporation," *Aeronautical Engineering Review,* 1 (Nov. 1942).

Hoff, N. W., "Thin Shells in Aerospace Structures," *Aeronautics and Astronautics, 5,* No. 2 (Feb. 1967).

Hoover, Herbert, Jr., "Radio on the World's Airlines," *Aero Digest, 18,* No. 1 (Jan. 1931).

Hunsaker, J. C., "Forty Years of Aeronautical Research," *Smithsonian Report, 1955,* No. 4237 (Washington, D. C., 1956).

Kaman, C. H., "The Kaman Aircraft Corporation," *Christian Science Monitor* (July 1-3, 1958).

Lippincott, Harvey, "The Navy Gets an Engine," *Journal of the American Aviation Historical Society, 6,* No. 4 (Winter 1961).

McCarthy, C. J., "Naval Aircraft Design in the Mid-1930's," *Technology and Culture, 4,* No. 2 (Spring 1963).

Martin, Glenn L., "The Development of Aircraft Manufacture," *Aviation Engineering, 5* (Dec. 1931).

Moffett, William A., "Twenty Years of Naval Aviation," *Popular Aviation, 3* (Dec. 1928).

Neville, J. T., "The Story of Wichita," *Aviation, 29,* Nos. 3, 5, and 6 (Sept.–Dec. 1930).

"North American Aviation, Inc.," *Aero Digest, 24,* No. 2 (Feb. 1934).

Northrop, John K., "Aviation History, 1903–1960," address before the National Air Council, Washington, D. C., Nov. 3, 1948.

Peale, Mundy I., "The Story of Republic Aviation," *Christian Science Monitor* (Feb. 10–13, 1959).

Philmus, Lois C., "The Airplane: The Only Way to Fly," *Engineering Opportunities, 4,* No. 10 (Oct. 1966).

Price, Wesley, "Merchant of Speed" (Kindelberger), *Saturday Evening Post, 221,* No. 34 (Feb. 19, 1949).

Seely, Victor D., "Boeing's Pacesetting 247," *Journal of the American Aviation Historical Society, 9,* No. 4 (Winter 1964).

Simonson, G. R., "The Demand for Aircraft and the Aircraft Industry," *Journal of Economic History, 20,* No. 3 (Sept. 1960).

———, "Missiles and Creative Destruction in the American Aircraft Industry, 1956–1961," *Business History Review, 38,* No. 3 (Autumn 1964).

Taylor, C. Fayette, "Aircraft Propulsion: A Review of the Evolution of Aircraft Powerplants," *Smithsonian Report, 1962,* No. 4546 (Washington, D. C., 1963).

————, "Twenty-Five Years of Engine Development," *Aviation, 40* (Aug. 1941).

Wright, T. P., "50,000 Planes a Year," *Aviation, 39,* No. 7 (July 1940).

"Wright Engines. The First Quarter Century," *Aero Digest, 47* (Nov. 1944).

List of Airplane Types Referred to in Text

Number and Name	Company	Number and Name	Company
A-17	Douglas	Boeing 307, Stratoliner	Boeing
A-20, Havoc	Douglas	Boeing 377, Stratocruiser	Boeing
A-31 and A-35, Vengeance	Vultee	Boeing Model 40	Boeing
AD Series	Douglas	Boeing 200, Monomail	Boeing
A3D, Skywarrior	Douglas	Boeing 707	Boeing
A4D, Skyhawk	Douglas	BT-13	Vultee
AT-6, Harvard	North American	C-46 (see CW-20)	Curtiss-Wright
B-1	Boeing	C-47 (see DC-3)	Douglas
B-9	Boeing	C-54 (see DC-4), Skymaster	Douglas
B-10	Martin		
B-17, Flying Fortress	Boeing	C-61, Forwarder	Fairchild
B-18	Douglas	C-69 (see L-049)	Lockheed
B-19	Douglas	C-74, Globemaster	Douglas
B-24, Liberator	Convair	C-82, Packet	Fairchild
B-25, Mitchell	North American	C-97	Boeing
		C-119	Fairchild
B-26, Marauder	Martin	C-124	Douglas
B-29, Superfortress	Boeing	C-130, Hercules	Lockheed
B-32	Consolidated	C-133	Douglas
		CW-20	Curtiss-Wright
B-36	Convair		
B-45	North American	DC-1	Douglas
		DC-2	Douglas
B-47	Boeing	DC-3	Douglas
B-50	Boeing	DC-4	Douglas
B-52	Boeing	DC-5	Douglas
B-57, Canberra	Martin	DC-6	Douglas
B-58	Convair	DC-7	Douglas
B-70	North American	DC-8	Douglas
		DC-9	Douglas
B-314, Clipper	Boeing	DT-1	Douglas
Beechcraft 17	Beech	DWC, World Cruiser	Douglas
Beechcraft 18	Beech	F-24	Fairchild
		F-84, Thunderjet	Republic

Number and Name	Company	Number and Name	Company
F-86, Sabrejet	North American	P-26	Boeing
		P-29	Boeing
F-89, Scorpion	Northrop	P-35	Republic
F-94, Starfighter	Lockheed	P-36	Curtiss
F-101	McDonnell	P-38, Lightning	Lockheed
F-102	Convair	P-39, Airacobra	Bell
F-104, Starfighter	Lockheed	P-40	Curtiss
F-105	Republic	P-47, Thunderbolt	Republic
F-111	General Dynamics	P-51, Mustang	North American
F2A, Buffalo	Brewster	P-59	Bell
F3D, Skynight	Douglas	P-61, Black Widow	Northrop
F4D, Skyray	Douglas	P-63, Kingcobra	Bell
F4F, Wildcat	Grumman	P-80, Shooting Star	Lockheed
F7U, Cutlass	Chance Vought	P2Y-1	Consolidated
F9F	Grumman	P5M-1, Marlin	Martin
F28-1	Boeing	PBM, Mariner	Martin
FB6	Boeing	PBY, Catalina	Consolidated
FC-1	Fairchild		
FD-1, Phantom	McDonnell	PT-1	Consolidated
FJ-1, Fury	North American		
FR-1, Fireball	Ryan	S-1	Lockheed
JN, Jenny	Curtiss	SB2U-1	Chance Vought
KC-135, Stratotanker	Boeing		
L-10, Electra	Lockheed	SBD-1, Dauntless	Douglas
L-14, Super Electra	Lockheed	S-38	Sikorsky
L-18, Lodestar	Lockheed	S-40	Sikorsky
L-049, Constellation	Lockheed	S-42, Clipper	Sikorsky
L-133	Lockheed	T-33	Lockheed
L-188, Electra	Lockheed	TBD-1, Devastator	Douglas
M-1	Ryan	TBF, Avenger	Grumman
M-1, M-4	Douglas	U-2	Lockheed
M-130, China Clipper	Martin	V-1	Vultee
MB	Martin	V-11	Vultee
MB-3	Thomas-Morse	Vega	Lockheed
		VS-300	Sikorsky
NC	Curtiss	X-1	Bell
O-2	Douglas	XB-15	Boeing
O-19	Consolidated	XB-35	Northrop
		XB-48	Martin
O-47	North American	XP-59A	Bell
		XFM-1, Airacuda	Bell
O2SU, Corsair	Chance Vought	XPB2M-1, Mars	Martin
Orion	Lockheed	XPY-1, Commodore	Consolidated

Index